Drumbeat

As the twenty-first century unfolds society is confronted with the normalization of warfare and political violence and their growing allure for the young. Current global political events highlight the extent to which young people have become the target of both State and non-State actors in the prosecution of war and terror. The conduct of what we can refer to as "social war" has increasingly come to target the young through media (social media, the internet and video games) and more directly through acts of violence (the massacre of children, the reliance on child soldiers, and the use of children in martyrdom operations) as legitimate forms of conduct. The appropriation of the young as political and military materials through the processes of both radicalization and militarization warrants close examination. *Drumbeat* examines these issues within the context of the ongoing process of militarization and the establishment of a state of perpetual warfare. The book distinguishes between radicalization, which refers to the application of propaganda and ideological methods by non-State agents, and militarization, which refers to the application of propaganda and ideological methods by State agents in order to effectively prosecute war. The focus of this book will be an examination of the mechanisms through which forms of media and other digital and web-based artefacts – social media, video and video games – assist in the militarization and radicalization of the young.

There is a growing body of evidence which points to the effectiveness of various forms of media in both the recruitment of young people and the promotion of ideological frames. For example, non-State actors (extremist religious groups and the Alt-Right) have been highly effective in appropriating new media to project their propaganda messages and their appeal to young people.

The book also argues that militarization has become a powerful societal force, which is re-configuring the daily conduct of life in the West. Just as radicalization seeks to prepare the young for the conduct of war, militarization also functions to position the broader society for war. This is a new form of the "civilizing process" to which Norbert Elias referred. In this context new media provides the conduits through which this process is legitimized, celebrated and promulgated.

John Martino is a Senior Lecturer in the College of Education at Victoria University, Australia. He is the author of *War/Play: Video Games and the Militarization of Society* (2015).

Drumbeat

New Media and the Radicalization and Militarization of Young People

John Martino

NEW YORK AND LONDON

First published 2021
by Routledge
52 Vanderbilt Avenue, New York, NY 10017

and by Routledge
2 Park Square, Milton Park, Abingdon, Oxon, OX14 4RN

Routledge is an imprint of the Taylor & Francis Group, an informa business

© 2021 Taylor & Francis

The right of John Martino to be identified as author of this work has been asserted by him in accordance with sections 77 and 78 of the Copyright, Designs and Patents Act 1988.

All rights reserved. No part of this book may be reprinted or reproduced or utilised in any form or by any electronic, mechanical, or other means, now known or hereafter invented, including photocopying and recording, or in any information storage or retrieval system, without permission in writing from the publishers.

Trademark notice: Product or corporate names may be trademarks or registered trademarks, and are used only for identification and explanation without intent to infringe.

Library of Congress Cataloging-in-Publication Data
Names: Martino, John (Lecturer in education), author.
Title: Drumbeat : new media and the radicalization and militarization of young people / John Martino.
Description: New York, NY : Routledge, 2021. | Includes bibliographical references.
Identifiers: LCCN 2020049669 | ISBN 9781138043268 (hardback) | ISBN 9781138043275 (paperback) | ISBN 9781315173245 (ebook)
Subjects: LCSH: Internet and youth—Political aspects. | Internet and terrorism. | Youth—Political activity. | Violence in video games—Social aspects. | Radicalization. | Militarization.
Classification: LCC HQ799.9.I58 M37 2021 | DDC 004.67/8083—dc23
LC record available at https://lccn.loc.gov/2020049669

ISBN: 978-1-138-04326-8 (hbk)
ISBN: 978-1-138-04327-5 (pbk)
ISBN: 978-1-315-17324-5 (ebk)

Typeset in Garamond
by Apex CoVantage, LLC

To my friends, I couldn't have written this without you.

Contents

	Preface	viii
1	Introduction	1
2	The Social War: Hybrid-Warfare and the Application of Social Media as Perceptual Weaponry	9
3	Playing@War: Video Games, New Media and Modern Warfare	27
4	*GoPro*-War, Live Streaming and the Gamification and Cinematic Construction of Terror and Armed Conflict-Themed Media	50
5	"Toughen Up": Cultural Politics and the Hardening of Youth	63
6	The Corruption of Language: "Radicalization"	84
7	"Hell Is Empty. And All the Devils Are Here.": Apocalyptic Thinking and the Emergence of "Death Cults"	103
8	Habitus and the Mechanics of Militarization	126
9	Militarization: The New "Civilizing Process"	145
10	Conclusion: The *Drumbeat* – Perpetual Social War	159
	Index	168

Preface

> The true hero, the true subject, the center of the Iliad is force. Force employed by man, force that enslaves man, force before which man's flesh shrinks away. In this work, at all times, the human spirit is shown as modified by its relations with force, as swept away, blinded, by the very force it imagined it could handle, as deformed by the weight of the force it submits to. For those dreamers who considered that force, thanks to progress, would soon be a thing of the past, the Iliad could appear as an historical document; for others, whose powers of recognition are more acute and who perceive force, today as yesterday, at the very center of human history, the Iliad is the purest and the loveliest of mirrors.
>
> Simone Weil (1965). *The Illiad, or the Poem of Force*.

Recently I revisited a classic depiction of warfare, Stanley Kubrick's 1987 film *Full Metal Jacket* (Twentieth Century Fox). It reminded me of how hard it has traditionally been to break down the civilian persona and to then replace it with a mental framework that one character in the film describes as signifying being "born again hard". The opening sequence of the film depicts the initial stages of the process the military calls *"soldierization"*. Kubrick begins his movie on Parris Island, South Carolina – a Marine Corps Recruit Depot, where *"Marines are Made"*. He chose to begin the first third of his film with a depiction of the initial stages in the creation of a Marine, we follow the process of dismantling the civilian mental framework of the recently arrived military recruit. The film is set in 1968, at the height of an increasingly unpopular South East Asian conflict – the Vietnam War. In the film's opening sequences, we see the main characters, as well as the other members of the unit having their civilian haircuts literally shorn off like sheep. This is the beginning of a process of "de-humanization", of breaking down the civilian sense of self, only to be replaced by the "Marine" psyche.

The scene which follows the haircutting event, focuses on the initial introduction of the newly formed unit to their Gunnery Sergeant, the lead training Non-Commissioned Officer (NCO). The Sergeant played by Lee Emory proceeds to insult, humiliate and assault the recruits as part of his welcome to basic training. This scene further extends the notion that the initial training of new recruits centers on breaking down their sense of self, of who they are, as well as introducing them to a whole new world – where the rules are not those of the civilian life, but are the product of centuries of military practice at hardening youth. The recruits are being welcomed into one of the five types of "Total Institution" that Erving Goffman wrote in 1961 – the "Army barracks" (Goffman, 1961). In the 21st century the process of soldierization does not need to take place within a "total institution" such as Parris Island – it can begin, online, in the bedroom, the lounge room or the college dorm. The internet is able to help project images, online experiences, a sense of community that help to weaken an individual's sense of self and their position in the world.

The purpose of this book is to examine how new forms of media and technology have facilitated in many cases the process of the breaking down of the self into a more malleable mental framework, or schema, that had not existed previously. Whilst the individual is not physically cut off from society, as in Goffman's total institutions of the asylum or the military barracks, a similar process of ideological envelopment does take place. It is digital, it is facilitated by the internet and enables the creation of a form of mental bubble in which thoughts and social and political dispositions are manipulated and fed. It is a new form of personalized propaganda that is at the call of both State and non-State actors, institutions, markets and cultural forms.

Whether it is the projection of a particular set of world views – religious, in the form of "jihad" or racial and cultural in the shape of White supremacism and neo-fascist ideology; or even the sanctioned State recruitment of youth into the military; there is a global drumbeat calling youth to arms. It is facilitated through the digital veins of the internet and the massive reach of the algorithms of Google and Facebook. The creation of animosity and open hatred at a communal and sectarian level – unheard of in Europe for decades or in the case of the United States not since its Civil War.

When I began writing this book my focus was going to be on the comparison between the way *Jihadi* groups such as the Islamic State recruited their young followers, with how State-agents targeted the same groups – young people – in an effort to recruit them. History, unlike the triumphalist assertion of Francis Fukuyama, did not end in 1989, instead we have witnessed the rebirth of the class, religious sectarian, and communal hatreds once also thought of as having disappeared. The focus necessarily changed with the re-emergence of extremist neo-Nazi and White supremacist groups – in Europe, the United States and elsewhere. As the writing progressed the similarity between the way extremist groups and State- and non-State agents were harnessing and weaponizing social media and the internet began to become evident. Coupled with this was a new awareness that many elements in popular culture and its dissemination have over the past decades become tinged with a desire to witness and celebrate violence and in many ways to cheer on a "dystopian future".

War and the preparation for war has over the history of modern society been an activity that humans have more often than not engaged in enthusiastically. At least initially in the heat of nationalism or the perception that an enemy has encroached on the territory or interests of the nation. Such enthusiasm vanished in the mud of the Somme or in the hell of the Eastern Front. Despite this, the lessons of war have never been learnt – consequently the need to have a population willing to actively engage in violence and war. As society has become more sophisticated so has the mechanism to prepare for war. This book will examine how modern sophisticated societies of the West are engaged both in the conduct and preparation for new forms of war. I will also examine how young people are attracted to the military machinations of both State and non-State actors.

These forces and processes have melded into what I am referring to as a global drumbeat – calling both the young and the old to war. This drumbeat not only beckons individuals to actively participate in war – through State and non-State military formations – it mesmerizes the population through the spectacle of the "shock and awe" of real or virtual violence. In the late 20th and continuing into the 21st century we are witness to the transformation of society into a militarized playground. Where algorithms and new forms of technology (both social and hardware based) can amplify the corrosive and base aspects of human nature – and as a consequence have reshaped what it means to be human and what constitutes a sane society.

I feel compelled to restate my complete disavowal of notions of liberal triumphalism and the subsequent dismantling of the post-Second World War social compact. The ease with which non-State and State actors have been able to dismantle any lingering sense of social solidarity which was built in the mid-20th century defeat of fascism has been awe inspiring. The 21st century is characterized by a techno-amplified neo-liberal political form that turned the planet into a playground for a vast military-industrial complex.

The pandemic that wracked the globe in 2020 was made worse in its impact and reach by the dominance of the neo-liberal political form and the creation of what I refer to in the book as the "hardening" of our culture.

Chapter 1

Introduction

The drumbeat referred to in the title of this book is a metaphor for the manner in which new forms of media have been used to attract young people to participate formally or informally in extremist actions. When I first conceived of this book the political impact of social media was only just becoming apparent. This was the drumbeat – Berger (2015) calls it a "carrier wave" – that first piqued my interest. Much of the initial academic and security analysis of this emerging trend focused on "radical" religious-oriented extremists. In commencing my work on the topic, it became increasingly obvious that it was not intellectually honest to simply focus on how one group of violent extremists had made use of the affordances presented by new forms of media and the underlying architecture of the web to project their message to a global audience. They are not alone in doing so. The period from 2015 onwards saw the dramatic application of technology such as social media to conduct information warfare and to project political messages by State and non-State actors (Audrey & Clifford, 2019; Berger, 2015; Brooking & Singer, 2016).

In this book I will examine the means through which new ideological formations such as the "Islamic terror" movement and extreme right-wing political formations have achieved a global level of recognition and often stunning propaganda successes through the manipulation of new forms of media and information technologies. As a consequence this book will not simply focus on technologically savvy Jihadist groups – no, what follows will present a nuanced discussion of how non-State agents and movements (Jihadist and the Alt-Right) as well as State actors (such as the formal military formations of the West, as well as Russian State-sponsored forces) have inserted themselves into the contemporary highly mediatized social, cultural and political landscape in an effort to engage in information and hybrid warfare in order to extend their appeal to the disaffected and alienated segments of Western societies and to inflict "perceptual" damage on their opponents.

Groups such as Islamic State (IS) have demonstrated their ability to shape minds and to attract followers to a global terror war through a sophisticated grasp of the principles of modern propaganda and a high level of media and digital literacy. However, as recent events have highlighted the use of new forms of media to achieve political goals and to engage in information warfare is not restricted to the work of religious extremists but is also an effective tool of the nascent neo-Fascist/nationalist movements – Alt-Right of the West, as well as by State actors. The term Alt-Right was first coined by the American right-wing writer Richard Spencer to encapsulate "a variety of right-wing voices at odds with the conservative establishment, including *paleocons*, libertarians, and White nationalists" (Lyons, 2017). It is important to cast a critical lens over the actions of these groupings as well as to highlight and contextualize in a sociological manner the acts of powerful State forces.

My Approach

Before I continue, I would like to mark out the conceptual starting point for this book. In an earlier work, *War/Play: Video games and the Militarization of Society* (Martino, 2015), I analyzed the emergence of militarized video games and their role in the expansion and projection of the militarization of Western society. In writing that book it was necessary to establish the standpoint from which I was viewing this phenomenon. The dominant political form in the nations of the West can be described as neo-liberal and these societies exist within the framework of what Hardt and Negri referred to as *"Empire"* (Hardt & Negri, 2001).

"Empire"

The extension of militarization, as well as the emergence of the global phenomenon of the radicalization of young people through social media/the internet, either by religious extremists (Islamic State) or nationalist ideological extremists (Alt-Right) has been made possible through and by the existence of what Hardt and Negri (2001) have described as the *"Empire"*. Australia and Europe form constituent elements in this globe spanning political, cultural, economic and military hegemon. The *"Empire"* functions as it does in the 21st century as a result of the extension of new forms of technology; in particular the growth and widespread use of the internet. The internet has enabled the flow and reach of ideas in ways that are unparalleled in human history. As well as the extension in the reach of information, the internet has enabled individuals and groups to make contact, to organize and to create virtual political and social communities.

These communities are virtual spaces, manifested and facilitated by and through advances in information technology – and have created "bubbles" where likeminded people are able to organize, socialize, educate and "radicalize". Within these spaces political activists have been able to radicalize disaffected youth and prepare them either to enter formal military structures as with Islamic State in Iraq and Syria or to conduct actions at home, in their own locations. The *Empire* to which Hardt and Negri first referred has created within its borders a set of flows: economic, cultural, ideological and informational. These flows amplify both the reach of contemporary neo-liberal capitalism, but also the extent to which both State and non-State agents can disseminate their world view and recruit followers.

For the purposes of this book the globe spanning *Empire* and its networks of power and ideology will provide the backdrop for our understanding of the reach and impact of militarized thinking.

Theory

This book draws inspiration from the approach adopted by the critical thinkers – such as Horkheimer and Adorno – who still have much to tell us about the workings of advanced capitalist society. A critical theory stance is the only approach that made sense to me in grappling with these massive social forces – militarization and the reconfiguring of Western society. We have entered a period akin to the "Dark Times" that Hannah Arendt (1968) once wrote about. The first half of the last century led to slaughter on an industrial scale and the potential – through technological advances – for the complete obliteration of the human race. The Cold War that lasted till the late 1990s had in a sense prevented global conflict through the existence of a "balance of terror". Our century is as complex and troubled as the last – it is perhaps even more at risk of a drift into the ultimate conflict. Arendt's phrase "Dark Times" resonates in a profound and existential way in our own era.

In the book I also draw on a broader set of thinkers' concepts which help me to make sense of this decades-long set of processes and their impact on young people and the broader society. Where appropriate I will also make reference to the writing of Virilio and his argument concerning media, perception and warfare (Virilio, 2006; Virilio & Lotringer, 1997; Virilio & Richard, 2012) in order to understand the relationship between new media, video games and warfare. I have also used a range of sociological and historical studies such as the work of Elias (2000) to build my analysis. For the purpose of this book I will draw on and add to the arguments that emerged from my earlier work (Martino, 2015) in order to analyze the relationship between social media, video games and forms of digital and popular culture (Doueihi, 2011), extremism and the process of militarization and their implications for young people.

I am not arguing that we should use a tick-box approach to social theory in order to study the re-configuring of society. I reject the argument that every new or emergent theoretical notion should be added to the lexicon of Critical theory. I wish to assert that the tradition of Critical theory has not lost its power to provide a useful set of explanatory tools. It does need to be more effectively tuned to the nature of the information-rich form of contemporary capitalist society. However, in also referring to other "critical" approaches I am not rejecting the essential project of Critical theory – understanding the nature of humanity under the conditions of advanced capitalism.

The decades long retreat into the academic debate and study concerning notions of identity or other hyper-individualist matters has rendered much of social science impotent in the face of the emergence of nascent forms of fascism and the expansion of extreme forms of exploitation and economic disparity. Contemporary societies are today split along class lines – much as they have been over the past 150 years. What is different today is that until quite recently the debates in the social sciences have all but ignored the gaping chasm that exists between those social groups who have benefitted from the expansion of neo-liberal social, economic and political manifestations and have the time, resources and energy to engage in the quest for individual fulfilment, and the social groups within society who struggle simply to exist. This blindness to the political and the economic can no longer be sustained nor defended.

Critical Theory: What Is Old Is New Again

For many years as an intellectual and keen observer of the nature of the contemporary, I have been concerned that we have not been intellectually prepared for the emergence of extremist forces and practices under capitalism in the 21st Century. The pyrrhic victory of the West over the authoritarian pseudo-socialist states of the East ushered in a brief period of self-congratulation. The West had won – the evil of "existing communism" was vanquished – much as Frodo defeated the Eye of Sauron in the *Lord of the Rings*. There was only one problem – without an ideological adversary capitalism has lurched in the direction of the extremism of neo-liberalism (with the dismantling of the welfare state; the crushing of organized labor and the complete capitulation to the needs and desires of the global "One Percent"). It also created an ideological vacuum that didn't really make itself clear until the mid-2010s. Into that vacuum extremists of the religious and non-religious type asserted themselves. In the Middle East they grasped the coat tails of the popular pro-democratic movements of the Arab Spring and helped topple dictators. These leaders' erstwhile client states of the American Empire were replaced by equally heinous regimes and movements – as in Egypt, or in the territory once controlled by the Islamic State, for example in Syria.

In the West and the former states of the Soviet Union populist movements have emerged this century to fill the gnawing hole in the political psyche of the working class and those who feel left behind. Trump, Orban (in Hungary) and others spoke to and on behalf of the politically disenfranchised – those who have lost hope that there could be an alternative to the militarily hardened contemporary neo-liberal State. Segments of the population in the West are now weary of war and weary of the effects of the constant disruption and destruction embedded in contemporary neo-liberalism. They crave certainty, they crave a sense of the imagined tranquility and stability of the past – the prosperity of their childhood and the post-War halcyon days of economic growth and personal freedom.

The emergence of the seductive siren song of the extremists (religious and non-religious) and the populists of Europe and North America has taken many thinkers and analysts by surprise. Trump – it was said – was doomed. He could never get elected. It is my contention that we have been caught with our intellectual pants down. Whilst progressive thinkers within and outside of the academy fell in love with the language games and pastiche of the postmodern turn, history re-asserted itself – with a thump. It is in this context – grappling with the growing shadow of authoritarianism, neo-fascism and the insanity of the IS "Death Cult" that Critical theory has once more gained traction as an analytical set of tools. For many long decades to even contemplate using the term Critical theory would open one to derision and muffled guffaws.

It is now not only important but essential that we find the tools and the intellectual disposition and fortitude to examine, critique and hopefully ultimately prevail over the extremist, anti-democratic and neo-fascist ideologies now set loose in the contemporary political landscape. There is a shadow over the minds of segments of the populations of the West. Irrational thought, disbelief in and disregard for the truth now occupy every corner of structures such as the internet and in popular discourse in general. Ideas which were thought long buried – such as anti-Semitism – are now openly expressed, both on the left and the right (BBC, 2019; Cose, 2018) – the blood of the innocents is all but forgotten.

Capitalism exists, it is not a word game. The economic structures that govern our lives are structured to benefit the few and not the multitude (Hardt & Negri, 2006). The social and political systems put in place to govern and reproduce this structure are real. The rise of extremist movements – both religious, such as the Islamic State, and non-religious, such as the neo-fascist Alt-Right, are a logical expression of a system that generates increasing levels of alienation and that is based on exploitation and imperialism, and is structured to maintain the wars that have continued both hot and cold since the mid-20th century.

As Fuchs (2015) has pointed out:

> the neoliberal mode of capitalism [has] resulted in [the] worldwide dramatic [rise] of inequality and precarious life and labor, which [has] culminated in a new global economic crisis that started in 2008.

> Coming to grips with class, inequality, and capitalism again became a crucial dimension of the social sciences. This development has resulted in a rising importance of critical theory approaches both in the social sciences in general and media and communication studies in particular. Critical theory is an approach that is of crucial importance for understanding contemporary society and political communication.
>
> (Fuchs, 2015)

The intellectual tools and the framework which have come to be described as "Critical theory" are the product of a tradition that traces its origins back to the work begun by Karl Marx in the mid-19th Century. Drawing on both the work of Marx and other significant thinkers, such as Freud, the *Institute for Social Research (Institut für Sozialforschung, IfS)* was established in Frankfurt in 1923. From that point on its members – Max Horkheimer, Theodor Adorno and Herbert Marcuse, to name some of the best-known thinkers in the *Institute* – began a project that had at its core the goal of explaining both the nature and structure of capitalism, but also of understanding how it was manifesting itself in the psyche of the inhabitants of modern societies such as Germany. The Frankfurt School was forced to move to America in the 1930s as a result of the rise of the German Nazi Party. The use of the term "critical" to describe the work of the Frankfurt school after their escape from Europe in the 1930s should be seen in the context of needing to disguise their work amidst the anti-Marxist intellectual and political atmosphere that has dominated Western thinking from the mid-century onwards (Held, 1980).

In applying an analytical lens to this set of problems I have, as I said earlier, drawn on Critical theory, and a number of sociological perspectives which whilst not strictly "Critical theory" have added to the toolbox of critical analysis of advanced capitalism. Here I am referring to Hardt and Negri (Empire), Virilio (perceptual damage), Bourdieu (habitus), and Elias (civilizing). One theoretical framework or approach cannot do justice to the complex nature of this advanced form of capitalism that now governs the planet, unchecked. When I use the term Critical theory, I am drawing on all the above.

Aims of the Book

This book will examine the way new forms of technology have been harnessed both by State and non-State actors to attract new followers and recruits into political/military endeavors and formations. In the chapters which follow, new forms of technology and social media, as well as forms and genres within popular culture, will be examined and placed within the context of the emergence of the process of militarization. It will be asserted that the decades-long process of militarization emerged out of the establishment of the Military-Industrial Complex – an offshoot of the Total War economy and political form established in the mid-20th century as part of the struggle to defeat the Axis. The vast array of visible and invisible relations of production and political and cultural formations strategies and tactics never went away (Martino, 2015). This machinery has re-configured capitalist society and has had a vast array of new tools – digital technology – to further entrench itself within the fabric of everyday life.

The book also aims to help the reader to think through how new forms of media and technology have contributed to what I have referred to as the hardening of youth and the entrenchment of perpetual warfare in the form of a digital "social war" – amplified and extended by and through the internet and social media. Violent video games and new streaming platforms that present unrestrained images of violence and brutality have also helped create a distinctly less humane stage in our social evolution. This is not a moral stance, or a version of the oral panic that has been met by many new forms of technology and media. I am arguing that we have entered a stage in our social and cultural development in which violence, military ideas and actions (terrorist- and State-sanctioned) are an acceptable element in our everyday lives. State and non-State actors compete for our attention and allegiance in a data- and media-drenched environment.

In understanding where we find ourselves today the thoughts of great thinkers such as Hannah Arendt can help to sustain us in our quest for understanding. Writing about the darkness that engulfed the world in the mid-20th century, Arendt argued that

> even in the darkest of times we have the right to expect some illumination.
>
> (Arendt, 1968)

References

Arendt, H. (1968). *Men in dark times*. Houghton Mifflin Harcourt.
Audrey, A., & Clifford. B. (2019). Doxing and Defacements: Examining the Islamic State's Hacking Capabilities. *CTC Sentinel, 11*(4), 7. Retrieved from https://ctc.usma.edu/app/uploads/2019/04/CTC-SENTINEL-042019.pdf
BBC (2019). Ilhan Omar: US House votes amid anti-Semitism row. Retrieved from https://www.bbc.com/news/world-us-canada-47488272
Berger, J. M. (2015). The metronome of apocalyptic time: Social media as carrier wave for millenarian contagion. *Perspectives on Terrorism*. Retrieved from http://terrorismanalysts.com/pt/index.php/pot/article/view/444
Brooking, E., & Singer, P. (2016). War goes viral. Retrieved from x-devonthink-item://D1882583-9A5B-4F2C-BCE0-2498D59581E5
Cose, E. (2018). One year after Charlottesville, Trump has normalized racism in America. *USA Today*. Retrieved from https://www.usatoday.com/story/opinion/2018/08/10/white-supremacists-neo-nazis-charlottesville-unite-right-rally-trump-column/935708002/

Doueihi, M. (2011). *Digital cultures*. Harvard University Press.
Elias, N. (2000). *The civilizing process: Sociogenetic and psychogenetic investigations*. Oxford, UK and Malden, MA: Blackwell Publishers.
Fuchs, C. (2015). Critical theory. In G. Mazzoleni, K. G. Barnhurst, K. I. Ikeda, H. Wessler, & R. C. Maia (Eds.), *The international encyclopedia of political communication* (Vol. 1). John Wiley & Sons.
Hardt, M., & Negri, A. (2001). *Empire*. Harvard University Press.
Hardt, M., & Negri, A. (2006). *Multitude*. Penguin Books.
Held, D. (1980). *Introduction to critical theory: Horkheimer to Habermas* (Vol. 261). University of California Press.
Lyons, M. N. (2017). Ctrl-alt-delete: The origins and ideology of the alternative right. Somerville, MA: Political Research Associates, January, 20.
Martino, J. (2015). *War/play: Video games and the militarization of society*. New York: Peter Lang.
Virilio, P. (2006). *Speed and politics*. Los Angeles: Semiotext(e).
Virilio, P., & Lotringer, S. (1997). *Pure war* (Rev. ed. H1 – British Library H2 – DSC m02/26332 H1 – British Library H2 – HMNTS YC.1999.a.2298 ed.). New York: Semiotext(e).
Virilio, P., & Richard, B. (2012). *The administration of fear* (Vol. 10). London: Semiotext(e).

Chapter 2

The Social War

Hybrid-Warfare and the Application of Social Media as Perceptual Weaponry

The Social War and the Tools of Perception

In early December 2016, Edgar M. Welch from North Carolina travelled to Comet Ping Pong pizzeria in Washington D.C., not far from the University of the District of Columbia. Welch was not looking for a slice of pizza. On his arrival he opened fire with a military grade assault rifle, an AR-15 (Kang & Goldman, 2016). No one was killed or hurt in the attack, but it was nevertheless a frightening act of domestic terrorism. What was it that sparked this attack? What was it that led a father of two to decide to get in his car and literally launch an assault on the pizzeria and its customers? Simply put, Welch had read a feed on the internet that claimed that the Comet Ping Pong pizzeria was a front for a Democrat-run sex slave operation. Stories had been circulated on Facebook and Twitter alleging that Hillary Clinton, the Democrat candidate for President in the 2016 election, was running the venture (Kang & Goldman, 2016). According to court testimony, Welch surrendered peacefully when he discovered that there were no "children . . . being harbored in the restaurant" (Kang & Goldman, 2016). This attack was the consequence of the unparalleled use of social media to transmit "fake news" in order to influence the thoughts and actions of American voters. What happened in the United States in 2016 was, in my thinking, part of a larger set of processes which have had the effect of using information to both persuade and attack. Information has been weaponized as part of what I will refer to as the Social War. The 2016 US Presidential election campaign has been highlighted as an example of the way new forms of media can reach and influence populations through the manipulation of, or at least the "gaming" of, the algorithms which lie at the heart of social media and the web.

Fake news as it emerged in 2016 is one example of the conscious manipulation of the social media landscape as a form of perceptual weaponry. Fake news can be defined as a form of internet content generated by groups and individuals in order to influence the political consciousness of specific populations. Examples of fake news and social media manipulation from that period and the impact that these technologies have had on setting the tone and agenda of political discourse have been examined in detail by others (Enli, 2017).

What occurred during that period was the culmination of a sustained political intrusion into the American political process (Allcott & Gentzkow, 2017). The use of fake news is only one example of the weaponization of information as part of a broader campaign of mis-information – and what we will refer to as "Information Warfare" within Western societies (Boatwright, Linvill, & Warren, 2018; Boyd et al., 2018; Brooking & Singer, 2016). The application of information in this manner in the period leading up to the 2020s has set the tone for how politics is now conducted in Western societies. Politics in Western nations is now a site for political warfare engaged in by both State and non-State actors.

It is my assertion that this is not politics as usual. The Information Warfare strategies developed in the post-Cold War period by the United States and successfully applied in the 1990s (Ganley, 1991) and the first decades of this century have now been turned upon Western nations by both State and non-State actors. Information Warfare strategies, augmented by the new social technologies such as Facebook, TikTok and the wide array of communication tools, for example *Signal* and *Telegram* (there are many more), have been harnessed to disrupt, manipulate and delegitimize institutions, political norms and practices within the democracies of the West (Shead, 2019; Singer & Brooking, 2018). This is what I have described as a new form of war: a "social war".

The Social War and Information "Intangibles"

When I am using the term social war I am referring to the manner with which State and non-State actors are able to use new forms of media and digital technologies to transcend national boundaries and narrowcast their message directly to individuals through the algorithmic technologies underpinning social media applications and the search engines that are used to navigate the internet. The term social war refers to "intangibles" (internet, social media, video games and streaming media) as providing the technological affordances that enable State and non-State actors to use information in order to engage in algorithmic based perceptual warfare.

For the purposes of this discussion the term information refers to an array of what Toffler and Toffler (1997) described as "intangibles". In this context information encompasses

> knowledge, in its broadest sense [to include] ideas, innovation, values, imagination, symbols, and imagery, [and] not just computer data . . . being a product of or being transmitted by a range of technologies.
> (Toffler & Toffler, 1997)

The intangibles Toffler and Toffler (1997) describe are crucial to our understanding of this new form of warfare. "Ideas, innovation, values, imagination, symbols, and imagery" are at the center of this set of practices and technologies. When the Tofflers were writing they had not envisaged the complex social web and molecular levels of information dissemination made possible through the internet, social media, video games and streaming media. The globalized nature of these technologies has, as Friedman (2003) argued, flattened out the world. What happens in one corner of the world has immanence across the globe. In many ways war and terror have been amongst the greatest beneficiaries of these technologies. An idea or an illness can travel at lightning speed across the globe. Speed and connectivity have enhanced the capacity for information to become in a sense another form of weaponry – in many ways almost as lethal as traditional kinetic weapons, and capable of inflicting harm – social, cultural and psychological upon one's enemy (Floridi, 2014).

The use of information as a weapon is as I have asserted no longer the preserve of State actors – social media and the internet have in effect democratized the tools and strategies of propaganda, or at least made it possible for non-State actors to also engage in Information Warfare. At the core of this democratized form of Information Warfare is the application of relatively easy to access forms of technology such as *GoPro* cameras, *iPhones* and microblogging platforms such as Facebook and video publishing platforms such as YouTube as well as video games. These forms of technology comprise what can be described as "perceptual weaponry". The combination of these technologies enables the projection of political propaganda in new and far reaching ways.

War by Other Means: Information Warfare in the 21st Century

Information Warfare has existed in various forms for decades – what has emerged as a new set of practices in the period after 2015 has been the ability to manipulate the underlying algorithms of software such as Facebook and Twitter to project political propaganda through the weaponization of social and new media forms (Boatwright et al., 2018; Brooking & Singer, 2016; Gardner, 2018). This is not to argue that information technology had not been used creatively before to accomplish political goals. The collapse of the former Soviet Union for example was helped along the way by computer bulletin boards and the "low-tech" facsimile machine (Ganley, 1991) through the spreading of a counter narrative to State-controlled media.

The extent to which information is now seen both as a threat and also as an asset is illustrated by the establishment of the US Cyber Command. The Cyber Command was created to deal with the emergence of a set of new information technology-based threats to the United States and its allies. According to the Cyber Command:

> Cyberspace threats are growing. They transcend geographic boundaries and are usually trans-regional in nature. States possess resources and patience to sustain sophisticated cyber campaigns to penetrate even well-protected networks, manipulate software and data, and destroy data, computers, and systems. Russia, China, Iran, and North Korea invest in military capabilities that reduce our military's competitive advantages and compromise our national security. Some of these states have demonstrated the resolve, technical capability, and persistence to undertake strategic cyberspace campaigns, including theft of intellectual property and personally identifiable information that are vital to our defenses. Disruptive technologies will eventually accelerate our adversaries' ability to impose costs.
>
> (Command, 2018)

Beyond the threat posed by global competitors such as China and Russia, the US Cyber Command has highlighted the threat posed by non-State actors in the new digital battlespace. According to the US Cyber Command:

> Aggressive non-state actors like terrorists, criminals, and hacktivists pose lesser threats than states but can still damage our military capabilities and critical infrastructure, as well as endanger American lives. Violent extremist organizations, such as the Islamic State of Iraq and Syria, al-Qaida, and affiliated groups, are destabilizing whole regions, attacking our global interests, and endangering our homeland and citizens around the world. These groups use cyberspace to promote their ideology, inspire followers, and control operations that threaten our allies and us.
>
> (Command, 2018)

Whilst the US Cyber Command posits a clear distinction in the threat level posed by State and non-State actors – the confluence of activities engaged in by these groups has created a new form of warfare. This is not a World War, nor is it a "Total War" in the sense that we understood this to mean in the 20th century (Baumann & Hellmann, 2001). As I pointed out above, there is a new phenomenon emerging, one which is multi-faceted and not easily defined. It comprises elements of the "low-intensity conflicts" of the Cold War, with the newly emergent hybrid and Information Warfare carried out by State and non-State actors. I am referring to this complex set of interlocking practices, technologies and military/political strategies as "the social war". It is my assertion that the use by State and non-State actors of the tools of Information Warfare – tools honed during the long decades of the Cold War – has been augmented by the widespread use and application of social media and other forms of internet-based technologies. Thus creating a new hybrid form of warfare, which is something I'd like to refer to as "social war".

War is no longer simply, as Margaret Mead argued, the condition "in which defined groups engage in purposeful, organized and socially sanctioned combat involving killing each other" (Mead, 1968). In the 21st century a form of warfare has evolved which employs a much more complex and fluid set of strategies and practices than traditional forms of war – Hybrid-warfare. Hybrid-warfare blends informational and traditional forms of war into a new and less conventional approach to conflict. Hybrid-warfare has been defined as encompassing

> full spectrum wars with both physical and conceptual dimensions: the former, a struggle against an armed enemy and the latter, a wider struggle for, control and support of the combat zone's indigenous population, the support of the home fronts of the intervening nations, and the support of the international community.
>
> (McCuen, 2008)

The North Atlantic Treaty Organization (NATO) in 2011 described the emergence of a range of "hybrid threats" consisting of, "a wide range of overt and covert military, paramilitary, and civilian measures [. . .] employed in a highly integrated design" (Aaronson, Diessen, De Kermabon, Long, & Miklaucic, 2011).

Hybrid-warfare has been the preserve of State actors – sovereign military formations and or their proxies, as in the Russian-initiated conflict in Ukraine (Monaghan, 2015). For the purpose of this book I wish to adapt or add to the formal military definitions of Hybrid-war to encompass a much broader set of militarized activities. These activities are not confined to territorial conflicts but encapsulate a wide array of emergent low-intensity conflicts – including but not limited to acts sanctioned by State actors – (sovereign military formations) and/or their proxies.

Here I am referring to the idea of a social war – a social media and internet amplified form of Informational warfare. This form of warfare does not include the kinetic aspects of Hybrid-warfare as practiced by the Russian Federation in the Ukraine (Monaghan, 2015; Rožukalne & Sedlenieks, 2017; Thiele, 2015). But it has become a weapon and has at its core the weaponization of information as a tool to be applied to both military and civilian populations. The example – though now from some time ago – with which I began this chapter reflects the capacity for information to spread fear and to encourage civil conflict. I refer to this as creating an "architecture of fear" and thus helps build the acceptance of militarization as the key organizing principle of the advanced societies of the West.

Weaponizing Social Media and Information

The advent of social media has enabled non-State actors to engage in a form of global perceptual conflict. The size of the organization is irrelevant. The tools of social media and the algorithms embedded within the search engines of the internet, enable the amplification of messages. This is an extension of the modern dominant form of asymmetrical warfare. New forms of media enable small groups to add to their arsenal of weapons through the application of perception as a form of weaponry. The use of perception as a weapon has enabled these groups to amplify both their message, as well as their impact. These new tools enable groups such as Islamic State and the Alt-Right to impact their adversaries in ways that are far beyond their actual political–military power. These new tools enable them to affect perception – to create a propaganda message that rivals that of the large well-organized military political formations of State actors. In fact, the new forms of technology have enabled groups such as the so-called Islamic State and individuals to challenge nation states, alliances and undermine social cohesion in a way other similar terror groups were never able to do.

Social media and the internet have been harnessed to meet the needs of a range of groups, institutions and individuals engaged in new hybrid forms of warfare. As I have argued elsewhere these groups can be either State or non-State actors – they are able to make use of this technology to both inform and to also influence populations. Specifically, this influence has taken the form of the weakening of social cohesion – pitting populations against each other through fake news – or the weakening of institutions such as what occurred in the Brexit campaign of 2016 and the US Presidential election held in the same year.

One of the prime uses made of social media, for example, is in the dissemination of negative and apocalyptic thinking. This form of thinking has been at the core of the ideological message being disseminated by extremist groups of both the religious and non-religious type. In a study of the propagation of apocalyptic thinking by groups such as the Islamic State, Peter Berger has identified the way social media has been utilized.

Berger (2015) has argued that

> social media has inherent utility to amplify and facilitate the transmission and inculcation of apocalyptic beliefs through three key mechanisms: 1. Temporal compression: A belief that prophesied events preceding or accompanying the end of history are imminent or already underway, and that the clock is literally running out. Social media helps accomplish this through the pace of postings and updates relative to older forms of media. 2. Social contagion: Intense social contact and prolonged interaction spreads apocalyptic memes in an impactful, life-changing manner. Social media empowers such contact over wide geographical areas and also makes contact with potentially violent

people safer for the curious. 3. Immersion: The diminishment and eventual replacement of normal existence with a heightened experience of an alternate interpretation of reality. This is achieved through both the volume of ISIS's media output, combined with the always-on transmission of that output online, and its content.

(Berger, 2015)

For the purpose of this book I am going to use the term "social war" to distinguish a set of practices and strategies within the broader construct which has been described as Hybrid-warfare. Both the terms Information Warfare and Hybrid-warfare do not capture the specific contours of what has emerged as a new and potent political–military strategy. Both concepts describe the application of non-kinetic weaponry (Information War) and a continuum from propaganda activities to the application of kinetic weapons (Hybrid-war). In the case of Information Warfare here I am referring to actions such as the Stuxnet attack on Iran's nuclear capability (Falliere, Murchu, & Chien, 2011). The form of Hybrid-war that I am referring to has been successfully applied by the Russian Federation in Ukraine, as mentioned previously (Thiele, 2015).

The amalgam of Information-War and Hybrid-war in the mid-2010s has created the circumstances in which it is often difficult to discern whether an act of cyber-war, cyber-espionage or "Trolling" has occurred. In this context it can be difficult to identify if the actions of State or non-State actors are responsible for an attack or an intervention (here I am referring to the initially non-identified subversion of the United States Presidential elections of 2016 (Boyd et al., 2018)).

The Russian "Troll Factory"

The term "non-linear" warfare has been applied to describe the methods and strategies used by State sponsored actors such as the Russian "Troll factory" – the Internet Research Agency (Boatwright et al., 2018; Gardner, 2018). Gardner (2018) has described the origins of the concept of non-linear war in a work of fiction written by a Russian confidant of Vladimir Putin. In a work of dystopian fiction, Vladislav Surkov, writing under the pseudonym Nathan Dubovitsky, described a conflict scenario where a non-linear war breaks out. In his story Surkov describes the scenario:

> It was the first non—linear war. In the primitive wars of the 19th and 20th centuries it was common for just two sides to fight. Two countries, two blocks of allies. Now four coalitions collided. Not two against two, or three against one. All against all (as cited in Pomerantsev, 2014, para. 3).

(Gardner, 2018)

Though this was a work of fiction it contains the germ of what we are now witnessing. Today State and non-State actors have been able to engage in this social war to militarize, radicalize and recruit followers or to attack the social cohesion of their enemy. We have witnessed the growing ability of State and non-State actors to harness the technologies of modern communication to engage in the now decades-long permanent war that began in the 1990s (Bacevich, 2010; Betts, 2012). I am also interested in the way Alt-Right groups have been energized by the potential of social media and the internet to both recruit new activists and supporters, but also to engage in Information Warfare against minority groups, the State and other non-State actors, in particular those on the left.

Non-State actors such as the Islamic State, as well as other modern political movements – the Alt-Right for example – as well as nation-states, have been able to employ social media to engage in this new social war. The concept of a social war is people-centric – it depends on both human subjects becoming a target for its activities and also its collateral damage. The social war is promulged through the technology affordances embedded in social media and the web.

The term social in this context refers to the information based mechanisms used by State actors such as national militaries (Command, 2018; Martino, 2015), and also by non-State actors such as the Islamic State (Chung, 2016; Goracy, 2016) and the Alt-Right (O'Callaghan, Greene, Conway, Carthy, & Cunningham, 2016) to engage in a form of conflict which heavily leverages social media and the web. These groupings rely on the ability of the affordances that new technologies offer to create a form of "sociality" (Cetina, 1997) through objects, and to weaponize information. The notion that objects in contemporary society can act as a mechanism for the creation of new forms of sociality was first promulgated by Cetina (1997). It is my contention that the ability of objects to foster a new form of sociality is at the core of the 21st century's unique form of warfare – the social war.

Cetina (1997) was writing at the turn of the century in an era in which the identity politics of today first emerged but had yet to gain widespread acknowledgement and cultural and political significance. According to Cetina (1997) the new technologies made possible through the expansion of the internet were creating spaces in which new identities and forms of community could emerge. At the time Cetina also argued that

> the modern untying of identities has been accompanied by the expansion of object centered environments which situate and stabilize selves, define individual identity just as much as communities or families used to do, and which promote forms of sociality (social forms of binding self and other) that feed on and supplement the human forms of sociality studied by social scientists.
>
> (Cetina, 1997)

In this context identity and the forms of community that these new technologies began to make possible began a process that has led to the creation of technology-dependent relationships. Cetina describes this as "objectualization" and argues that a

> strong thesis of "objectualization" would imply that objects displace human beings as relationship partners and embedding environments, or that they increasingly mediate human relationships, making the latter dependent on the former.
>
> (Cetina, 1997)

The sociality inherent in new forms of communications technology has meant that both State and non-State actors are able to create links and a type of social connection hitherto unknown. Social media, the web, and other forms of new media as well as various strands within popular culture provide conduits or mechanisms that radicalize and militarize people. Young people in particular have been the focus of the radicalization and militarization processes. They are both the target of these practices and some have become participants or materiel in a new form of warfare.

The notion of social war shares some of the strategies and practices previously referred to as Hybrid-war (Hoffman, 2009; Jasper & Moreland, 2016; Monaghan, 2015; Thiele, 2015). However, the strategies and practices underpinning social war have been augmented and more broadly applied than the examples of Hybrid-war described earlier. Both Hybrid-warfare and social war draw upon new forms of media and technology which have been added to the existing kinetic elements essential to the conduct of traditional forms of war. Here I am referring to social media, the web, video games and the pro-war/violent strains within popular culture (such as Mixed Martial Arts – MMA), which have helped extend the reach of and augment traditional State and non-State forms of propaganda and war fighting.

The Social War: Beyond Simple Propaganda

For centuries propaganda has been used in times of war as an effective adjunct to armed conflict and as a means of maintaining public support. Governments have now gained new affordances through the harnessing of advances in digital technology in their efforts to shape attitudes. Traditional forms of propaganda have utilized existing and dominant modes of communication to disseminate political-ideological messages. New forms of technology such as social media, the web and the proliferation of information technologies have extended the reach of governments and others interested in shaping opinions and promoting ideological positions.

The term propaganda is complex and has no clear definition. It has been used to describe processes where information is communicated to populations as a method of promoting particular ideological or political objectives (Jowett & O'Donnell, 2011; Lasswell, 1995). Jowett and O'Donnell have described propaganda as

> the deliberate, systematic attempt to shape perceptions, manipulate cognitions, and direct behaviour to achieve a response that furthers the desired intent of the propagandist.
> (Jowett & O'Donnell, 2011)

During the last major global conflict (the Second World War), contemporary media – in particular film – was used as a highly engaging vehicle for the communication of propaganda messages. One of the most effective examples of this tactic from the time was Frank Capra's Second World War US Army propaganda film series, *Why We Fight*, which was produced in order to promote America's involvement in the war and to canvass the core values of the American-led "Free World" (which in the latter phase of the war morphed into the United Nations) in opposition to the "Slave World" of the Axis.

As a work of propaganda *Why We Fight* was a masterpiece and played a significant role in positioning the United States for its successful participation in the Second World War. The use of modern forms of media to project national interests in time of war proved highly successful in the last century. The practice of adapting new technologies to the needs of the nation – both in times of "hot" and "cold" wars – has endured into our own century. For example, early in the 2000s it became apparent that video games offered a new space within which national political interests could be both played out – via games scenarios – and also utilized to generate pro-military ideas in the population as part of the process of "militarization" (I will devote a considerable portion of the book to examine this idea).

Here I am referring to the First-Person Shooter (FPS) genre of video games, such as *America's Army*, and other military-themed games, for example the *Call of Duty* series, both of which share a realistic aesthetic with *Why We Fight*. This is not the *Yankee Doodle Dandy* (1942) form of propaganda – it is not a Hollywood song-and-dance film like those popular at the time. *Why We Fight* set out the case for war and reported on its progress in unblinking realism. *America's Army* depicts realistic training and combat scenarios and has serious intent just as *Why We Fight* had had in the previous century. First Person Shooters, such as the US Army-produced *America's Army* or *Call of Duty*, share another facet with *Why We Fight*: they project American power (albeit in a "soft" form) and are a form of perceptual weaponry. Frank Capra was consciously crafting a propaganda message. The message he crafted was tailored to respond to the powerful Nazi-propaganda vehicle, Leni Riefenstahl's *Triumph of the Will* (1935).

America's Army was created at a time of war in the period after 9/11 both as a means of recruiting individuals but also as a way of reaching out to America's adversaries to display – in a form readily accessible to young people – examples of the power and prestige of the American military in the 21st century. Admirers of *America's Army* were quick to compare it favorably to Capra's propaganda films. In the early years of Gulf War II and Afghanistan the case was made that these conflicts were part of a global struggle similar to the Second World War (Au, 2002, 2004). In a piece written for *Salon.com* at the time of the creation of *America's Army*, game critic and designer Wagner James Au (2002) made the case for the adoption of FPS games as ideological weapons in the "War on Terror" and drew a connection between the Capra films and this form of gaming. According to Au:

> *America's Army* and *Delta Force: Black Hawk Down* are the "Why We Fight" for the digital generation. Though not explicitly doctrinaire in an ideological sense, by showing the very young how we fight, applying the moral application of lethal force on behalf of liberal values, these games create the wartime culture that is so desperately needed now. One hopes they'll inspire the best gamers to consider a career of military service, while preparing them for the battles to come. There are even indications that playing these games provide useful experience for when they do go into real-world combat. All to the good: it will aid them in the war to conclude what is truly the unfinished business of 1945.
>
> (Au, 2002)

The creation of the "wartime culture" that Au describes was essential to the prosecution of the wars in Iraq and Afghanistan. The statement made by Au illustrates how firms within the technology, entertainment and gaming industries became active participants in the conflict. Their weapons were tools for the construction of popular culture.

America's Army and other military themed First-Person Shooters such as the *Call of Duty* series have helped to transform popular culture by embedding military themes and concepts within the daily lives of millions. Playing games such as *Call of Duty* or *America's Army* does not simulate real warfare – it does, however, reinforce the broader socio-political process of militarization. Militarization refers to "the contradictory and tense social process in which civil society organizes itself for the production of violence" (Geyer, 1989). The First-Person Shooter has been added to the repertoire of mechanisms available for the reinforcement of propaganda messages and the extension of militarized "war culture" and the organization of the "production of violence".

The use of social media and other forms of technology by non-State actors such as the Islamic State (and more recently by the nascent neo-Nazi

Alt-Right global movement) signals its utility, effectiveness and capacity as a means of disseminating propaganda. Social media has in the early decades of the 21st century become "weaponized" (Singer & Brooking, 2018) and is now able to shape perception, sway political processes – through "fake news" and the manipulation of the algorithms underpinning the search technology of the internet – as well as direct military actions/attacks through the direct messaging to and radicalization of individuals, and as a general mechanism through which violence is incited globally (Chung, 2016; Gardner, 2018).

The application of new forms of media to the process of opinion formation is no longer restricted to traditional nation states. Contemporary non-State military formations such as the so-called Islamic State that emerged out of Syria and Iraq in 2013–2014 (Glenn, 2016) have been able to use social media and other forms of new media to amplify their political and military message. In the case of the Islamic State, in 2014 it was able to harness social media and the internet to project its political message that they had created a Caliphate, and to then follow this with a global call for its followers to engage in violent action to destabilize the West (Chung, 2016; Gorka, 2015; Muñoz, 2016).

The ability to manipulate the thinking of populations in the interests of nations and political movements is not something new. For example, the mass-mobilization of populations to engage in "Total War" during the Second World War was fundamental to both Axis and Allied powers (Horne, 2019; Mackay, 2018). A key tool used in the creation of pro-war thinking and the mass-mobilizations essential for the Total War stance adopted by both the Axis and Allied forces was "propaganda" (Lasswell, 1995).

According to the French intellectual Jacques Ellul, writing in the late 1960s, we can understand propaganda as a product of the "scientific analyses of psychology and sociology" (1965). The scientific approach to understanding how people think and how society is organized has, since the early part of the 20th century, been put at the disposal of political and economic structures such as the nation State and "the market". Drawing on the growing awareness of how to effectively manipulate the political attitudes of populations, leaders were able to create the conditions necessary for the mass-mobilizations of both the First and Second World Wars. The key to these mobilizations was the advent of new forms of media and through them the projection of a propaganda message targeting the civilian population and harnessing their fear and anger for the effective prosecution of war. All parties in both conflicts engaged in one form of propaganda or another.

There is no agreed upon definition of the term "propaganda", for the purpose of this book we will consider it in its political manifestations. Here I am referring to the use of a range of tools and practices which are employed both by State and non-State actors as a method of promoting particular ideological and political actions (Jowett & O'Donnell, 2011; Lasswell, 1995). Two of the most important writers on the topic of propaganda, Jowett and O'Donnell, have argued that propaganda is "the deliberate, systematic attempt to shape perceptions, manipulate cognitions, and direct behavior to achieve a response that furthers the desired intent of the propagandist" (Jowett & O'Donnell, 2011).

In the 20th century, the creation of new forms of media and modes of communication helped to strengthen the capacity of State and non-State actors to influence populations and to more effectively present their specific world view or narrative. The propagandist has always been able to draw on printed materials, pamphlets, newspapers or art (posters, art works, etc.), however, the advent of film, audio and radio technologies in the early part of the century massively expanded the reach and influence of the modern propagandist. Perhaps the best example of modern propaganda from the 20th century was the work of the German Nazi Party (*Nationalsozialistische Deutsche Arbeiterpartei* – NSDAP or Nazi Party) and specifically the films of Leni Riefenstahl. Her body of work from the pre-war Nazi era can, I argue, be part of a broader process, the militarization of the German people through highly sophisticated propaganda vehicles such as the Nazi-era documentary *Triumph of the Will* (Riefenstahl, 1935). This is not to say that the Allies in the Second World War did not also produce sophisticated propaganda artefacts – the work of John Capra in the US Government-commissioned film series *Why We Fight* (1943) is a notable example of this.

The documentary *Triumph of the Will* (Riefenstahl, 1935) was commissioned by the Nazi Party to both document and celebrate the 1934 Party Congress in Nuremberg. From its sweeping opening depicting the arrival of the Führer's airplane delivering Hitler to Nuremberg (the spiritual home of the Nazis), the *Triumph of the Will* showcased the way in which imagery, sounds and music could be harnessed to project a coherent political message and help to construct a particular political narrative. In this case the narrative was one of Germanic unity, purity and the messianic nature of their new political leader and his movement. The documentary showcased the newfound *völkisch* (folk) unity of the German people to the world at large. The film crafted a vision of the power and capacity for national unity and war that the Nazi movement was able to marshal.

Prior to the 20th century, print media in the form of newspapers, pamphlets, books and magazines had been used as tools for propaganda. As had the various forms of art such as paintings, posters and murals. The harnessing of this relatively new media (motion pictures only became "talkies" in 1927 with the film the *Jazz Singer*) by the Nazis in the early 1930s demonstrated the role that new forms of media could play in the formation of people's attitudes and their political allegiances. This is a lesson that has remained as significant for us today as it was in the last century – technology harnessed to create new forms of media to manage the formation of people's attitudes has become another weapon in the arsenal of war and in the repertoire of control mechanisms at the disposal of political movements and governments.

Pop Culture Propaganda: Gaming, Social Media – the Case of the Islamic State

Using social media to disseminate ISIS propaganda has allowed the message to become diffuse. It is widely available to anyone who wishes to view it. Although there is a constant battle going on between the content managers who pull the content or disable the accounts and those who are continuously uploading more content, Twitter is still commonly used by ISIS supporters to disseminate and recruit. It is easy to read the feeds without having to sign in and until quite recently we have been readily able to access a multitude of accounts through the "suggestions" box that pops up. Al-Hayet Media Centre is the official ISIS media channel. It was a WordPress site where tweets and videos had been uploaded. The use of social media by IS and its supporters helps to advance the message of the empowered individual. The concept of the "foot soldier" has been very prominent in IS propaganda and although there is a strong sense of brotherhood/community/oneness, the use of social media allows the individual to assert their power and agency by allowing their voice to be heard.

In an article in the *New Yorker Magazine* in 2014, Jay King pointed out the game-like quality of IS propaganda. He argued that

> In *Halo, Call of Duty, Gears of War*, and pretty much every other F.P.S. sold today, when your first shot misses, the scope button will help you to home in on your target. The edges of the screen blur to black, the red dot jumps to simulate the shooter's heartbeat, and, when you hit the trigger button, the reaction—the gush of blood, the facial contortions, and the man's slow exit from view—is registered, frame by frame. The sequence is so familiar that, while watching the ISIS video, I, who only play such games on occasion, could feel the rhythm of the controller's commands. Right trigger (missed shot), hold down left trigger to bring up scope, orient the crosshairs, right trigger again, watch your handiwork as it falls out of the frame. The similarities between ISIS recruitment films and First-person-shooter games are likely intentional. Back in June, an ISIS fighter told the BBC that his new life was "better than that game Call of Duty."
>
> (King, 2014)

The use of the various forms of new media both as a set of propaganda and perceptual weapons, as well as a means of recruitment, has been a constant element in the military strategy of the United States in the past decades. The pioneering work of the US Army at the turn of the century set the pattern for others to follow. As pointed out in various parts of this book, the creation of *America's Army* was part of a broader strategy constructed to project a weaponized form of American culture to both attract local potential enlistees in the military as well as to strike directly at friends and foe.

Non-State actors have been adept at learning from how the United States has conducted this form of Information Warfare, as have other global rivals such as the People's Republic of China and the Russian Federation (Boyd et al., 2018; Vasu et al., 2018). Where non-State actors have added a novel and extreme variant to this set of propaganda tools and practices is in their willingness to use images and content featuring brutality and micro-level violence in projecting their messages and in creating media content which appeals to puerile "horror movie"-like appetites. In this context media creation technologies such as GoPro cameras and the easy access to a global audience provided by streaming media-capable platforms such as Facebook, YouTube and TikTok are central. These technologies have added what I have described as democratizing aspect to Information Warfare – any individual or group is capable of reaching a global audience and in inflicting perceptual damage to enemies and a wide audience.

In this context "brutality" and violence as the content of the products created and disseminated by these groups is an informational micro-version of the classic American strategy known as "Shock and Awe".

Conclusion: The Social War – Information Warfare in the 21st century

> Political language—and with variations this is true of all political parties, from Conservatives to Anarchists—is designed to make lies sound truthful and murder respectable, and to give an appearance of solidity to pure wind. One cannot change this all in a moment, but one can at least change one's own habits, and from time to time one can even, if one jeers loudly enough, send some worn-out and useless phrase—some jackboot, Achilles' heel, hotbed, melting pot, acid test, veritable inferno or other lump of verbal refuse—into the dustbin where it belongs.
> George Orwell, "Politics and the English Language" (Orwell, 1946).

It is my contention that both State and non-State actors have been highly effective in making use of social media, video games and the internet as a set of mechanisms through which weaponized forms of information and communication are projected. These technologies have been harnessed in the waging of a form of Information Warfare (González, 2015a, 2015b; Gorka, 2015) – what I have described earlier as a social war. The social war reaches into almost every corner of the globe. It is able to turn individuals into instruments of carnage – as internet soldiers – such as the "Lone Wolf" attackers, for example the neo-Nazi mass murderers in Norway in 2011 and New Zealand in 2019 or the myriad Jihadis. It has also democratized the tools which had once been the prevue of nation-States. Individuals and groups can now shape and project an information bullet designed to undermine and sow confusion.

The "fake news" and "Post-Truth" period led up to the 2016 American Presidential election and the Brexit campaign and has continued on beyond. The pandemic of 2020 also highlighted the extent to which malicious actors, both State and non-State, are now able to access and use these new "democratized" forms of information weaponry to sow civil disorder and to undermine social and political institutions. The mass civil unrest that followed the killing of George Floyd also was, it appears, in part amplified by the same sophisticated information weapons – contributing to the social and political situation that followed (Scott, 2020). This was straight from the information warfare playbook that has evolved over the past decade. Misinformation is injected into the debate and acts as a mechanism with which to amplify discord and to push particular ideological and political stances.

The weapons of perception which had been successfully applied by America in the Cold War and in the decades which followed have now been directed at the United States itself. The tools that they developed coupled with the logistics afforded by new technology have matured and have now caused disruption on a massive scale.

References

Aaronson, M., Diessen, S., De Kermabon, Y., Long, M. B., & Miklaucic, M. (2011). NATO countering the hybrid threat. *Prism, 2*(4).

Allcott, H., & Gentzkow, M. (2017). Social media and fake news in the 2016 election. *Journal of Economic Perspectives, 31*(2), 211–236.

Au, W. J. (2002). Weapons of mass distraction. *Salon.com, 4*.

Au, W. J. (2004). America's arming. In America's Army PC Game Vision and Realization.

Bacevich, A. J. (2010). Washington rules: America's path to permanent war: Macmillan.

Baumann, R., & Hellmann, G. (2001). Germany and the use of military force: ,"Total war", the ,"Culture of restraint", and the quest for normality. *German Politics, 10*(1), 61–82.

Berger, J. M. (2015). The Metronome of Apocalyptic Time: Social Media as Carrier Wave for Millenarian Contagion. *Perspectives on Terrorism.* Retrieved from http://terrorismanalysts.com/pt/index.php/pot/article/view/444

Betts, R. K. (2012). From cold war to hot peace: The habit of American force. *Political Science Quarterly, 127*(3), 353–368.

Boatwright, B. C., Linvill, D. L., & Warren, P. L. (2018). Troll factories: The internet research agency and state-sponsored agenda building. *Resource Centre on Media Freedom in Europe*.

Boyd, R. L., Spangher, A., Fourney, A., Nushi, B., Ranade, G., Pennebaker, J. W., & Horvitz, E. (2018). Characterizing the Internet Research Agency's social media operations during the 2016 US presidential election using linguistic analyses. *PsyArXiv. October, 1*.

Brooking, E. T., & Singer, P. W. (2016). War goes viral: How social media is being weaponized across the world. Retrieved from http://www.defenseone.com/ideas/2016/10/war-goes-viral/132233/

Cetina, K. (1997). Sociality with objects: Social relations in postsocial knowledge societies. *Theory, Culture & Society, 14*(4), 1. Retrieved from http://www.ncbi.nlm.nih.gov/entrez/query.fcgi?db=pubmed&cmd=Retrieve&dopt=AbstractPlus&list_uids=14218374918110723545related:2T1Q5afQUcUJ

Chung, A. (2016). Jihadism 3.0: The Islamic State's agenda of borderless radicalisation through the use of #social media. Retrieved from http://papers.ssrn.com/abstract=2760618

Command, U. S. C. (2018). *Achieve and maintain cyberspace superiority*. Retrieved from https://www.cybercom.mil/Portals/56/Documents/USCYBERCOM%20Vision%20April%202018.pdf?ver=2018-06-14-152556-010

Ellul, J. (1965). *Propaganda: The formation of men's attitudes* (1st American ed.). New York: Knopf.

Enli, G. (2017). Twitter as arena for the authentic outsider: Exploring the social media campaigns of Trump and Clinton in the 2016 US presidential election. *European journal of communication, 32*(1), 50–61.

Falliere, N., Murchu, L. O., & Chien, E. (2011). W32. stuxnet dossier. *White paper, Symantec Corp., Security Response, 5*(6), 29.

Floridi, L. (2014). The latent nature of global information warfare. *Philosophy & Technology, 27*(3), 317–319.

Friedman, T. L. (2003). The lexus and the olive tree: Understanding globalization. *International Research Journal of Arts and Humanities, 38*.

Ganley, G. D. (1991). Power to the people via personal electronic media. *The Washington Quarterly, 14*(2), 5–22.

Gardner, B. (2018). Social engineering in non-linear warfare. *Journal of Applied Digital Evidence, 1*(1), 1.

Geyer, M. (1989). The militarization of Europe, 1914–1945. In J. R. Gillis (Ed.), *The Militarization of the Western World* (pp. 65–102). New Brunswick: Rutgers University Press.

Glenn, C. (2016, December 20, 2017). Timeline: Rise and spread of the Islamic State.

González, R. J. (2015a). Seeing into hearts and minds. *Anthropology Today, 31*(4), 13–18.

González, R. J. (2015b). Seeing into hearts and minds: Part 1. The Pentagon's quest for a 'social radar'. *Anthropology Today, 31*(3), 8–13.

Goracy, N. (2016). Lone wolf, the young lion, and the impressionable American: The impact of social media platforms on homegrown Islamic extremism. Ris database.

Gorka, S. (2015). The Islamic State and information warfare. Retrieved from the Threat Knowledge Group website.

Hoffman, F. G. (2009). *Hybrid warfare and challenges*. Washington DC: Institute for National Strategic Studies.

Horne, J. (2019). A world at war: 1911–1949: Conclusion. In *A World at War, 1911–1949* (pp. 279–305): Brill.

Jasper, S., & Moreland, S. (2016). ISIS: An adaptive hybrid threat in transition. *Journal Article| October, 29*(8), 56am.

Jowett, G. S., & O'Donnell, V. (2011). *Propaganda and persuasion*: Sage Publications.

Kang, C., & Goldman, A. (2016). In Washington pizzeria attack, fake news brought real guns. *The New York Times*, 5.

King, J. C. (2014). ISIS's call of duty. *The New Yorker*.

Lasswell, H. D. (1995). *Propaganda*. Basingstoke: Macmillan.

Mackay, R. (2018). Half the battle: Civilian morale in Britain during the Second World War.

Martino, J. (2015). War/play: Video games and the militarization of society. New York: Peter Lang.
McCuen, J. J. (2008). Hybrid wars. *Military review, 88*(2), 107.
Mead, M. (1968). Alternatives to war. In *War: The anthropology of armed conflict and aggression*, ed. Morton Fried et al., 215–228.
Monaghan, A. (2015). The'war'in Russia's' hybrid warfare'. *Parameters, 45*(4), 65.
Muñoz, C. (2016). Islamic State perfects art of self-radicalization, confounds counterterrorism officials. *Washington Times*. Retrieved from https://www.washingtontimes.com/news/2016/dec/21/isis-perfects-art-of-self-radicalization-confounds/
O'Callaghan, D., Greene, D., Conway, M., Carthy, J., & Cunningham, P. (2016). An Analysis of Interactions within and between Extreme Right Communities in Social Media. 88–107. doi:10.1007/978-3-642-45392-2_5
Orwell, G. (1946). Politics and the English Language. *Horizon*.
Rožukalne, A., & Sedlenieks, K. (2017). The elusive cyber beasts: How to identify the communication of pro-Russian hybrid trolls in Latvia's internet news sites? *Central European Journal of Communication, 10*(1 (18)), 79–97.
Scott, M. (2020, June 1, 2020). Russia and China target U.S. protests on social media. *Politico*. Retrieved from https://www.politico.com/news/2020/06/01/russia-and-china-target-us-protests-on-social-media-294315
Shead, S. (2019). TikTok used by Islamic State to spread propaganda videos. Retrieved from https://www.bbc.com/news/technology-50138740
Singer, P. W., & Brooking, E. T. (2018). *LikeWar: The weaponization of social media*. Eamon Dolan Books.
Thiele, R. D. (2015). Crisis in Ukraine: The Emergence of Hybrid Warfare. *ISPSW Strategic Series*(347), 1–13.
Toffler, A., & Toffler, H. (1997). Foreword: The new intangibles. In J. Arquilla & D. Ronfeldt (Eds.), *In Athena's Camp* (1 ed., pp. xiii-xxiv): RAND Corporation.
Vasu, N., Ang, B., Teo, T.-A., Jayakumar, S., Raizal, M., & Ahuja, J. (2018). *Fake news: National security in the post-truth era*. RSIS.

Chapter 3

Playing@War

Video Games, New Media and Modern Warfare

Playing@War

Preparation for war has traditionally involved soldiers engaging in endless drill, marching in formation, following commands, target practice and the completion of obstacle courses. Modern warfare requires a different set of skills and characteristics. On the modern battlefield the soldier needs to be a thinker, a problem solver and a specialist in applying the necessary level of violence. The modern training regime within the US Army and similar advanced military formations has evolved beyond the "boot camp" approach that has been popularized in films such as *Full Metal Jacket* and *Tigerland*. However, the enculturation into military thinking is no longer simply the preserve of State actors and organizations preparing for traditional forms of conflict. In the contemporary context the preparation for armed conflict has gone beyond traditional State-sanctioned activities designed to recruit and train young people for war. Non-State agents are also heavily engaged in the recruitment of young people for their conflicts – insurrectionary as localized actions or exported to foreign soil as al-Qaeda and Islamic State did in the post-9/11 era. Both State and non-State actors are in a sense actively recruiting from the same pool of young people. One claims national sovereignty and legitimacy over the recruitment of young people for armed conflict, the other groups – non-State actors – equally claim legitimacy and point to their religious roots and goals as a justification.

I am in no way arguing that extremist groups have any legitimacy in their goals nor in their often bloody acts. Simply stated, both State and non-State actors are using new forms of media and technology to appeal to young people – often disaffected and un-moored socially and psychologically – to sign up for their causes (Almohammad, 2018; Gagnon, 2010). In this chapter I will examine how video game culture has influenced both State and non-State actor tactics and methods through both gaming and social media to attract young people, as well as to use these technologies as forms of "perceptual weaponry" (Arquilla & Ronfeldt, 1997; Brooking & Singer,

2016; MacDonald, 2014). Weaponry which is capable of projecting power and ideology in order to inflict perceptual damage. To project their propaganda messages, and to engage in a ruthless struggle for the "hearts and minds" of young people and the broader population.

Creating this predisposition for the necessity of sustaining military power and the imminence of its application depends on the establishment of specific social, psychological, cultural forms and the affordances presented by new technologies. In this book I have written about the role played by the weaponization of information and its application through social media – but here I wish to extend that train of thought to an analysis of how a specific form of new technology has been harnessed to enhance the decades long process of militarization. Specifically, I will examine video games (in particular, the First Person-Shooter) and their pedagogic characteristics. Games have been used for centuries to educate and to entertain humans – in fact it has been argued that "play makes us human" (Huizinga, 2003).

The *Xbox*, the *PlayStation* and the First-Person Shooter are more than simple technological platforms and forms of entertainment. Just as social media has become a weaponized form of communication and "entertainment", video games in the form of the First-Person Shooter (though other forms of gaming also fit within this construct) are useful in both recruitment and training. Video games have been used to project particular ideological tropes and propaganda messages such as the "Digital Arab" (Šisler, 2008) as the universal enemy. They have also been useful in the development of skills that are applicable to full-fledged military technologies such as drones (DiRomualdo, 2007; D. Nieborg, 2009; Rayner, 2012). As one military official stated in the 2010s:

> the younger generation of Video gamers is well-suited for real military combat. In fact, the controller for some surveillance drones is modeled after a Video game controller . . . [and] many of the objectives look and function the same. The real military use a touchscreen notebook to control drones; you can land one by touching an airstrip, and the drones essentially fly on their own.
>
> (Brandon, 2012)

Video games have had a long connection with military organizations and have been used both in the development and "gaming" of military plans and doctrine, as well as training tools. At their core, modern video games (here I am specifically referring to First-Person Shooter games) have both propaganda messages – as in the *Call of Duty* series or simply as skill development tools – both in basic military notions such as how to enter a room or how to take a "head-shot". The games do not make you a soldier, nor do they prepare you to actually handle a weapon or engage in real combat. But they do attune the player to military ways of thinking and to the culture of violence (though simulated).

Play

If we accept the argument that "play" is an important part of what makes us human, we use it to entertain ourselves, we use it to teach and to learn. Then it is not a long stretch to assert that the highly political games of the post-9/11 21st century are more than simple entertainment. Human and animal alike participate in play. Puppies frolic with one another just as groups of young children do. Animal play can include the simple romping of young dogs or more sophisticated demonstrations such as those associated with mating rituals. Johan Huizinga writing in the mid-20th century provides us with a powerful analysis of the significance of play in human society.

Huizinga has argued that when we study play, we observe an activity that has meaning that goes beyond basic physiological and psychological imperatives. Huizinga asserts that "all play means something"; it has social and cultural meaning (2003). In his book, *Homo Ludens* Huizinga (2003) states that "play gives us culture" (Huizinga, 2003). It is in this context that video game play and militarization coalesce. Military-themed and oriented video games act as both training mechanisms and a tool for "enculturation" into the dominant aspect of contemporary western society and culture – militarization. This process of enculturation occurs through the creation of a habitus that both extends militarization and helps build on extrinsic processes also working towards that goal.

Before explaining at least how I see this process working, it is necessary to briefly examine a key form of video game that I have already referred to in this chapter and within this book – the First-Person Shooter (FPS). Why have I singled this game genre out for close examination? Simply put it is the First-Person Shooter that contains within it both the elements of enculturation and skill formation and thus embodies the form of habitus that I am interested in. It presents a distillation of the wider process of societal militarization through its focus on the use of violence as the prime tool for problem solving and achieving political goals. More broadly it helps develop a set of "soft skills" (D. Nieborg, 2009) that, as I have argued earlier, are not immediately applicable to actual combat, but are nevertheless useful for the preparation and actual training for military service and combat (Martino, 2015; D. Nieborg, 2004).

The First-Person Shooter

America's Army and other military-themed First-Person Shooters such as the *Call of Duty* series have helped to transform popular culture by embedding military themes and concepts within the daily lives of millions. The playing of games such as *Call of Duty*, *America's Army* or *Fortnite* does not simulate real warfare – it does however reinforce the broader socio-political process of militarization. As previously stated, "militarization" refers to "the contradictory and tense social process in which civil society organizes itself for the production of violence" (Geyer, 1989). The First-Person Shooter has been added to the repertoire of mechanisms available for the reinforcement of propaganda messages and socialization necessary for the maintenance and extension of militarized "war culture" and the organization of society for the "production of violence".

Getting people to accept war and conflict, as we have in the 21st century, was no simple process. The "peace dividend" supposed to have been delivered in the 1990s by the collapse of the Soviet Union and the end of its eastern Empire and global reach never eventuated. Instead from the early to mid-1990s a gradual shift and re-orientation occurred within the United States and then flowed on to the rest of the world (Bacevich, 2010). This shift took the United States and its allies and client states from "Cold War" to Imperial maintenance. No longer was the American Empire confronted by an equally powerful and dangerous adversary. Instead the United States found itself in charge of a global Empire that did not require the large-scale mass mobilizations of the Second World War and the subsequent

Figure 3.1 Screenshot from *America's Army: Proving Grounds*

conflicts of the Cold War, Korea and Vietnam (Bishai, 2004; Hardt & Negri, 2001). War became, in the late 1900s and into this century, small scale, low-intensity and asymmetrical (Betts, 2012; Hall, Hendrickson, & Polak, 2013). Instead of the mass call up of the Second World War or the Cold War conflicts, a trickle in comparison of manpower was needed for the all-volunteer military that defeat in Vietnam had brought about. In this context the media and in particular forms of entertainment media have aided in enhancing and maintaining the militarization of everyday life and the construction of a cultural setting where violence – actual or virtual – is both expected and normalized (Benson-Allott, 2018; Bernazzoli & Flint, 2010; Betts, 2012; Delwiche, 2007).

Games as Weapons of "Perceptual Damage"

The capture of particular forms of videogaming by the military is well documented (Burston, 2003; Delwiche, 2007; Der Derian, 2009) – the close alignment with both the technology industry and the entertainment establishment (Turse, 2008) have created the conditions necessary for the deployment of a type of "soft power" (D. Nieborg, 2009). Games are able to present new sites or "fronts" where conflict with a digital enemy (the "Digital Arab" (Šisler, 2006, 2008)) are conducted. This reflects a shift in military doctrine to reflect the understanding that warfare in the 21st century is not limited to the physical landscape. The United States now operates under the assumption that even the media offers "a decisive theater of operations. Virtual conflict and 'perceptual damage' are as important as real conflict and real damage" (Defense Science Board, 2004, 2008; Department of Defense, 2003; Peters, 1997).

The identification of perception as a potent weapon in the conduct of war presages the position adopted by the US Army as part of its military doctrine (Defense Science Board, 2008). The political scientist Paul Virilio, writing in the 1980s about the relationship between war and cinema, pointed to the manner in which perception – generated through sight or sound – had in effect become a weapon. According to Virilio (1989),

> [t]here is no war . . . without representation, no sophisticated weaponry without psychological mystification. Weapons are tools not just of destruction but also of perception – that is to say, stimulants that make themselves felt through chemical, neurological processes in the sense organs and the central nervous system, affecting human reactions and even the perceptual identification and differentiation of objects.
> (Virilio, 1989)

Virilio refers to the manner in which one of the earliest mechanized terror weapons – the German *Stuka* dive bomber of the Second World

War – could, through the sound it generated, demoralize combatant and non-combatant alike (Virilio, 1989). Its piercing sound was the embodiment of *Blitzkrieg* and created sheer terror without actually having to drop a bomb. The ability to create the perception of being vulnerable and under attack became a potent weapon. The First-Person Shooter is able to generate a perception of the power and reach of the neo-liberal war machine.

Traditional notions of war focus on the physical aspects of conflict – the occupation of territory, the destruction or capture of enemy forces or materiel (Virilio, 1989). Video games offer a new theatre within which war can be waged, where perception can be harnessed to inflict damage. The neo-liberal war machine has, in a sense, done away with the need to physically destroy the enemy. Whilst not as directly lethal as other militarized technologies – such as "Drones" – this soft power is an ideological weapon at the service of the neo-liberal hegemon. Gamers are not soldiers – though whilst logged into an FPS they are operating as though they were at war.

The history of *America's Army* for example represents the successful projection of United States power into the digital domain and has helped extend the reach of American "soft-power" (D. Nieborg, 2009). It inflicts a form of "perceptual damage" through its depiction of US Forces in combat scenarios. Both the content of the game and the procedural aspects of how to engage in fighting are representations with political and ideological meaning. The missions that the player is tasked with, the conduct – "Rules of Engagement" – embedded in the games (shooting a fellow GI or civilian is penalized) help project a preconceived image of what the neo-liberal war machine can is capable of doing (Løvlie, 2008). Without firing a shot, the power and prestige of the US military is projected globally and is capable of inflicting damage.

Playing *America's Army* is not the same as engaging in real combat, but it does have a ring of truth to it. *America's Army* and other realistic First-Person Shooters extend the boundaries of modern warfare. They act as conduits for the extension and reach of the neo-liberal war machine and its assemblage of techniques and technologies and as such they are capable of inflicting perceptual damage. *America's Army* and other First-Person Shooters, such as the *Call of Duty* and *Battlefield* series, facilitate the deployment of this soft power. Asymmetrical warfare has literally jumped the boundaries between the real and the simulated. Games in the form of the First-Person Shooter provide a space within which the political military objectives of the neo-liberal State formation can be played out in both subtle and not so subtle ways.

State Actors and the Recruitment of "Human Materiel"

It has been the legitimate purview of State actors to craft tools with which to recruit young people for military service, but also to train and to prepare them for the horrors that they will experience when and if

> **THE SOLDIER'S CREED**
>
> I am an American Soldier.
> I am a Warrior and a member of a team.
> I serve the people of the United States and live the Army Values.
>
> > I will always place the mission first.
> > I will never accept defeat.
> > I will never quit.
> > I will never leave a fallen comrade.
>
> I am disciplined, physically and mentally tough, trained and proficient in my Warrior tasks and drills.
> I always maintain my arms, my equipment, and myself.
> I am an expert and I am a professional.
> I stand ready to deploy, engage, and destroy the enemies of the United States of America in close combat.
> I am a guardian of freedom and the American way of life.
> I am an American Soldier.

Figure 3.2 The Soldier's Creed – United States Army

they rotate into a war zone. The perpetual state of war that the West has been enmeshed in since the end of the Second World War, through the Cold War and into the current "Global War on Terror", has necessitated a constant stream of new recruits in the post-war era particularly. In the Vietnam war this was accomplished through compulsion – "the Draft". With the defeat of the United States in Vietnam the idea that a modern society could produce large numbers of young people who would take to "soldiering" or would willingly accept the rigors of armed conflict was proven to be erroneous and politically dangerous (Abney, 2019; Erikson & Stoker, 2011). In the post-Vietnam period Western nations such as the United States, Australia and the Europeans quickly abandoned compulsory military service.

In place of compulsion the notion of military service as a gateway to future careers became one of the dominant recruitment strategies. Military service provided job-oriented skills or access to higher education or training after one had completed their military obligations.

Modern military training methods, at least those used in the US Army, are designed not to produce the near robotic infantryman of the past. Drill and punitive forms of discipline, once the bedrock of the military training regimen, are no longer seen to be useful or appropriate. As Gill (2009) points out, the shift

> within infantry training and strategy has sprung from the realization that discipline – being trained through drill and physical exercise for strict obedience to hierarchical structures – often breaks down on the battlefield. No matter how accurately a soldier can shoot, how willing to obey orders, or how loyal to the nation and officers he or she might be, factors such as fear, the effect of killing, and generalized confusion at unforeseen events often override all sense of discipline in the heat of the moment.
> (Gill, 2009)

The falling out of favor of the traditional drill and physical discipline approach to "soldierization" (the transformation from a civilian to a soldier) has led to a paradigm shift in both the preparation for and the conduct of modern warfare. The nature of modern war – its asymmetrical and extended temporal characteristics – has forced the reorganization of the training of the armed forces to encompass a new basis for the mental framework of the soldier.

The modern soldier must draw on a set of thought processes, values and methods of working, which are not in accordance with the drill and punishment approach that had previously dominated the process of soldierization. The modern soldier has morphed into what we can describe as a performative subject. It is a soldier's ability to perform in complex scenarios, often through a process of immersive simulation – both physical and digital – that performance is measured. The modern soldier is expected to be creative, intuitive and able to deal with diversity. The postmodern mantra of performativity is now an essential characteristic of life in a modern army. Problem solving, the ability to change and the skills to work collaboratively, are crucial features of the modern soldier's make-up.

In this context playing games – simulating how to solve complex battlefield scenarios – in a simulator like the Dismounted Soldier Training System (DSTS), a digital simulated combat system, has become a powerful training mechanism (Bymer, 2012). Playing at war has always been part of military training and the socialization of young males. Computer technology has amplified the capacity and effectiveness of play as a means of preparing new recruits and soon-to-be-deployed soldiers in specific military scenarios. The First-Person Shooter genre and other military video games present the player with similar scenarios and "Rules of Engagement" that official training applications such as the DSTS have embedded within them. *America's Army* for example cannot be successfully played unless the player adheres to the "Warrior Code" of the US Army and engages in the game as a team player. In this way games such as *America's Army* and the more realistic FPS games such as *CoD* and *Battlefield* can easily become training tools for the military, enabling civilian and military players to realistically simulate complex battle scenarios in order to rehearse the intricacies of modern combat in diverse settings.

The notion that using modern forms of new media could bridge the gap between playing at war and actually engaging in war was highlighted in the early 2000s by the United States military. Drawing on ideas from science-fiction, specifically the "Battle Room" featured in the novel *Ender's Game* (2014) by Orson Scott Card, where young children played at war without realizing that they were actually fighting an alien enemy, was the quintessential model of the ludic military habitus (M. Macedonia, 2002, 2005; M. R. Macedonia & Herz, 2002). Dr. Michael Macedonia, as the chief scientist and technical director for the US Army Simulation, Training, and Instrumentation Command in the early 2000s, argued that preparing for war could take on a game-like aspect. Referring to the plot and main character in the book, Macedonia states that

> Andrew "Ender" Wiggin is drafted into Battle School. Although only a child, Ender tackles increasingly difficult simulator missions against an alien race. After he wins the brutally difficult final scenario, Ender realizes that the simulated battle he has just fought was no sim, but the real conflict's ultimate conclusion. Thus, did Card envision the emergence of simulations and games for training and the power of the Internet to influence ideas and change. Ender Wiggin's bizarre world is no longer fiction. The military is already using the simulation technology of first-person thinkers to help soldiers learn how to fight the three-block war, learn the language of allies and adversaries, heal mental scars, and even save the lives of others.
>
> (M. Macedonia, 2005)

The term "first-person thinker" used by Macedonia gives us an interesting insight into where we are in the 21st century in the context of video games, particularly the First-Person Shooter games and their role in the creation of the ludic based military habitus. These games are part, or have become part, of a process which seeks to create military "First Person Thinkers" and "Full Spectrum Leaders". The contemporary asymmetrical "Battlespace" requires not simply that a soldier can use a weapon or follow orders – these are easy things to inculcate in a young person. What purpose-built video game military simulators – and I argue civilian-focused, military-themed or oriented video games – are capable of is creating a set of skills, a way of thinking that is highly adaptable in the context of conflict situations.

The language, game play (multi-player, head shots and kill points), high-tech weapons and gear (armor, uniforms and insignia which adorn game avatars) and other military elements of this form of gaming extend and amplify the process of militarization and helps constitute a ludic based military habitus. This emergent military habitus coupled with the immersive and realistic war simulation at the heart of the First-Person Shooter helps construct a foundation upon which entry into and effective participation within military organizations becomes easier to facilitate. We can begin to understand how this process takes shape by referring to the concept of "anticipatory socialization". Neil Stott describes anticipatory socialization as a process through which young people are able to rehearse and test future roles and occupations. In this context playable media such as the *Call of Duty* series become more of a simulation than a form of entertainment and assist in the extension of the process of militarization.

"Fire Rates"

Getting people to kill other people in war has never been an easy process. Military organizations such the US Marines pride themselves in being able break down the civilian in order to build the "warrior" from the ground up. Despite the popular misconception, this does not mean that these organizations are able to create hardened killers who are willing and able to fully engage in the dirty business of armed combat. In this context the work of the military specialist S. L. A Marshall, who pioneered the methodology to document and analyze combat experiences (the After-Action Review), has been adopted in most armed forces. Marshall's work during and after the Second World War was to examine rates of fire or, more precisely, combat fire ratios. The data collected by Marshall documenting the combat fire ratios,

> particularly . . . in World War II [indicates that] less than 25 percent of American combat infantrymen in battle fired their weapons.
> (Field, 2012)

Marshall published his initial results in his 1947 book, *Men Against Fire*. The work was begun by Marshall in the last years of the Second World War and was built upon during the Korean War. In both settings he applied his methodology to the after-action group interview with enlisted men. Marshall concluded that in combat less than half the front-line soldiers were firing their weapons. Even when they were firing their weapons the evidence Marshall produced indicated that US forces were not trying to kill the enemy (Field, 2012).

Writing about the Second World War Marshall argued that "the average and healthy individual has such an inner and usually unrealized resistance toward killing a fellow man that he will not of his own volition take life if it is possible to turn away from the responsibility". He thought moreover that the relief felt by US troops when they went into a quiet sector "was due not so much to the realization that things were safer there than to the blessed knowledge that for a time they were not under the compulsion to take life" (Field, 2012).

Marshall's analysis and his approach to gathering data has had an enduring influence over the thinking of the US military. It's arguable that they have been working towards identifying how to overcome the "pro-social" tendency of their young recruits ever since Marshall identified this aversion to killing (Field, 2012). It's important to note that according to Marshall the single most important factor in getting soldiers to fight is their commitment to their unit, and their unwillingness to let their comrades down.

The relationship between this unit or group dynamic to the willingness of soldiers to fight – to confront great adversity and to cohere as a fighting force – has had a profound impact on military training doctrine. The parallels between real life military behavior as described by Marshall and the popularity of online multi-player versions of First-Person Shooters is highly significant.

A study on "prosocial" attitudes in the military conducted by Field in 2012 found that people on the whole are far more altruistic and unwilling to kill others than either social science or popular conceptions would lead us to believe. The US Army for decades took this onboard and modified its training methods in an effort to overcome such prosocial behavior. According to Field,

> what military trainers struggled with is a more or less universal human aversion to the close range killing of other conspecifics, an aversion with biological as well as cultural roots. To say that this is more or less universal is to say that it is observed across cultures, but also to acknowledge that, with respect to this trait as well as many others, there are variations among individuals in the strength of the predisposition. It is also to acknowledge that effective conditioning can largely suppress the inhibition (as reforms in military training undertaken in response to Marshall's writings have confirmed) and that even in the absence of explicit conditioning, there are circumstances that will defeat it.
> (Field, 2012)

Field's study and subsequent work substantiated the claims made by Marshall that soldiers did not easily engage in the killing at the heart of a combat scenario. Different methods of training would be needed to overcome such prosocial behavior and attitudes.

Getting People to Kill

So, if it was difficult to get soldiers to kill the enemy, at least according to the work of Marshall, how have modern armed forces dealt with the problem? A technological fix for the problem was sought. First, we have seen the introduction of increasingly sophisticated simulators and detailed simulations such as those discussed earlier in this chapter. These forms of technology have evolved a great deal since the early wooden flight simulators of the Second World War, or even the 1980s strategic computer simulator depicted in the film *WarGames* (Badham, 1983). Since the early part of the last decade, military simulations have become highly effective learning tools.

At the same time, we have seen games and game-like simulators adopted by the military to help both train soldiers prior to a military engagement as in the DSTS technology and also through *America's Army* and other FPS games to inure the civilian population to the nature of modern warfare. This is a crucial point. It's not that using this technology helps you to learn how to shoot better or react in the same way as you would out in the field in real combat, under real fire. But, like a boxer becomes immersed in the culture of the ring, in the smell and feel of the fight, so that his body becomes wired for the fight, so too the young recruit and increasingly the gamer are immersed in these simulated war experiences, and the culture of war. The aversion to killing is watered down well before they see a Drill Instructor. Technology has progressed to the point where it offers these affordances – the capacity to think like a soldier, to solve a military problem and to engage in virtual combat in a safe and secure environment. The *Xbox* is a potent military simulator when loaded with the right kind of software.

In this context the video game genre known as the First-Person Shooter adds to this process of militarization and has become something of a "military training tool" for the military (through virtual simulation applications), not just for its personnel but for society as a whole thus extending the process of militarization. It is my view that the language, game play (head shots and kill points), high-tech weapons and gear (armor, uniforms and insignia) and other military elements of this form of gaming extend and amplify the process of militarization through what I referred to earlier as the creation of a military habitus.

New forms of media such as video games help to create what I have referred to as a form of military habitus. The war simulation that is at the core of many video games, specifically First Person Shooter games, help construct a youth culture which is militarized. Whilst these forms of new media do not create soldiers or give the player skills that are directly transferable to war settings, they do facilitate what Neil Stott describes as "anticipatory socialization". The player is in effect prepped for potential military functions – the games act as a test bed for militarized thinking and action. Using an Xbox controller doesn't make you a soldier – but an Xbox-like controller is at the core of many modern military weapons systems. Being familiar with how to control simulated war fighting technologies in a game setting does help one to actually use similar technology in the cauldron of real warfare.

Another way of thinking about how this process occurs is to re-consider the idea of pedagogy and pedagogical practices. The creation of a militarized societal predisposition to engage in war or to accept the application of violence as a political tool and as normal has been achieved through the embedding of militarization within the political form of neo-liberal capitalism. Militarization has become the dominant pedagogic principle since the Second World War. I have expanded on the way militarization has come to shape and become embedded within the structure of our society in more depth elsewhere in this book.

This application of pedagogic practices within the context of the shift of Western society towards a militarized pro-war social, psychological and political stance has, as I have argued earlier, been facilitated by new forms of technology and media. Militarization as a social process has been amplified by the digital revolution of the post-Second World War era. The application of new media and technology to the shaping of individuals and societies through militarization has not been limited to State actors. In a sense the creation of new relatively inexpensive mechanisms through which opinion can be shaped, individuals trained for conflict or incited to violence, has been due to the "cat being let out of the bag". New technology and forms of media have enabled non-State actors to make use of a set of tools that in the context of asymmetrical warfare have had a leveling effect. The adoption of these new technologies and media forms by non-State actors has meant that warfare is extended into the perceptual realm – but also gives the less powerful the means to inflict harm globally and in an asynchronous manner.

In the next section I will examine how non-State actors, both Islamic and Alt-Right, have harnessed particular forms of technology and new media to project their messages, gather recruits and inflict perceptual damage. Specifically, the main focus will be an examination of how play – in the context of video games and the First-Person Shooter genre – have been harnessed to achieve the political and military goals of non-State actors.

Non-State Actors

YouTube contains numerous examples of the visual representation of armed conflict and the adoption by many of the groups producing this content of elements of particular video game aesthetics. For example, an image from the phone camera of an Islamic State recruit was part of a propaganda video. It is framed in a manner intended to mimic the aesthetics of the First-Person Shooter genre; it is game like in nature (Bittanti, 2006; Klevjer, 2006). The application of game aesthetics and game culture to online propaganda messages is part of the broader appropriation of popular culture by armed groups – video games, social media and YouTube (but not limited to those platforms) have all been harnessed for this purpose (Lakomy, 2019; Simon, 2016). The First-Person Shooter genre has provided a rich and easily assessible means with which to project perceptual damage and recruit youth to their cause (Al-Rawi, 2016). Games modelled on *Call of Duty* are not only designed so that the player is able to take on the enemies of the Islamic State – they also help to project the power and the ideology of the movement (Dauber, Robinson, Baslious, & Blair, 2019).

Non-State actors such as the Islamic State have been highly effective in appropriating visual aspects of new forms of media to both recruit and train their soldiers. They have also used the concept of "spectacle" to both harden and enculturate their new recruits. A 2015 report: *How ISIS Abducts, Recruits, and Trains Children to Become Jihadists* describes the use of video to instruct young Yazidi children who had been kidnapped in how to behead a person. They were then given dolls and a sword and shown how to correctly hold the weapon and conduct the beheading. This was a crude yet effective use of video technology to train their new recruits – after they had been in effect "brainwashed". The use of filmed executions as part of a training regime help to desensitize the new recruits to violence and also act to socialize them into the culture and ideology of the Islamic State (Danner, 2015).

According to research conducted by Bloom (2019) these video depictions of brutal violence were shown at public forums where I argue a sense of "community" was created around the application of violence and its normalization. The use of the "routine spectacle of such events internalizes and normalizes the violence. Although some children may get physically ill from attending the beheadings, the vast majority becomes immune to violence" (Bloom, 2019). Bloom drawing on the work of Bandura points to how this process of desensitization unravels the existing socialization that young children had experienced in their previous life. According to Bandura:

> In early phases of child development conduct is largely regulated by external dictates and social sanctions. In the course of socialization people adopt moral standards that serve as guides and major bases for self-sanctions regarding moral conduct. [. . .] In the face of situational inducements to behave in inhumane ways, people can choose to behave otherwise by exerting self-influence.
>
> (Bloom, 2019)

As Bloom points out, in the case of the Islamic State and its young recruits their ability to self-correct, to "self-influence", has been removed along with their past life. This breaking down of the individual and then re-modeling them in the image of the "jihadi" is a similar process to that used by all military training organizations – though without the horror and exposure to filmed or actual killings. The military of all nations break down the civilian persona and generate a new militarized person capable of following orders, engaging in armed combat and participating in active service in precarious situations (Black, Britt, Lane, & Adler, 2018; Knight, 2007). The Islamic State has adapted elements of the "soldierization" process and added the "hardening" of children and young people through particularly savage means.

Jihadi "Mods"

Just as State actors such as the United States military had seen the potential of new forms of media technology earlier this century, such as video games, and then subsequently set about creating their own militarized variant of a video game, non-State actors have followed suit. The Islamic State – as well as other Middle-Eastern armed/terror groups, for example Hezbollah (Eid, 2018) – have made use of militarized video games in the dissemination of their propaganda messages and as tools in the projection of perceptual damage (Defense Science Board, 2004). Not simply adopting the aesthetics of the First-Person Shooter as in the YouTube video screenshot described above, groups such as the Islamic State have created their own versions of games within this genre (Al-Rawi, 2016; Dauber et al., 2019; Simon, 2016).

The terror groups have as far I am able to discern not created their own video games from scratch. They have continued in the well-worn path of video game enthusiasts who "mod" games (D. B. Nieborg & Van der Graaf, 2008; Sotamaa, 2010). The "modding" of video games refers to "the practice of nonprofessionals altering or adding to games" (Kretzschmar & Stanfill, 2019). This is a technically illegal activity in that it breaches copyright law and involves the manipulation of intellectual property that has been created by gaming and entertainment companies. Breaking the law has never really been a concern of terror groups or even "fan-boys" obsessed with specific titles.

A mod can for example alter the rules of a game so that a player can progress through the game's narrative rapidly or add new features. Mods add new elements such as specialist weapons, decals, body armour and unique elements of characterization.

In 2014 it was reported that the Islamic State had produced its own version of the game *Grand Theft Auto* (GTA) – a trailer for the game was posted to YouTube. The modification (Abramson & Modzelewski) of the game was given the name *Salil al-Sawarem* which is Arabic for *The Clanging of the Swords* (Al-Rawi, 2016). In the cover description of the Islamic State game its authors boldly assert that "Your games which are producing from you, we do the same actions in the battlefields!!" (Al-Rawi, 2016). Al-Rawi – who has made a detailed study of the game and terror inspired games in general – argues that the Islamic State is making it clear that they see

> the types of real armed confrontations ISIS is engaged with [as being] similar to the virtual wars produced in Western video games. Further, the name itself given to the game is also supposed to project the idea of strength, fearlessness, and resilience at times of war. It is alleged that ISIS adapted another first person shooter game called *ARMA III* which

is developed for Microsoft as well as another version of the famous *Call of Duty*.

(Al-Rawi, 2016)

The use of video games as a recruitment tool has been a supplement to the continuing distribution of "snuff" films and pop culture inspired videos on YouTube and more recently the TikTok platform (Shead, 2019).

State Actors

State actors are able to draw upon the ongoing process of militarization – a process that emerged out of the necessity of waging a "Total War" to win the Second World War. Militarization has embedded itself within the social, cultural, economic and political fabric of modern Western society. It has in effect become the dominant political/economic form of the advanced societies of the West. It both facilitated and extended the post-Second World War conflict between the Eastern and Western political blocs and continued to undergird these societies well beyond the end of that conflict ever since. Militarization has in effect become a socio-technical apparatus with which the economy, the political process, the culture and in effect the whole of society has been reconfigured to help conduct war. What we understand as modern society is today constituted by and through the mechanism of militarization and its ability to construct structures and processes that facilitate the production of violence.

Unlike non-State actors, who operate usually in clandestine ways in their recruitment activities, the State has no need to do this surreptitiously (Shead, 2019). The militarization of society facilitates the recruitment of young people into the military through its penetration of everyday life and the normalization of war (Lutz, 2002; Torres & Gurevich, 2018). This, as I will expand upon later in the book, is today the end result of the need to have a steady stream of potential war fighters without the need to resort to conscription. State actors are able to rely on their untrammeled access to potential recruits through both the underlying process whereby everyday life has been militarized – through media, advertising, social practices – and the high status afforded to the military in societies such as the United States. In this context easily accessible forms of media help State actors to project their political messages and to recruit young people. In the United States examples include the *Army vs Navy* football game (Butterworth & Moskal, 2009), advertising (Enloe, 2000), Hollywood portrayal of the military (Espiritu & Wolf, 2013), new media such as video games, for example *America's Army* (Allen, 2011; DiRomualdo, 2007), Facebook and online information dissemination (Singer & Brooking, 2018).

Fortnite

At this point in the discussion of play in its relationship to military themes and attitudes in video games, it is important to briefly look at a game that appeared on the scene in the late 2010s. Here I am referring to the massively popular multiplayer online "Battle-Royale" styled First-Person Shooter video game, *Fortnite*. A Battle-Royale styled video game involves the player competing with other players in a confined geographic location (imaginary or based on realistic locations). Over the period of play the gamer must kill their opponents using a variety of weapons and gather loot (either that appear in game randomly or are the possessions of their vanquished foes). The Battle-Royale genre maintains

> dramatic tension through the intersection of uncertainty and inevitability. Uncertainty is reinforced by randomness of the game world and hidden information of player statement. Inevitability is emerged from the level design with choke point, and restriction of playable field over time. From this mechanism, Battle Royale genre establishes the gameness which derives players' meaningful choice and maintains players' tension until the end of the game.
>
> (Ahn, 2017)

This style of game maintains a high level of tension for the player as the playing field narrows and narrows and the room to outrun or outmaneuver one's opponents shrinks. There are a number of these types of game – *Player Unknown Battle Grounds* (PUBG) was one of the first to garner a global following and player base. For the purpose of this chapter I want to focus though on *Fortnite,* which has had a much more widespread level of awareness and has meshed with a variety of popular culture forms and "franchises". For example both Marvel and Disney have lent their intellectual property in the form of the *Marvel Avengers* (Skrebels, 2020) and the *Star Wars* (Statt, 2019) characters to special in-game events or seasons. The willingness from these other popular culture franchises to engage with the game and its fanbase is indicative of its cultural and economic status. The game is free to download and contains in-game micro-transaction purchases for mods and "bling". *Fortnite* has grown from its 2017 launch to have 350 million (Statista, 2020b) registered players in May 2020 with over 62% of users aged 18–24 years (Statista, 2020a).

Fortnite was a runaway global success with children and adults since its launch, which was I think in part due to its design – it contains comic style game animation and is extremely colorful, loud and engaging. The game play is frenetic, and the tension referred to above is incessant. Stepping back from the noise, color and spectacular weaponry and scenery, the game has been able to mask its underpinning militaristic foundations. Unlike *Player*

Unknown – which makes no pretense at being anything other than a brutal militaristic survival game – *Fortnite* attempts to mask this foundation.

The game uses its colorful images and cartoonish characters to make the killing and destruction embedded in the game play appear to be harmless. As I have argued in this book and elsewhere, my critique of the game is not based on a moral stance – in fact it is not a question of right or wrong here. What I wish to highlight is the link between militarization in its broadest sense and games such as *Fortnite* (and PUBG). *Fortnite* is not a First-Person video game – it is a Third-Person Shooter where the player is a two-dimensional character within the game space. It is nevertheless military themed in that the object is to build defensible spaces and to hunt down one's opponents and kill them.

As I have argued elsewhere (Martino, 2012, 2015), playing a military-themed or oriented video game does not transform the player into a soldier or a violent person. However, it is my assertion that games such as *Fortnite* (and PUBG) fit within the framework of mechanisms that enhance military thinking and attitudes. The games are not about problem solving or working collaboratively to battle a zombie horde. They involve individual and squad based strategies and tactics – in the case of *Fortnite* in a cartoonish world, but in *Player Unknown* within a realistic landscape.

These games and other new forms of media and internet-based communications add to the general context of militarized media and cultural forms and I wish to argue assist in the attraction of young people to military causes and ensembles. They contribute to the recruitment of these young people into State and non-State military formations. I am not arguing that there is a direct link between playing *Fortnite* and signing up for the military. However, this game and other cultural forms described elsewhere in this book add to the pull or allure of military thinking and the elan of being part of a fighting force, even if it's only virtual. The work being done by *Fortnite* differs from the specifically designed recruitment-oriented video game *America's Army*. That game makes no pretense to its goal – to attract young people into the military. *Fortnite* on the other hand masks its militarized roots.

It is important to place this game and other militarized media forms within the context of a wider set of processes which both State and non-State actors have employed to attract recruits. *Fortnite* represents the embedding of militarization within the everyday life of young people and others. In contrast, the recruitment of young people to extremist causes cannot rely on something as banal as a video game – turbo-charged though it might be, such as *Fortnite*.

In the case of extremist groups, as Condis has argued,

> [m]odern internet-based recruitment efforts are designed around the creation of a frictionless pipeline that slowly inoculates potential

converts to hate – like putting a bunch of would-be Pepe the Frogs in a slowly boiling pot. Rather than waiting for targets to find them, recruiters go to where targets are, staging seemingly casual conversations about issues of race and identity in spaces where lots of disaffected, vulnerable adolescent white males tend to hang out. Those who exhibit curiosity about white nationalist talking points or express frustration with the alt-right's ideological opponents such as feminists, anti-racism activists and "social justice warriors" are then escorted through a funnel of increasingly racist rhetoric designed to normalize the presence of white supremacist ideology and paraphernalia through the use of edgy humor and memes.

(Condis, 2019)

Whilst the extremists must work very hard in many ways to attract their followers and to militarize them, both *Fortnite* and the general recruitment tactics of extremist groups act within this "frictionless pipeline" of the internet.

Conclusion

The origins of these forms of perceptual weaponry can be found in the close alignment between the military, its industrial base, and the entertainment establishment. In turn this alignment has fostered the militarization of society – a process that could not have had the success and unparalleled reach that it has without the affordances created by and through advances in digital technology. Creating gaming-based military training technologies and subsequently the bleeding of this technology into the civilian space through the popularity of war play as illustrated by the First-Person Shooter genre has had profound social, cultural and political consequences.

I think it's important to make it clear that this technology is part of an array of digital tools designed to extend the capacity for the waging of war. Training simulators, First-Person Shooter video games, *Xbox* and other forms of console gaming, whilst not capable of actually injuring someone, do have a perceptual impact. It is war propagated through other means. It is my assertion that there has been a conscious effort to harness gaming and game culture to appeal to young people, the origins of this being the desire to find new and better ways to train troops, but also since the 1990s to recruit young people through the widespread availability of militarized forms of gaming. This gaming technology has been augmented by the use of new forms of media to record military and terror attacks and thus amplify the impact of militarization and the construction of an acceptance of military thinking and military culture. I wish to assert that when viewed as whole these practices and processes are as deadly in intent as an advanced drone or a nuclear warhead.

References

Abney, W. (2019). *Random destiny: How the Vietnam War draft lottery shaped a generation*. Vernon Press.

Abramson, C. M., & Modzelewski, D. (2011). Caged morality: Moral worlds, subculture, and stratification among middle-class cage-fighters. *Qualitative sociology, 34*(1), 143–175.

Ahn, J.-K. (2017). A study on game dynamics of Battle Royale genre. *Journal of Korea Game Society, 17*(5), 27–38.

Al-Rawi, A. (2016). Video games, terrorism, and ISIS's Jihad 3.0. *Terrorism and Political Violence*. doi:10.1080/09546553.2016.1207633

Allen, R. (2011). The Unreal Enemy of America's Army. *Games and Culture, 6*(1), 38–60. doi:10.1177/1555412010377321

Almohammad, A. (2018). ISIS child soldiers in Syria: The structural and predatory recruitment, enlistment, pre-training indoctrination, training, and deployment. *The International Centre for Counter-Terrorism–The Hague, 8*.

Arquilla, J., & Ronfeldt, D. (1997). *In Athena's camp: Preparing for conflict in the information age*. Rand Corporation.

Bacevich, A. J. (2010). *Washington rules: America's path to permanent war*. Macmillan.

Badham, J. (Writer). (1983). *WarGames*. L. Goldeberg (Producer). USA: MGM.

Benson-Allott, C. (2018). On Platforms: They're coming to get you . . . or: Making America anxious again. *Film Quart, 72*(2), 71–76.

Bernazzoli, R. M., & Flint, C. (2010). Embodying the garrison state? Everyday geographies of militarization in American society. *Political Geography, 29*(3), 157–166.

Betts, R. K. (2012). From cold war to hot peace: The habit of American force. *Political Science Quarterly, 127*(3), 353–368.

Bishai, L. S. (2004). Liberal empire. *Journal of International Relations and Development, 7*(1), 48–72.

Bittanti, M. (2006). From GunPlay to GunPorn. A techno-visual history of the first-person shooter. URL: http://www.mattscape.com/images/GunPlayGunPorn.pdf. *12*(9).

Black, K. J., Britt, T. W., Lane, M. E., & Adler, A. B. (2018). Newcomer engagement and performance strategies in a high-risk occupational context. *Sport, Exercise, and Performance Psychology, 8*(3), 334–351.

Bloom, M. (2019). Weaponizing the weak: The role of children in terrorist groups. In *Research Handbook on Child Soldiers*, Mark A. Drumbl & Jastine C. Barrett (eds.). Edward Elgar Publishing.

Brandon, J. (2012). What's it like to pilot a drone? A lot like "Call of Duty". Retrieved from http://www.foxnews.com/tech/2012/11/26/whats-it-like-to-pilot-drone-lot-like-call-duty/

Brooking, E. T., & Singer, P. W. (2016). War goes viral: How social media is being weaponized across the world. Retrieved from http://www.defenseone.com/ideas/2016/10/war-goes-viral/132233/

Burston, J. (2003). War and the entertainment industries: New research priorities in an era of cyber-patriotism. *War and the Media: Reporting Conflict 24/7*, 163.

Butterworth, M. L., & Moskal, S. D. (2009). American Football, flags, and "fun": The Bell Helicopter Armed Forces Bowl and the rhetorical production of militarism. *Communication, Culture & Critique, 2*(4), 411–433.

Bymer, L. M. (2012). DSTS: First immersive virtual training system fielded. Retrieved from http://www.army.mil/article/84728/DSTS__First_immersive_virtual_training_system_fielded/

Card, O. S. (2014). *Ender's game* (Vol. 1): Tor Teen.
Condis, M. (2019). From Fortnite to Alt-Right. *The New York Times*.
Danner, C. (2015). How ISIS abducts, recruits, and trains children to become Jihadists. *Intelligencer*. Retrieved from http://nymag.com/intelligencer/2015/07/how-isis-abducts-recruits-and-trains-children.html?gtm=top&gtm=top
Dauber, C. E., Robinson, M. D., Baslious, J. J., & Blair, A. G. (2019). Call of Duty: Jihad – How the video game motif has migrated downstream from Islamic State propaganda videos. *Perspectives on Terrorism*, *13*(3).
Defense Science Board. (2004). *Strategic Communication*. Washington: US Government
Defense Science Board. (2008). *Strategic Communication*. Washington: US Government
Delwiche, A. (2007). From The Green Berets to America's Army: Video games as a vehicle for political propaganda. *The Player's Realm: Studies on the Culture of Video Games and Gaming*. Jefferson, NC: McFarland and Company, 91–109.
Department of Defense. (2003). *Information Operations Roadmap*. Retrieved from Washington DC:
Der Derian, J. (2009). *Virtuous war: Mapping the military-industrial-media-entertainment network*. New York: Routledge.
DiRomualdo, T. (2007). *US Army playing the recruiting game: How the U.S. Army has pioneered the use of game technology to recruit the Digital Generation*. Retrieved from Oxford: www.careerinnovation.com
Eid, J. (2018). New Hezbollah video game lets players annihilate IS fighters in Syria. Retrieved from https://www.france24.com/en/20180301-hezbollah-video-game-syria-lebanon
Enloe, C. H. (2000). *Maneuvers: The international politics of militarizing women's lives*: University of California Press.
Erikson, R. S., & Stoker, L. (2011). Caught in the draft: The effects of Vietnam draft lottery status on political attitudes. *American Political Science Review*, *105*(2), 221–237.
Espiritu, Y. L., & Wolf, D. (2013). The appropriation of American war memories: A critical juxtaposition of the Holocaust and the Vietnam War. *Social Identities*, 1–16.
Field, A. (2012). Prosocial behavior: Lessons from the military. Available at *SSRN 2085076*.
Gagnon, F. (2010). "Invading your hearts and minds": Call of Duty® and the (re) writing of militarism in US digital games and popular culture. *European Journal of American Studies* (2).
Geyer, M. (1989). The militarization of the Western world. In J. R. Gillis (Ed.), *The militarization of the Western world* (pp. 65–102). New Brunswick: Rutgers University Press.
Gill, Z. W. (2009). Rehearsing the war away: Perpetual warrior training in contemporary US Army policy. *TDR/The Drama Review*, *53*(3), 139–155.
Hall, B., Hendrickson, R. C., & Polak, N. M. (2013). Diversionary American military actions? American military strikes on Grenada and Iraq. *Comparative Strategy*, *32*(1), 35–51.
Hardt, M., & Negri, A. (2001). *Empire*. Harvard University Press.
Huizinga, J. (2003). *Homo ludens: A study of the play-element in culture*: Taylor & Francis.
Klevjer, R. (2006). The way of the gun. The aesthetic of the single-player First Person Shooter. *Bittanti, Matteo/Morris, Sue (Hg.): Doom. Giocare in prima persona*. Mailand: Costa & Nolan, 223–249.
Knight, D. J. (2007). *Transforming initial entry training to support a nation at war*. Carlisle Barracks, PA: Army War Collection.
Kretzschmar, M., & Stanfill, M. (2019). Mods as lightning rods: A typology of video game mods, intellectual property, and social benefit/harm. *Social & Legal Studies*, *28*(4), 517–536.

Lakomy, M. (2019). Let's play a video game: Jihadi propaganda in the world of electronic entertainment. *Studies in Conflict & Terrorism, 42*(4), 383–406. doi:10.1080/10576 10X.2017.1385903

Løvlie, A. S. (2008). *The rhetoric of persuasive games.* Paper presented at the Conference Proceedings of the Philosophy of Computer Games.

Lutz, C. (2002). Making war at home in the United States: Militarization and the current crisis. *American Anthropologist, 104*(3), 723–735.

MacDonald, M. (2014). *Black logos: Rhetoric and information warfare.* Paper presented at the Literature, Rhetoric and Values: Selected Proceedings of a Conference held at the University of Waterloo, 3–5 June 2011.

Macedonia, M. (2002). Games, simulation, and the military education dilemma. *Internet and the University: 2001 Forum*, 157–167.

Macedonia, M. (2005). Ender's game redux [computer games]. *Computer, 38*(2), 95–97.

Macedonia, M. R., & Herz, J. C. (2002). Computer games and the military: Two views. *Defense Horizons* (Number 11, April 2002).

Martino, J. (2012). Video games and the militarisation of society: Towards a theoretical and conceptual framework. In *ICT Critical Infrastructures and Society* (pp. 264–273). Springer.

Martino, J. (2015). *War/play : Video games and the militarization of society.* New York: Peter Lang.

Nieborg, D. (2004). America's Army: More than a game. In T. Erble (Ed.), *Transforming Knowledge into Action.* Munich: SAGSAGA.

Nieborg, D. (2009). Training recruits and conditioning youth: The soft power of military games. In I. Bogost, N. B. Huntemann, & M. T. Payne (Eds.), *Joystick soldiers: The politics of play in military video games* (pp. 53–66): Taylor & Francis.

Nieborg, D. B., & Van der Graaf, S. (2008). The mod industries? The industrial logic of non-market game production. *European Journal of Cultural Studies, 11*(2), 177–195.

Peters, R. (1997). Constant conflict. *Parameters, 27*, 4–14.

Rayner, A. (2012). Are video games just propaganda and training tools for the military? *The Guardian.* Retrieved from http://www.guardian.co.uk/technology/2012/mar/18/video-games-propaganda-tools-military?newsfeed=true

Shead, S. (2019). TikTok used by Islamic State to spread propaganda videos. Retrieved from https://www.bbc.com/news/technology-50138740

Simon, P. (2016). How Isis hijacked pop culture, from Hollywood to video games. *theguardian.com.* Retrieved from https://www.theguardian.com/world/2016/jan/29/how-isis-hijacked-pop-culture-from-hollywood-to-video-games

Singer, P. W., & Brooking, E. T. (2018). *LikeWar: The weaponization of social media*: Eamon Dolan Books.

Šisler, V. (2006). Representation and self-representation: Arabs and Muslims in digital games. *Gaming realities: A challenge for digital culture.* Athens: Ed. Fournos.

Šisler, V. (2008). Digital Arabs: Representation in video games. *European Journal of Cultural Studies, 11*(2), 203–220.

Skrebels, J. (2020). Marvel's Avengers getting a Fortnite crossover. *IGN.* Retrieved from https://www.ign.com/articles/marvels-avengers-fortnite-hulk-smashers-hulkbuster-pickaxe-style

Sotamaa, O. (2010). When the game is not enough: Motivations and practices among computer game modding culture. *Games and Culture, 5*(3), 239.

Statista. (2020a). Distribution of players of Fortnite in the United States as of April 2018, by age group. *Media & Advertising›Video Games & Gaming*. Retrieved from https://www.statista.com/statistics/865616/fortnite-players-age/

Statista. (2020b). Number of registered users of Fortnite worldwide from August 2017 to May 2020 *Media & Advertising›Video Games & Gaming*. Retrieved from https://www.statista.com/statistics/746230/fortnite-players/

Statt, N. (2019). How to watch Fortnite's exclusive Star Wars: The Rise of Skywalker clip this Saturday. *The Verge*. Retrieved from https://www.theverge.com/2019/12/13/21020843/fortnite-star-wars-the-rise-of-sykwalker-clip-exclusive-premiere-risky-reels

Torres, N., & Gurevich, A. (2018). Introduction: Militarization of consciousness. *Anthropology of Consciousness, 29*(2), 137–144. doi:10.1111/anoc.12101

Turse, N. (2008). *The complex: How the military invades our everyday lives* (1st ed.). New York: Metropolitan Books.

Virilio, P. (1989). *War and cinema: The logistics of perception*: Verso Books.

Chapter 4

GoPro-War, Live Streaming and the Gamification and Cinematic Construction of Terror and Armed Conflict-Themed Media

A Gamified Military and Terror Battlespace

The use of images, film and video to project political messages in the form of propaganda is an integral feature of political action both in times of war and also in peace. The digital revolution begun in the last decades of the 20th century has been augmented by and through the popularization of the internet and the exponential growth in social media platforms and their audience. These technologies have created both a domestic and a global audience for political messaging and propaganda. The affordances presented by these technologies have been utilized by both State and non-State actors to project political messages and to engage in Information warfare. In this chapter I will examine the use of video technology to in effect gamify terror and armed conflict as a result of the ubiquity of live-streaming and easily accessible publishing technology such as social media platforms. I will discuss the use of *GoPro* technology by both State and non-State actors to project their messages and to create a gamified military and terror battlespace.

GoPro War

In September 2015 the Russian Federation was formally invited to come to the aid of the Syrian government in its war with pro-Western rebels and the nascent Islamic State army which had swept into Syria from Iraq (Charap, Treyger, & Geist, 2019; Maher & Pieper, 2020). This entailed the movement of ground forces supported by Russian airpower out of Syrian government-held zones on the coastal fringe towards rebel- and Islamic State-held towns and cities. This incursion had a devastating impact on the Syrian government's opponents and in time would change the course of the war and effectively destroy opposition to the Syrian government and its allies. This new phase of the war was unique in its capacity to bring home to a global audience the application of unrestrained Russian military prowess. In order to project this new image of a post-Soviet, post-Afghanistan (of the 1980s) Russian Army, the range of new media then available was utilized. In particular, the use of *GoPro* cameras to document much of the action has become the leitmotif of this intervention.

This Russian incursion into Syria brought with it an adaptation of new media such as the *GoPro* technology and YouTube to the task of creating a global perception of Russian military success and capability. It also added another layer to the techniques developed and honed by the Islamic State which we can refer to as the gamification of war and terror. As discussed elsewhere in this book the Islamic State has drawn on video game culture in the construction of the *mise-en-scène* of their propaganda videos as well as in the creation of pro-Islamic State First Person Shooter video games.

The use of video technology in the battlespace was not an invention of the Russians – non-State actors such as the Islamic State and al-Qaeda had been used to record roadside bombings caused by Improvised Explosive Devices (IEDs), or to record infantry actions and ritual executions as depicted in the now infamous series of beheading videos transmitted by the Islamic State. However, the use of *GoPro* technology by the Russians and their government allies in Syria differed from how it had been used elsewhere. The Russians produced First Person *GoPro* videos of tank assaults and traditional house to house combat in an effort to assert their re-emergence as a potent military and political force.

First Person *GoPro* videos provided another tool in their growing hybrid-warfare toolbox. The Russians were drawing on this technology to create their own version of "Shock and Awe", as the Americans had with their devastating bombing of Iraq in the first decade of this century. The mediatization of modern warfare was in full swing, as it has been since at least the end of the Cold War. The application of video game culture to the propaganda videos of the opposing forces in both Syria and Iraq has been given impetus by the affordances embedded in the internet and streaming platforms, such as YouTube, and their proliferation.

The Russians and the Syrians were able to generate volumes of YouTube video footage – constructed in such a way that the conflict took on aspects of video game play – the conflict was gamified (Tarantola, 2014). *GoPro* and similar video technology gave the viewer a driver's seat vantage point of the carnage. For example, one image taken from a YouTube collage of videos highlights the Syrian/Russian liberation of the city of Darayya, Syria. In the video the *GoPro* camera was placed on the command turret of the tank and thus mirrors the First Person perspective adopted in many shooter games such as *Call of Duty* (Bittanti, 2006; Martino, 2015). As Bittani points out, the First-Person perspective

> is a digital application, originally created for recreational purposes, resulting from the interaction of four major components: computer, film, television, and military technology, with the latter informing

the previous three. The computer is both a production tool and a consumption space. Cinema and television provide the visual style and the narrative context of the FPS, whereas the military ethos supplies the ideological basis for the genre.

(Bittanti, 2006)

The construction of the video, and the many others posted by the Russian and Syrian governments, reflects the adaptation of the elements of film, television and military technology that First Person Shooter video games have used since the 1990s to the new medium of streaming video. The videos posted both by State and non-State actors in the Syrian conflict share a gamified aesthetic and the dual purpose of both entertaining and politicizing the viewer. This is representative of a shift away from "old forms" of media – the traditional network news-gathering services and their supplanting by the growth of multiple sources of news and information.

This emergence of new forms of media and digital technologies has helped to foster the mediatizing of warfare – this has, as Kaempf (2013) argues, created

> a structural shift from a multipolar to a heteropolar global media landscape, in which newly empowered non-state actors and individuals contest the hitherto state-policed narratives and coverage of war, and in which traditional media platforms have started to converge with digital new media platforms. Heteropolarity thus refers to the multiplication and simultaneous diversification of structurally different media actors. This current transformation of the global media landscape has, in turn, impacted heavily on and altered the traditional relationship between media and war, creating the conditions for contemporary media wars.
>
> (Kaempf, 2013)

This "sea change" (Kaempf, 2013) has been with us since the early part of this century but it has only been since first the rise of the Islamic State and then the reassertion of Russian military prowess in Ukraine and more recently in Syria, that both State and non-State actors have been able to fully realize the potential of these technologies.

The images generated by both State and non-State actors in Syria and then distributed using digital streaming platforms and the internet extends the same process of the democratization of political propaganda that social media has enabled. Both the conflict in Ukraine and in Syria (as well as the ongoing social war described in the previous chapter) are examples of hybrid-warfare.

One of the key characteristics of hybrid-warfare is the ability of both non-State as well as State actors to project political messages and inflict perceptual damage at the individual and societal level. War has become digital and mediatized. War is no longer distant or, in the case of the Western intervention in Afghanistan and then Iraq earlier this century, hidden and the subject of self-censorship by traditional news media (Zweers, 2016). These wars were the first large scale conflicts that the United States and its Allies had engaged in since their defeat in Vietnam. They were prosecuted under quite different circumstances than the Vietnam war – the War on Terror legitimized the conduct of military action in a clandestine or less opaque manner than other conflicts. The War on Terror ushered in an era where conflict became localized – the homeland could now become a theater of conflict (as it had been during the Second World War, for example, as had happened in the Blitz), through terror attacks. It was also different in that the commitment of ground forces first in Afghanistan and subsequently in Iraq, whilst public, was also opaque in its actual prosecution. Whereas in the 1960s and 1970s a constant stream of film and video was consumed by the general public through the evening news, a practice which made the war in Vietnam the first "Television War" and brought its horror into our living room, the War on Terror actively negated this type of transparency. Whilst individual soldiers recorded many aspects of these conflicts and posted them to personal vlogs and later on YouTube – this was never a conscious military or political strategy actively encouraged or engaged in by US forces and their allies (Christensen, 2016). When graphic gunsight video was leaked to a horrified global public by Wikileaks, the US military and political authorities were severely embarrassed by the exposure of the true nature of conflict in these settings.

Both the Islamic State and the Russian and Syrian forces have on the other hand adapted this new media landscape and its underpinning technologies to both project their political message and to inflict a form of perceptual damage to their opponents. A key element in this new mediatized form of warfare has been the promotion of a narrative which has at its core – at least in the case of the Russians in Syria – that they are an army of "Heroes", a modern version of the Red Army which had defeated the Nazis.

"Heroization"

Both State and non-State actors have evolved a propaganda strategy which packages the recording of combat footage (using a video game aesthetic in its production) to both project their political messages and also to inflict perceptual damage as part of a broader strategy of hybrid-warfare. Another aspect of what the form of hybrid warfare that the State and non-State actors engaged in, both in Syria, but also in the Russian intervention into Ukraine, can be described as fostering the process of the "heroization" of their forces (Classen, 2007). The process of "heroization" occurs

> through [a range of] social and communicative processes. These processes require a mediatized representation and are affectively and normatively charged. The specific forms of the processes of heroization depend on the actors involved and their motivations. Another aspect is the question of how and why the heroic is used as an attribute, and how it takes effect in the first place.
>
> (von den Hoff et al., 2019)

The videos that have been produced by both State and non-State actors in the Syrian conflict are an interesting example of the use of streaming technology and video to construct an image of their respective forces which amplifies the heroic nature of their role in the conflict. This is what I mean when I argue that they are engaged in the "heroization" process. They both seek to portray their forces as being on the side of the just. In the case of IS it is their Jihadi terror volunteers, and in the case of the Syrian and Russian forces, formal military formations and militia groups that are fighting the good fight.

The creation of *GoPro* propaganda footage highlighted above can be seen in the context of hybrid-warfare and the strategies and tactics that the Russians had perfected in Ukraine (Greenberg, 2018; Thiele, 2015). The strategy also reflects an understanding of the nature of digital culture and the role streaming technology now plays in the contemporary social and cultural landscape. It is also a recognition that this relatively new and cheap technology is a potent mechanism with which political imagery can be applied in waging information warfare.

It is my assertion that these new forms of media (streaming platforms and video technology such as *GoPro*) have provided a cultural and political space with which to disseminate political imagery in order to both appeal to potential supporters and purposely inflict perceptual damage to their foes. The live steaming of political violence has supplanted the cultural–political position once held by the still image. Streaming platforms and video technology such as *GoPro* have become a spark for political action and the means of projecting a political message that is easily consumable by the viewer. This was a place that the still image or newsreel footage once held.

Political Imagery: From Sontag to *GoPro*

At this point in the chapter I would like to briefly contrast the seminal discussion of the political power of photography in the 20th century that Susan Sontag wrote about in her classic book, *On Photography* (1977), with the application for political purposes of "streaming video" in the 21st century. Where the still image capturing the atrocities of war and conflict were in the 20th century amongst the most powerful political imagery, here Sontag talks about images from the Holocaust and the war in Vietnam.

In *On Photography* (1977) Susan Sontag argued that the still image in the 20th century had helped project political messages and led to many instances of political change. In her thinking, the still image was able to capture the historical moment much more effectively than the moving image in television and film had been able to. Sontag asserted that

> [p]hotographs may be more memorable than moving images, because they are a neat slice of time, not a flow. Television is a stream of under selected images, each of which cancels its predecessor. Each still photograph is a privileged moment, turned into a slim object that one can keep and look at again: Photographs like the one that made the front page of most newspapers in the world in 1972 – a naked South Vietnamese child just sprayed by American napalm, running down a highway toward the camera, her arms open, screaming with pain- probably did more to increase the public revulsion against the war than a hundred hours of televised barbarities.
>
> (Sontag, 1977)

The tragic images that Sontag describes in her book as both politicizing her at an individual level – images of a Nazi death camp and the napalm bombing of a young Vietnamese child – and in this case at a generational level differ in one key point. They were not constructed to inflict perceptual damage. The image of the Vietnamese child, though, did in fact do that – it fundamentally shifted people's perspective on the war and eroded much of what was left of public support for the war. The events captured by *GoPro* technology in Syria and posted to YouTube are intentional, they are not the product of serendipity as the Vietnam example was. They have been constructed to add a cinematic and mediatized angle of viewing for a global audience, in this context these new forms of media and their underpinning technologies are more like the propaganda vehicles constructed by the Allies in the Second World War – Capra's *Why We Fight* (Capra, 1942) series – or the Nazi propaganda vehicles such as the *Triumph of the Will* (Riefenstahl, 1935).

The Cinematic Construction of Terror and Armed Conflict

During the military incursions of the mid-2010s, IS was able to utilize media as both a weapon of terror and as a means of attracting recruits and supporters to their cause. A key element in the strategy adopted by IS was the construction of murder as performance. The countless variants of execution videos that were live streamed or posted to YouTube generated a global sense of fear, but also awe and empowerment amongst groups and individuals (Koch, 2018; Tinnes, 2015). The ritual slaughtering of captives, filmed in cinematic style then posted as slick, almost Hollywood-like productions, transmitted both fear and terror on a planetary scale. IS was able to harness new media and apply it as a weapon. Its message, transmitted through the web but also picked up by global media outlets and relayed to vast audiences, was truly terror inducing. To fully understand the working of social technologies such as social media in modern hybrid war, we need to expand our understanding of how messages that target the young specifically but that also attempt to project fear and panic in civilian populations, function.

As I pointed out earlier, video games and video game metaphors provide propagandists with a visual set of concepts and tools with which to craft their messages in a manner that is easily understood. Young people in particular are familiar with both the visual aesthetic of video game genres (particularly the First-Person Shooter) but more generally gamification is now embedded in the cultural landscape of the broader society. The gamic nature of some of the material produced by both State and non-State actors as part of the array of tools and methods used in contemporary propaganda has been facilitated by technologies such as YouTube and publishing platforms, for example Twitter and Facebook (Shammas, 2016; Stein, 2017; Tarantola, 2014). What these platforms have enabled is the creation of a new form of propaganda messaging – the *GoPro* live stream. The harnessing to live streaming of violence has enabled a new powerful perceptual and propaganda weapon. The live streaming of violent political acts is now an accepted tool in the array of propaganda weapons available to State and non-State actors. A report published by the Network of Excellence for Research in Violent Online Political Extremism and authored by Conway and Dillon (2019) included a description of a terrorist attack in Magnanville, France. As the report describes, on the 13 June 2016,

> around 8pm: policeman, Jean-Baptiste Salvaing has been stabbed to death outside his home. Forcing his way into the house, the attacker murders Jessica Schneider, who also worked for the police, by cutting her throat. The couple's three-year-old son is taken hostage by the killer, Larossi Aballa. Prior to a three-hour stand-off with police negotiators, Aballa turns to social media to broadcast and justify his actions, dedicating them to his 'Emir' Abu Bakr Al-Baghdadi (Hume et al 2016). It is the first time a terrorist has used a live-streaming service in the midst of an attack. It is unlikely to be the last.
>
> (Conway & Dillon, 2019)

As the report goes on to state, the use of visual technology to project a terror act to a global audience is not new. The massacre of the Israeli Olympic Team in 1972 was in effect the first terror attack recorded live and transmitted via satellite to a global audience (Silke & Filippidou, 2019). But what was unique and also instructive in this act was the use by the perpetrator of his easily accessible and operated technology – a mobile phone to project the propaganda message himself. He created a form of perceptual weaponry with which he generated an "information bullet" which was projected both at his supporters, but more particularly in the direction of his perceived enemies as well as bystanders. The Palestinian terrorists of "Black September" were reliant on the international media to both record their action but also to interpret their short statements to the world. The Magnanville terrorist and those who have followed his example are both the subject and producers of their propaganda message. Both during and after they commit their crimes, these non-State actors take the time to tell their audience what they are going to do and why. The technology enables them to project their message in an unfiltered and unmediated manner.

The New Zealand mosque massacres that took place in Christchurch in 2019 highlighted the extent to which media-savvy non-State actors are able to use new media technology to amplify both the propaganda value of their actions, as well as amplifying its horror and impact.

Using a *GoPro* to live-stream acts of terror and violence is the newest adaptation of what can be described as a "video game aesthetic" – taking elements from the First-Person Shooter genre to tailor this form of information bullet. These attacks tapped into the popular cultural practice of live streaming video game play to an audience who are watching this on platforms such as Facebook, YouTube and Twitch and made possible by the ubiquitous nature of the internet (Roose, 2019).

With the ability to by-pass traditional means of getting a political or propaganda message across to a target audience, new media has now constructed a potent means of information dissemination, at scale. An individual, a group or a nation are now all on an equal footing in their capacity and effectiveness in crafting a political message and having it delivered in a cost efficient and globe spanning manner.

The use of video game metaphors and aesthetics in the design of propaganda messages or as recruitment tools is not restricted to either State actors or Islamic extremists. The newly energized armies of the extreme right have taken on board similar militarized modes of representation and also the visual culture of the First-Person Shooter, and added another layer of horror to this approach (Russworm, 2018). Perhaps one of the most salient examples in recent history of the manner in which video game culture has been adopted as both a stylistic and cultural inspiration to extremist groups and individuals is the Christchurch massacre (Nguyen, 2019). As I pointed out earlier in this chapter, the 2019 mass killing of Muslim people in Christchurch, New Zealand, had distinct new media and video game elements in how the shooter conducted himself and how he projected his violent message onto the global internet. Using *GoPro*-like cameras he filmed himself getting ready for the attack and then the actual attack. This was live streamed to the internet and was rapidly shared across the web.

GoPro cameras have been used to record military actions by State actors such as the Israeli military and in Syria by both Syrian government forces and their Russian Federation allies for a number of years (Stein, 2017; Tarantola, 2014). *GoPro* technology along with drones carrying these cameras have also been used extensively by non-State actors such as the Islamic State who have recorded First-Person video like footage of combat for their media operations (Shammas, 2016). The Christchurch murderer adopted a similar strategy to the Islamic State, and it seems added his unique touch in that he live-streamed the shooting. This live streaming via Facebook and subsequently the uploading of copies of the footage to YouTube and other sites was facilitated by the growing ubiquity of the internet. Easy access to high speed broadband has meant such a crime was not only possible but inevitable.

Footage streamed by the killer has the look and feel of a First-Person Shooter video game, in fact he has made a great deal of the inspiration and affordances made available by these games in both his preparation and execution of his crime. It is clear from accounts of what he published in his 75-page online manifesto that he was "trolling" his audience when he stated that "Fortnite trained me to be a killer" (Roose, 2019). He is referring to one of the most popular online First-Person Shooter video games. Of course, this statement sent the traditional media, the social media world and conservatives globally into a frenzy. Once again video games were causally linked to an actual act of violence.

As Megan Condis pointed out in *The New York Times*: "the shooter who live-streamed himself killing 50 worshipers in two mosques in Christchurch, New Zealand, ... was not being serious when he wrote that 'Spyro the Dragon 3 taught me ethno-nationalism' or that *Fortnite* prepared him to kill" (Condis, 2019). As a number of commentators have pointed out, the Christchurch killer was in effect generating a "meme" (Condis, 2019; Roose, 2019). He was trolling his global audience. This nevertheless does not negate the point I have been making in this chapter and the rest of the book – video games, much of popular culture and the general cultural undercurrent in our society is oriented to creating the conditions that are conducive to the "production of violence". At the same time these new forms of media are able to be used asymmetrically to amplify and engage in perceptual warfare and the carrying out of acts of perceptual violence.

If the concentration camp was the product of the age of mass production and industrialization then it would not be overstating the point to argue that the live-streaming social media-savvy killers of recent times are the product of the digital age. They were schooled in the culture of the web. They think in terms of "likes", doing things for the "LOLs" and numbers of "retweets". They tailor their actions to fit the technology and construct their acts of violence in a performative manner. They are streaming to their audience live through Facebook or asynchronously via the other social media platforms or YouTube. Just as the Situationists of the 1960s and 1970s constructed their political actions with a national and international audience in mind, the terror groups and nation-state actors of the 21st century construct their armed assaults in person or via a drone with a clear goal of reaching the global 24/7 audience and the 24/7 news cycle (Beck, 2015; Bourg, 2005).

Live streaming through such technology as *GoPro* has added one more element to the array of perceptual weaponry that new media has placed at the disposal of both State and non-State actors. *GoPro* technology provides non-State actors with a cheap and effective means with which to capture their armed assaults. It has also been utilized as I pointed out earlier to document recent State-actor violence in places such as Syria and also Ukraine. State actors have also made use of the recording of armed assaults through drone-mounted video to document attacks on terror hideouts or the targeted assassination of terror leaders and their followers. Whilst the use of live-captured video streams by State actors is not usually constructed to mirror a First-Person Shooter – they still have a game-like quality to them in that the camera is controlled by "joysticks" and also often through *Xbox*-like controllers (Orvis, Moore, Belanich, Murphy, & Horn, 2010; Salter, 2013; Shaw, 2013; Zulaika, 2013).

The adoption of game metaphors from the First-Person Shooter genre is illustrated by, for example, the way the social media-savvy killers we have seen in New Zealand and elsewhere have mounted a camera on their head gear or gun barrel in order to capture the footage of the attack in a manner that mirrors the *mise-en-scène* of the First-Person Shooter. The game-like nature of these attacks is also reflected by the assailants decorating or "modding" their weapons – for example the New Zealand killer painted neo-Nazi slogans and images on his gun. These assaults have also by their very nature mirrored the accepted practice amongst gamers of live streaming game play through Twitch and other video streaming platforms, thus enabling these killers to tap into the audience for live game action. What they have added into the mix is that it is real – it is not simulated and thus the "body count" and "head shots" of the First-Person Shooter are visceral. The snuff movies of the past that existed in the dark corners of the web or on disk or tape, whispered about and sold on "black markets", have now been mainstreamed and projected to a vast global online audience. The "society of the spectacle" that Debord (1992) wrote about lives and breathes in the 21st century.

Through his actions the New Zealand killer illustrates how the Alt-Right are also making use of the same strategies that the Islamic State has adopted to recruit young people to their cause – by creating a vivid live-action depiction of his ideology at work (Besley & Peters, 2020). This was a clear attempt to tap into the broader gamer culture. As I have pointed out earlier, the new technology amplifies the capability of groups such as neo-fascists of the Alt-Right as well as groups such as the Islamic State. In a piece written not long after the shootings, Duff (2019) pointed out that in his manifesto the killer refers to a range of cultural tropes such as "The Great Replacement" and also

> mentions videogames, the name of a massively popular online YouTube gamer, and leaves what are known as 'easter eggs' – gaming terminology for a hidden message or image that reveals a work's 'true' meaning.
> (Duff, 2019)

From the understanding gleaned from his manifesto and manner in which he constructed the live streaming of the shootings it is possible to argue that the killer and the broader Alt-Right that fostered his development are making use of similar tactics and strategies to those used by the Islamic State. These include "using fabricated narratives and false concepts designed to deceive, with messages deliberately targeted to different online platforms" (Duff, 2019).

Conclusion

What draws together all of these strategies and tactics is the application of game-like metaphors, approaches and experiences. The Alt-Right, the Islamic State and State actors share an interest in the application of gaming to both recruit new followers and to project their political message by the weaponization of these new forms of media technology. These groups share a commitment to use play – specifically war play – to accomplish this. Playing at war, either in a game or through the witnessing of live streamed game-like attacks, enables these groupings to project their ideological and perceptual weaponry into a range of settings. They can project their messages and display their corporeal power through the generation of video game-like footage which is distributed by existing or emergent streaming platforms. The various forms of social media and streaming technology act like a "force amplifier" for both State and non-State actors by giving them a platform – an unregulated one at that – from which to launch these perceptual attacks (Roose, 2019).

References

Beck, C. J. (2015). *Radicals, revolutionaries, and terrorists*. Cambridge, UK: Polity.
Besley, T., & Peters, M. A. (2020). Terrorism, trauma, tolerance: Bearing witness to white supremacist attack on Muslims in Christchurch, New Zealand. *Educational Philosophy and Theory, 52*(2), 109–119. doi:10.1080/00131857.2019.1602891

Bittanti, M. (2006). From GunPlay to GunPorn. A techno-visual history of the first-person shooter. URL: http://www. mattscape. com/images/GunPlayGunPorn.pdf. 12(9).

Bourg, J. (2005). The Red Guards of Paris: French Student Maoism of the 1960s. *History of European Ideas*, 31(4), 472–490.

Capra, F. (Writer). (1942). *Why We Fight*. U. S. A. S. S. Division (Producer). USA: US War Department.

Charap, S., Treyger, E., & Geist, E. (2019). *Understanding Russia"s intervention in Syria*. RAND.

Christensen, C. (2016). Images that last? Iraq videos from YouTube to WikiLeaks. In *Image operations*. Manchester University Press.

Classen, C. (2007). Thoughts on the significance of mass-media communications in the Third Reich and the GDR. *Totalitarian Movements & Political Religions*, 8(3–4), 547–562. doi:10.1080/14690760701571171

Condis, M. (2019). From Fortnite to Alt-Right. *The New York Times*.

Conway, M., & Dillon, J. (2019). Future trends: Live-streaming terrorist attacks? *VOX-Pol*. Accessed October, 8.

Debord, G. (1992). *The society of the spectacle*. 1967. Paris: Les Éditions Gallimard.

Duff, M. (2019). Gaming culture and the alt-right: The weaponisation of hate. *Stuff*. Retrieved from https://www.stuff.co.nz/national/christchurch-shooting/111468129/gaming-culture-and-the-alt-right-the-weaponisation-of-hate?cid=app-iPhone

Greenberg, A. (2018). Darkness at midnight: Could Russia be using Ukraine as a lab for global cyberwar? *The Age*. Retrieved from http://www.theage.com.au/world/hunting-the-hackers-how-ukraine-became-russias-test-lab-for-cyberwar-20171017-gz2dtx.html?btis

Kaempf, S. (2013). The mediatisation of war in a transforming global media landscape. *Australian Journal of International Affairs*, 67(5), 586–604.

Koch, A. (2018). Jihadi beheading videos and their non-Jihadi echoes. *Perspectives on Terrorism, 12*(3), 24–34.

Maher, D., & Pieper, M. (2020). Russian intervention in Syria: Exploring the nexus between regime consolidation and energy transnationalisation. *Political Studies*, 0032321720934637.

Martino, J. (2015). *War/play: Video games and the militarization of society*. New York: Peter Lang.

Nguyen, K. (2019). Accused Christchurch mosque shooter used same radicalisation tactics as Islamic State, expert says. Retrieved from https://www.abc.net.au/news/2019-03-17/brenton-tarrant-in-court-*suspect-face-must-be-pixelated.-only/10908862

Orvis, K. A., Moore, J. C., Belanich, J., Murphy, J. S., & Horn, D. B. (2010). Are soldiers gamers? Videogame usage among soldiers and implications for the effective use of serious videogames for military training. *Military Psychology, 22*(2), 143–157.

Riefenstahl, L. (Writer). (1935). *Triumph of the Will*. L. Riefenstahl (Producer). Berlin, Germany: Leni Riefenstahl-Produktion Reichspropagandaleitung der NSDAP (as NSDAP Reichspropagandaleitung Hauptabt. Film).

Roose, K. (2019, March 19, 2019). A mass shooting of, and for, the internet, online. *The New York Times*. Retrieved from https://www.nytimes.com/2019/03/15/technology/facebook-youtube-christchurch-shooting.html

Russworm, T. M. (2018). A call to action for videogame studies in an age of reanimated white supremacy. *Velvet Light Trap, (81)*, 73–77.

Salter, M. (2013). Toys for the boys? Drones, pleasure and popular culture in the militarisation of policing. *Critical Criminology*, 1–15. doi:10.1007/s10612-013-9213-4

Shammas, J. (2016). Chilling footage shows ISIS terrorists using DRONES and GoPro cameras to film battles in Iraq. Retrieved from https://www.mirror.co.uk/news/world-news/chilling-footage-shows-isis-terrorists-7102106

Shaw, I. G. R. (2013). Predator empire: The geopolitics of US drone warfare. *Geopolitics, 18*(3), 536–559. doi:10.1080/14650045.2012.749241

Silke, A., & Filippidou, A. (2019). What drives terrorist innovation? Lessons from Black September and Munich 1972. *Security Journal*, 1–18.

Sontag, S. (1977). *On photography*. New York: Farrar, Straus and Giroux.

Stein, R. L. (2017). GoPro occupation: Networked cameras, Israeli military rule, and the digital promise. *Current Anthropology, 58*(S15), S56-S64.

Tarantola, A. (2014). Terrifying GoPro video from tanks in Syria"s war zone. Retrieved from https://gizmodo.com/incredible-footage-from-tanks-in-syrias-warzone-is-utt-1548084560?IR=T

Thiele, R. D. (2015). Crisis in Ukraine: The emergence of hybrid warfare. *ISPSW Strategic Series, 347*, 1–13.

Tinnes, J. (2015). Although the (dis-)believers dislike it: A backgrounder on IS hostage videos–August-December 2014. *Perspectives on Terrorism, 9*(1).

von den Hoff, R., Asch, R. G., Aurnhammer, A., Bröckling, U., Korte, B., Leonhard, J., & Studt, B. (2019). *Heroes–Heroizations–Heroisms. helden. heroes. héros.*, 2.

Zulaika, J. (2013). Drones and fantasy in US counterterrorism. *Journal for Cultural Research*, 1–17. doi:10.1080/14797585.2013.851853

Zweers, A. (2016). *The propaganda model and the news coverage on the War on Terror*. The Netherlands: Radboud University.

Chapter 5

"Toughen Up"
Cultural Politics and the Hardening of Youth

Violence, Cruelty and Evil

The American sociologist Jack Katz writing in his classic book the *Seductions of Crime* (Katz, 1988) developed an interesting argument concerning why crime and also particular acts of evil occur. In his book, Katz argued that these acts embodied what he calls the "pleasures of evil". Criminal and violent acts, according to Katz, embody a form of sensuality and seductiveness. For Katz, crime enables perpetrators to act out evil – to do things that in the normal state of affairs would not be countenanced. But when acting in a criminal manner violence, cruelty and evil become options. They become avenues through which perpetrators can experience evil as a form of pleasure. It is my contention that we have over the past few decades witnessed the gradual colonization of our social, political, economic and cultural landscapes by these "pleasures of evil". Since the publication of Katz's insightful study into the allure of criminality we have experienced the emergence of an obsession with depictions of violence and crime as a staple of popular culture and the bread and butter of all forms of sensationalist news coverage. As I will expand upon later in this book, this obsession with violence is part of a broader process which has at its core the normalization of war within the context of the militarization of society.

It will be argued in the pages that follow that there is an obsession with violence and cruelty in contemporary Western culture. This is not to deny that our culture is rich with examples of violence in both history and fiction. The real and the imagined have always had a strong tinge of violence. What I think is different to the literary description of violence or the historical analysis of war and revolution is the access to simulated and real depictions of violence and cruelty that new forms of technology now afford us. We can think of this easy access to the depiction of violence and cruelty as being part of a process of what I will refer to as the "hardening" of Western culture and society. This is reflected in a range of cultural forms, social and political processes that act to reinforce the "toughening up" of the population in general and young people in particular. We no longer need mass armies, or large bodies of reserve personnel to engage in military action, nor do we need military-like structures such as the boy scouts, or even the Hitler Youth, to prepare populations for possible conflict. Instead new forms of media have provided a "soft" form of preparation for war.

The focus of this chapter will be an examination of how this process of hardening, and the embracing of the pleasures of evil has emerged. Whilst it would be possible simply to examine these developments from the perspective of society as a whole, I intend meshing this broader view with insights into how young people fit within this set of emergent social, political and cultural processes. I will now elaborate on these statements.

New Forms of Media, Popular Culture and the "Hardening" of Youth – Some General Remarks

New forms of media such as YouTube, Facebook, Twitter and the explosion in streaming platforms have enlarged the cultural landscape upon which violence, cruelty and acts of degradation are witnessed, simulated and disseminated. Exposure to images and vision of violence both real and scripted has become much more accessible and commonplace (A. L. Hall, 2013; Malhara, 2017). Since the advent of these new platforms and modes of delivery and consumption the ability of individuals and groups to create and disseminate still images, video and memes depicting violence and acts of cruelty and degradation has become in a sense "democratized". As Deleuze and Guattari (Deleuze, Guattari, & Massumi, 1986) argued, it defeats the purpose of these acts of violence to spill large amounts of blood; new forms of digital technology enable the application of an "economy of violence". Digital media platforms such as Facebook and YouTube for example have created digital spaces within which violent and extreme acts can be played out for a global audience in real-time and created with very low-cost technology. State actors are no longer the sole purveyors of propaganda or fear – this is what I mean by the "democratization" of digital forms of cruelty or of terror.

Young People as "Materiel" and Audience

The easy access to violent videos produced by groups such as the Islamic State and more recently the live streaming of violent attacks on two mosques in New Zealand should be seen within a broader context of the normalization of violence and cruelty as cultural commodities. These commodities are available for consumption 24/7 through the conduit of high-speed, high-definition media and information technologies. This is an evolution of what has been a part of the seedy undercurrent of Western culture for decades. The enactment and depiction of violent acts for the voyeuristic consumption of individuals and groups.

For example, since the late 1990s there has existed a voyeuristic subculture of video fights depicting people being pitted against each other and forced to fight – often homeless people or prisoners are used. These fights were videoed for distribution, initially in the last century this was done on videocassette or later compact disc/DVDs but now in the 21st century they are distributed through the internet. Salter and Tomsen (2011) have argued that the internet enabled the amplification of

> sadistic and voyeuristic interests that were previously sublimated in cultural life are now more openly nurtured in online representations of violence. A quick internet search can find many amateur films of 'underground' fight matches and conflicts in bars, on the streets or in schools. The phenomenon of 'happy-slapping' in the form of physical assaults between young people that are planned with the intention of distributing the digital recording online has emerged with the advent of mobile phone cameras.
> (Salter & Tomsen, 2011, pp. 308–309)

Since the period in which Salter and Tomsen (2011) were writing we have seen the expansion of what is tolerated in the everyday consumption of violence. The mass executions, beheadings and slaughter documented and distributed through the internet by extremist groups such as the Islamic State took this form of cultural debasement to new depths. The violent internet propaganda of groups such as the Islamic State are oriented specifically to the recruitment of young men (Barr & Herfroy-Mischler, 2017). Young people are both the subject of, and key consumers of, these forms of cultural product. Young men and women are also readily enculturated into a violent culture of cruelty through the internet and social media (Schils & Pauwels, 2014).

Young men and women are being "toughened-up" or "hardened" in a range of ways, some explicit and some more or less subliminal. This hardening occurs both through the engagement of young people in violence – in real life and virtually through affordances made by new forms of media. It will be argued this acculturation to violence occurs through the exposure of young people to mediatized forms of violence by the means of playing video games such as the First-Person Shooter *Call of Duty* (Martino, 2015) and easy access to streaming violence-themed video through YouTube and series such as *Game of Thrones* available through *Netflix* and other similar platforms (Elwood, 2018; Ferreday, 2015; Gierzynski A, 2015; Malhara, 2017). Another source of this culture of "hardening" is the proliferation of, and popularity of, forms of Mixed-Martial Arts now easily accessible for viewing through the internet, cell phone apps and traditional cable television. The mediatization of violence and thus its ready accessibility in a variety of forms (and consequently its normalization) can be understood within a broader frame, a frame that encapsulates the notion of a growing culture of cruelty and the conscious hardening of youth.

Parallel to the emergence of this culture of cruelty has also been a hardening of attitudes towards the young – this is most clearly in evidence when we hear the public mantra of the need for "boot camps" (Mills & Pini, 2015) and more discipline in order to deal with entrenched social problems such as intergenerational unemployment and juvenile crime (Gascón & Roussell, 2018; Williams, 2016). This attitude towards the young is underpinned by the notion that there are growing sections of the population that are "disposable" (Giroux, Di Leo, McClennen, & Saltman, 2012). The disposable populations can be the young, the unemployed or the dispossessed. As the American sociologist Henry Giroux has pointed out, for decades American society and, I would add, those nations within the Anglosphere such as the United Kingdom and Australia have embraced the creation of what he calls the "punishing state". This is particularly the case for young people as

> more and more [of them] are caught in the punishing circuits of surveillance, containment, repression, and disposability. As a result of what can be called the war on youth, young people no longer are seen as part of the social contract and appear to have been banished from the everyday social investments, imagination, and future that once characterized the American dream.
>
> (Giroux et al., 2012)

Whilst at the same time as many young people are being marginalized and left out of "the American Dream", it is my contention that the cultural landscape of contemporary society has evolved to promote particular spaces where young people are welcomed and, in a sense, directed towards. Here I am referring to digital spaces that provide a virtual location within which young people are exposed to particular cultural forms and messages (Martino, 2015). These digital spaces are comprised of online forums, YouTube channels, *Discord* channels (a gaming dedicated form of social media which combines text and voice) and a variety of Twitch channels (and its alternatives). Within spaces such as Twitch, Twitter and Facebook (and the various other social media platforms), young people are able to explore their identities, to act out particular roles and to communicate in ways that make meaning for themselves and other young people. It is in these digital "safe spaces" (enabled through their smart devices) – the internet, social media and gaming culture – that young people are exposed to the violent cultural messages now sanctioned within contemporary advanced societies, but also to the political and cultural messages of non-State agents (Almohammad, 2018; Danner, 2015; Horgan, Taylor, Bloom, & Winter, 2017; Winter, 2015).

These digital spaces and the forms of social, cultural and political messages that permeate them can be seen within the broader context of the societal process known as "militarization". From the perpetual war in various theaters of operation both "kinetic" and "digital", to the creation of militarized forms of schooling and the expanded use of young people in conflicts, to the celebration of unbridled cruelty and individualism in the media and in the economy – the "hardening" of youth and the broader culture and society has gained pace. It is my assertion that these processes, practices and cultural forms have at their core the celebration of cruelty and violence. These dominant social and cultural practices have helped to engender what I have referred to as the hardening of youth and the privileging of violence, "toughness" and the celebration of cruelty. This idea should also be considered within the context of the ongoing process of militarization and the privileging of military action, military expenditure and the celebration of war (Geyer, 1989; Martino, 2015; Shadiack, 2012; Torres & Gurevich, 2018). In this context young people are positioned as both "materiel" – to be drawn upon and utilized in the preparation for new forms of war and as the audience for emergent forms of media and propaganda designed to promote the process of hardening.

It is to state the obvious to say that some of the major consumers of popular culture are young people. That is not to assume that it is young people alone who are the target audience for the forms of cultural production that I have described briefly so far in this chapter. It is, though, young people who are significant targets for the consumption of these products and are also often the central protagonists within some forms of popular content with a narrative structure. The gratuitous violence embedded in particular genres such as "slasher" and other horror-themed movies and streaming media are marketed towards young people and often focus on the violent and gruesome demise of groups of young people (Pearson, 2017; Tamborini, Weber, Bowman, Eden, & Skalski, 2013). Films such as *Halloween* and *Friday the 13th* have become cultural icons and have evolved through their various sequels to have an intergenerational appeal (Alford & Scheibler, 2018; Hitchcock, 2016).

Violence-themed media products such as the slasher genre of movies and streaming series are distinguished by their graphic depiction of violence (González, 2018; Jones, 2018). The unrelenting attempt to shock the audience through ever more elaborate forms of murder and mayhem is now a mainstay of popular culture. As well as this fictional depiction of violence we have witnessed the growth in popularity of the transmission (through cable and Pay-Per-View) of real violence in the form of Mixed-Martial Arts (MMA), specifically the Ultimate Fighting Championship (UFC) – the premier broadcast MMA competition. This differs from the tradition of broadcasting on television of contact sports such as boxing – in a boxing match blood is if possible minimized and not the prime focus of the contest. In the UFC, the spilling of blood is a central aspect of the entertainment appeal of the event and the sport of MMA (Green, 2016; Jensen, Roman, Shaft, & Wrisberg, 2013; Mayeda, 2011).

Augmenting the growing accessibility of formalized blood sports such as the MMA-style of fighting is the advent of internet-delivered streaming video. The advent of YouTube and Facebook have enabled easy access to the depiction of horrific violence by terror groups and individuals. In 2019 we achieved "peak digital violence" with the New Zealand live streaming of a lone-wolf terror attack. Coupled with this has been the emergence this century of entertainment being delivered via the internet as a digital stream. These new forms of delivery sit alongside traditional forms of media such as broadcast television and cable channels.

Violence, Fear and Spectacle

The emerging discourse concerning the need to discipline and toughen up young people is characteristic of a broader cultural phenomenon, one that is an outcome of the growing ascendancy of violence as a cultural form. Political violence and the drift into perpetual war appears to be the dominant feature of daily life in the 21st century (Kohn 2009; Shadiack 2012). It often seems that, as in ancient Rome, our "bread and circuses" is heavily tinged with both real and simulated violence. Cruelty has emerged as a key aspect of daily life as illustrated by an obsession with millenarian "End of Times" religious and media tropes. This is evidenced by the prevalence of dystopian and savage cultural images, concepts and political movements both within neo-liberal societies and more broadly at a global level (Jones and Smith 2014; Phillips 2014).

In her classic work written at the time of the Nazi occupation of France, the eminent European literary figure Simone Weil describes the relationship between "force" and "violence" depicted in Homer's *The Iliad*. In the essay, Weil writes about one of the most iconic descriptions of violence as spectacle in Western culture. Weil emphasizes the impact of the concentrated application of force through violence on an individual. As Weil argues, if we seek to

> define force – it is that x that turns anybody who is subjected to it into a thing. Exercised to the limit, it turns man into a thing in the most literal sense: it makes a corpse out of him. Somebody was here, and the next minute there is nobody here at all; this is a spectacle the Iliad never wearies of showing us.
>
> (Weil and McCarthy, 1965, p. 6)

To make her point Weil quotes a passage from Homer's text:

> the horses Rattled the empty chariots through the files of battle, Longing for their noble drivers. But they on the ground Lay, dearer to the vultures than to their wives. The hero becomes a thing dragged behind

a chariot in the dust: All around, his black hair Was spread; in the dust his whole head lay, That once-charming head; now Zeus had let his enemies Defile it on his native soil.

(Weil and McCarthy, 1965, p. 6)

The concept of spectacle links both the real world and the events depicted within the domain of contemporary popular culture and the 24-hour news cycle, social media and the internet. Guy Debord and the Situationists had singled out the crucial role spectacle had come to play in advanced capitalist society (Debord, 1992; Wollen, 1989).

At the core of spectacle in modern society is the commodification of everyday life. The subsumption of everyday life into the commodity form has become the fundamental constant in capitalism. As Debord has argued, the

> spectacle is the moment when the commodity has attained the total occupation of social life. The relation to the commodity is not only visible, but one no longer sees anything but it: the world one sees is its world. Modern economic production extends its dictatorship extensively and intensively.
>
> (Debord, 1992)

The mechanism that helps facilitate this process in contemporary society is the cloud of digitally disseminated and amplified cultural form/s that envelope us and which are sustained through the creation of fear.

As Virilio (2012) has pointed out in his book, *The Administration of Fear*, our media drenched society presents us with a succession of fear-inducing images of events and catastrophes. Richard (2012), writing in the preface to the Virilio book, argues that "(c)limate chaos, stock market panics, food scares, pandemic threats, economic crashes, congenital anxiety, existential dread . . . Fear and fears: individual and collective, combining and reinforcing each other (the dynamic of fear itself), are charging through our world. Infiltrating it, jolting it, deranging it" (Richard, 2012), and all delivered to our smartphones via social media or the streaming platforms.

During the past decade we have also witnessed the concerted efforts of non-State agents engaged in terror activities and warfare to add to this climate of fear by producing graphic depictions of their treatment of opponents and non-combatants disseminated through social media platforms such as YouTube and Twitter (Koch, 2018; Winter, 2015). In a sense the violent extremists of the Islamic State took the American idea of "shock and awe" – introduced during Gulf War I – to the next logical level; they delivered live cinematically produced politically motivated acts of brutality. Designed to both horrify and appeal to the prurience inherent in some of the online forms of digital culture that have emerged in the past decades.

Much of the spectacle that we witness through the myriad of screens that now infest our daily lives helps compose a distinct form of culture – what Doueihi has described as comprising a form of "digital culture" (Doueihi, 2011). Digital culture has been characterized as a set of "discursive practices, with their own conventions and norms that tend to fragilize and disturb well-established categories and values" (Doueihi, 2011).

Streaming media such as the HBO series *Game of Thrones* (Benioff, 2011–2019) reached an unparalleled global audience through the graphic depiction of sex, violence and sexual violence. From beheadings, to massacres and rape – violence, and in particular sexual violence, was a key element in the series from its inception (Elwood, 2018; Ferreday, 2015; Malhara, 2017). As Elwood, writing about the series from a legal perspective points out, "[t]here is a tremendous amount of sexual violence in the show, and the portrayal of such violence is uniformly and hyperbolically disturbing, if controversial. Viewers voyeuristically witness these disturbing scenes of sexual violence—as entertainment" (Elwood, 2018).

A similar commitment to representing increasingly graphic images of violence can be traced back to the action movie genre – specifically to Sam Peckinpah's *The Wild Bunch* (1969), which was perhaps the first mass audience production which portrayed and, it could be argued, celebrated gratuitous violence and the realistic depiction of cinematic blood – in slow motion and wide-screen (Bani-Khair, Alshboul, Al-Khawaldeh, Al-Khawaldeh, & Ababneh, 2017; Rødje, 2016). The film can be read as a response to the social, cultural and political context in which it was made. America was at war in Vietnam, a war which saw the dropping of more bombs on that small country than had been dropped in the entire European theater of operations in the Second World War.

Examples of this enduring cultural obsession with violence can also be found in contemporary military themed or oriented video and computer games (slow motion headshots, kill points and the gamification of simulated killing); X-sports and the new violent forms of competitive had-to-hand combat sports such as Ultimate Fighter Championship (UFC) and other combat sports or Mixed Martial Arts (MMA) (Jensen et al., 2013; Mayeda, 2011; Weaving, 2014). These new forms of "sport" can be viewed as examples of the growth of a "culture of cruelty" or the emergence of a process of "de-civilizing" (García & Malcolm, 2010; Wouters, 1986) and part of the "toughening-up" of Western society and in particular of young men.

The aim of UFC for example is the pinning to the mat, or "KO"ing – (knocking out) of one's opponent in an octagon-shaped ring – using a variety of martial arts, boxing and wrestling techniques to achieve this. UFC is a very popular sporting event which has drawn heavily on social media, streaming and pay-per-view technologies to grow its fan base. It is a unique amalgam of East and West in that it draws on martial and contact sport traditions from Asia as well from Europe and North America.

The spilling of blood in UFC/MMA contests is an acceptable and celebrated aspect of a match – unlike wrestling and boxing it is not usually a cause for the match to halt. In fact, it is part of the ritual of the fight and adds, literally, to the color of the contest. It is informative to briefly examine one event run by the Ultimate Fighting Championship – *UFC 247*, a fight card comprising the main event between Jon Jones and Dominck Reyes that took place on February 8 2020 at the Toyota Center in Houston, Texas, United States. The UFC event featured male and female combatants and a series of Mixed Martial Arts matches. As a footnote before going into detail here, I have been observing UFC for a number of years. I have not completed a detailed sociological study of the franchise or of the broadcast events. This is my interpretation of a specific match I watched live on the day of its broadcast.

The level of violence and cruelty which was displayed would in any of the traditional sporting codes illicit a ban and perhaps even the intervention of law enforcement. During each of the matches leading up to the main event broadcast live to a global audience, the spilling of blood was cheered on and as one match ended and another began the volume, color and pattern of blood splattered on the floor of the "Octagon" took on an ever darker shade of red.

But this is the whole point of the UFC and the broader Mixed Martial Arts movement and the events which it holds; the spilling of blood is central to the enjoyment of the audience and the goal of physically dominating one's opponent is central to the sport. As a respondent in a 2013 study of MMA fighting stated, the entire focus of the match was "imposing your will . . . on the opponent" (Jensen et al., 2013). Central to this form of sport is physical domination of one's opponent – the assumption of the dominant position is achieved through a violent exchange that leaves the loser battered and bruised. A quintessential example of being hard, of winning through the application of brutality. As another un-named fighter in Jensen's study talking about the feeling of being in the Octagon puts it:

> I've been in there enough to where I've just been getting the crap beat out of me. But something in your body doesn't let you quit, you know, rather it's your heart or if it's just your will to win, your competitive side. You just keep coming and coming and coming and coming. And eventually, you know, you'll break the guy's will.
>
> (Jensen et al., 2013)

In many ways UFC is the embodiment of the cruelty that is central to the culture of neo-liberal societies. The hardening of society, despite the spontaneous outpouring of anger and grief at the killing of Black men in America, is a pattern that has consistently been exposed. The panic and catastasis demonstrated during the pandemic of 2020 overshadowed the days of rage that spread across America and beyond. Without the media dissemination of the series of police deaths I am convinced the selfishness and lack of empathy that was demonstrated during the panic surrounding "lockdowns" would have continued unabated (Ling & Ho, 2020).

The dissemination of this content is made possible through the advent of a new array of technologies that afford the easy access to paid and unpaid content. This form of media content is part of the broader developments within the domain of new media – in particular, the cable and internet streaming of television content. Much of which is delivered by emergent streaming platforms that have embraced programming which differs considerably from traditional network broadcasting. This new technology is an important element within the broader cultural transformation that has taken place since the turn of the century.

Popular culture in the form of new types of serial and episodic television drama (streamed through services such as *Netflix*) is riddled with examples of this "culture of cruelty". Episodic television drama such as, *Breaking Bad*, *The Walking Dead* and *Game of Thrones* make no effort to sanitize the most bestial forms of human behavior (Gierzynski, 2015; González, 2018; Malhara, 2017). "Accident porn" such as the *MTV* program *Ridiculousness* and the plethora of YouTube videos depicting stupid and often dangerous behaviors (such as "planking") flood the internet and cable networks.

What binds these new forms of media together is their non-sanitized depictions of cruelty and violence. There is no hesitation – often no sense of moralizing or the questioning of violence. It simply happens. The reader might pause here and ask the question: But isn't that what happens in real life? Doesn't violence often strike in an unannounced and often unprovoked form? In short, the answer to these questions is, yes. Violence in real life can occur in an unexpected way, one can be in the wrong place at the wrong time. But here I am wanting us to think through what the readiness to depict violence, especially in forms readily accessible to young people, tells us both about the culture within which these products are consumed and the values we willingly transmit to those young people. It is my assertion that the mediatization of violence embodies what Katz has so eloquently described as the celebration of the "pleasures of evil" (Katz, 1988).

At the same time, it is necessary to put the prevalence of violence in the daily media diet of the consumers of popular culture within the context of real and profound horrors. During the past decade we have been witness to visceral images of extreme violence that occurred in Iraq and the Levant in the period leading up to and following on from the emergence of the Islamic State in the mid-2010s. Here I am specifically referring to the Islamic State's policy of using extreme violence and documenting it online to engender fear and to spread their propaganda messages. The Islamic State was perhaps the first political terror organization to effectively make use of emergent digital and online tools to both construct and project their message. The 24/7 news cycle, the advent of YouTube and social media platforms presented these groups with the tools and spaces to project carnage to a global audience.

The hunger for fresh content to fill the 24/7 news cycle also played into the media strategy of the Islamic State as Barr and Hefroy-Mischler have argued:

> [the] . . . Imperatives within the global media to provide coverage of major or "newsworthy" events creates a threshold which terrorist groups seek to cross by engaging in acts of graphic violence and brutality.
> (Barr and Herfroy-Mischler, 2017)

The ability to generate content has, as I pointed to above, been facilitated by the advances in digital technologies that have "democratized" the ability to both produce and also disseminate content. The creation of violent videos – the beheading, burning and drowning as well as mass shooting of captives – was breathlessly reported on in the Western media. In creating their videos, groups such as the Islamic State "are able to . . . bridge the gap between professional and amateur media production, between objective coverage of an event and purposeful staging, as well as between actions undertaken for civic purposes and violence directed at creating and perpetuating a psychology of fear" (Barr and Herfroy-Mischler, 2017).

The Mediatization of Violence

Fear of the other and fear of the imminent collapse of society as we know it have become powerful social, cultural and political factors in contemporary life (Berardi, 2017; Featherstone, 2016; Karouny, 2014; Riedl, 2014). A key mechanism in creating this sense of fear and an enduring perception that we are on the cusp of the apocalypse is the process of "mediatization". For the purpose of this book the term "mediatization" refers to the

> transformation of everyday life, culture and society in the context of the transformation of the media — which, in the long run, organizes all symbolic operations of a society and culture.
> (Krotz, 2017)

Media through digital technology, such as computer networks, the internet, social media, smartphones and tablets, have had the effect of altering our perceptions of what is normal, and what is acceptable. These technologies and cultural forms have helped to re-configure our perceptions of the "symbolic operations" and nature of our everyday life. These digital mechanisms and artefacts have helped re-shape our understanding of society, culture and the motivations of fellow citizens. The rise of Trump, the Alt-Right and the Islamic State are, it can be argued, the products of the emergence of new forms of technology and the process of mediatization. The manipulation of new technology and cultural forms for political purposes is part of a broader corrosive cultural turn within advanced capitalist societies.

This corrosive cultural turn, I argue is underpinned by the ready access to and consumption of images and videos of violence in a digital form. The explosion of violent spectacle both simulated and real, onto screens of all sizes, has been enabled through innovations in both the delivery mechanisms – the internet, streaming services – and new technology. But at its core has been a growing acceptance of the depiction of violence and the manipulation of hatred, both cultural and political through new forms of media and advanced technologies.

Violence, Danger and the Fear of the Other

Violence has been a part of human existence since there were humans. However, in advanced societies there has been a steady reduction in levels of crime and violence. Despite the decline of crime and violence as social and cultural aspects of everyday life, the popular perception in societies such as the United States is the opposite – there is a general fear and perception that crime and violence are growing phenomena (Callanan & Rosenberger, 2015). Since at least the 1960s, political rhetoric in the United States and elsewhere has been peppered with assertions that crime and violence are out of control. This has often been articulated within a racialized public discourse which has had dire consequence for particular ethnic minorities, the poor and other marginalized groups (Anderson & Enberg, 1995; Gopnik, 2012; Scott, Gibson, Alomaja, Minter, & Davis, 2017). Life in pre-modern society was best described by the English philosopher Hobbes as being "Nasty, brutish, and short" – it was not the idyllic communitarian vision many people like to imagine.

Studies undertaken in the first part of this century have found that, rather than contemporary society being a place where violence has grown or is even very common, our societies and in fact life in general is safer, less violent and in many parts more convivial. This argument of course runs counter to the narrative expounded by the Alt-Right and conservative political critics who portray contemporary society as a very dangerous jungle-like environment. The political ideology of the contemporary Right, even before the emergence of the extremist Alt-Right, has relied on the creation of a sense of danger and a fear of the other – people of color, refugees, strangers, the unemployed and the homeless (Anderson & Enberg, 1995; Scott et al., 2017).

Contemporary multicultural societies such as the United States, Australia and Britain have been sites of open race baiting and the manipulation of public opinion to support increasing levels of policing, incarceration and a militarized approach towards civilian populations and crises (Graham, 2011, 2012; S. Hall, Critcher, Jefferson, Clarke, & Roberts, 2013; Schlosser, 1998). However, the reality is of declining crime rates and in particular a consistent reduction in murder rates in the developed world – these facts has been conveniently ignored in much of the political debate (Knepper, 2015; Weiss, Santos, Testa, & Kumar, 2016). As Steven Pinker (2011) has pointed out, humans are not more violent today than they were in past. As the accounts I referred to above, and the work of Pinker (2011; 2018) and others (Gat, 2008) has highlighted, humans are not becoming more violent.

According to Pinker (2011, 2018) and Gat (2008) human society has over time progressed to become a safer, less violent, more harmonious place to live. Pinker (Pinker, 2011, 2018) argues persuasively that critics of contemporary society and in particular those who hold a romanticized view of what human society was like in the past base their arguments on a misreading of the past. Pinker has argued in his classic account, *The Better Angels of Our Nature: Why Violence Has Declined*, that

> nostalgia for a peaceable past is [a] delusion . . . We now know that native peoples, whose lives are so romanticized in today's children's books, had rates of death from warfare that were even greater than those of our world wars. The romantic vision of medieval Europe omit the exquisitely crafted instruments of torture and are innocent of the thirtyfold greater risk of murder in those times. The centuries for which people are nostalgic were times in which the wife of an adulterer could have her nose cut off, children as young as eight could be hanged for property crimes, a prisoner's family could be charged for easement of irons, a witch could be sawn in half, and a sailor could be flogged to a pulp. The moral commonplaces of our age, such as that slavery, war, and torture are wrong, would have been seen as saccharine sentimentality, and our notion of universal human rights almost incoherent. Genocide and war crimes were absent from the historical record only because no one at the time thought they were a big deal.
>
> (Pinker, 2011)

The mantra that in the past humans lived in a peaceable, pastoral world where violence and conflict was restrained by the bonds of family and community is a powerful idea – it forms the bedrock of many forms of philosophy and religion. In particular it feeds the "cultural pessimism" that permeates contemporary Western society (Stern, 1974). This view also informs the nostalgia-imbued ideology of many social and political conservatives, and, when coupled with the contemporary fear of terrorism – a quite negligible threat when we look at the statistics (Pinker, 2018) – has become part of the dominant militarized liberal-capitalist political form.

"Cultural Pessimism"

Grappling with the horrors of the Nazi era and its failed global empire – the Third Reich – Fritz Stern tried to contextualize how such an important nation in the family of European nations could create this true apocalypse. Stern argued that the Nazi party was able to tap into an underlying sense of cultural pessimism that was embedded with the German culture and the German character to achieve its political ends.

In later years Stern applied his thinking to the United State and concluded that America also shared a deep-seated sense of cultural despair. According to Stern:

> [c]ultural pessimism has a strong appeal in America today. As political conditions appear stable at home or irremediable abroad, American intellectuals have become concerned with the cultural problems of our society and have substituted sociological or cultural analyses for political criticism . . . There is a discontent in the Western world that does not stem from economic want or from the threat of war; rather it springs from dissatisfaction with life in an urban and industrialized culture.
>
> (Stern, 1974)

The sense of cultural despair Stern is talking about is at the core of the growth in media and political discourses – the dominance of violent cultural themes and products that now dominate are an outgrowth of this deep-seated sense of foreboding and cultural despair. Fear of the apocalypse or the violent other – local or foreign – is a pattern that is repeated over and over in the media, in popular culture and the fevered outpourings of the dominant political class.

Despite the evidence that violence and war are not statistically more common than in the past, our culture projects images and messages that the reverse is true. That we are on the cusp of societal collapse (Virilio, 2012). It is a dominant media trope and haunts much of the explosion in media content on the emergent streaming platforms. Concurrently, virtual violence not only saturates popular culture but the fear of a violent world bleeds into our everyday existence. What makes the inhabitants of peaceful, well organized and rich societies act as though hordes of barbarians are, like Hannibal, at the gate? It is not overly simplistic to argue that the cultural artefacts described above have contributed in generating a sense of impending collapse and the notion that a dystopian future is just beyond the horizon.

The Covid-19 pandemic of 2020 and the civil unrest in the United States following the murder of George Floyd (the latest example of institutionalized racial violence) has helped create a concrete sense of doom and the possibility of civil collapse in America and beyond. Decades of building up media images and a cultural context steeped in a sense of the possibility of impending collapse lurking just beyond the visible became, for many in fact, a lived experience. Media, popular culture, digital technology and institutional structures, as well as an enduring sense of cultural despair have helped to facilitate what I have called the drumbeat of war. In the next section of this chapter (and elsewhere in the book) I want to flesh out in more detail how militarization has enabled the creation of the conditions in which military action is able to be engaged in an almost frictionless and unquestioned manner.

Militarization, Habitus and Social Discipline

Before expanding on my initial thoughts concerning the process of the hardening of young people in more detail, it is necessary to briefly restate the role played by "social discipline" and how it meshes with the notion of habitus. Habitus is the key sociological concept underpinning my analysis of the militarization of society and the mechanics of how this has evolved. It is my contention that social disciplining is the outcome of the habitus that is formed in families, institutions and the broader society. Habitus in its many forms is in a sense the main cog in the machinery of militarization and helps produce a form of social discipline which consists of the acceptance of power structures, adherence to routine and to hierarchical structures, as well as rule following. In the previous chapter I went into more detail about the mechanics of militarization and the logistical role played by habitus in this process. When habitus and, in the case of my argument, a militarized form of habitus is deployed, the end result is a social discipline which is embedded in the subject population – it produces compliant citizens and prospective soldiers. Habitus creates in a sense an "Iron cage", as Weber might describe it, which binds humans to the desired form of social discipline.

In the remainder of this chapter I examine notions of hardness and toughness and their importance for the establishment and maintenance of the process of militarization which has reconstructed Western society over the past decades.

"Get Hard"

The process of hardening within the larger construct of militarization is both subtle and at times explicit components of our everyday experience of life. The process of hardening and the culture of violence embedded within militarization can be experienced or rehearsed by young people through games and simulations, or through militarized activities such as particular martial sports such as Mixed Martial Arts and "boot camps", both educational and sporting (De Avila, 2008).

Taken as a whole, these technologies and practices act as a form of pedagogy – they educate populations in both direct and indirect ways. The process of hardening takes place within a broad societal form of pedagogical work. The hardening of society has at its core the promotion of what has been described as militarization – and forms the kernel of a "soft approach" to preparing modern societies for the state of perpetual war and conflict we find ourselves inhabiting.

The process of militarization then in effect draws upon these technologies to accomplish its goals. The hardening of young people and of society in general can be thought of as a key factor in this broader development. Militarization is not simple or straightforward, it is in effect quite subtle in both its penetration of everyday life, but also in its application through various technologies, forms of media and propaganda. It is dependent on facilitating and maintaining this cultural shift to a cultural form which facilitates and normalizes violence, the preparation for conflict and the maintenance of a perpetual state of war. This is accomplished, I argue, through the constant project of hardening society and hardening youth through social discipline and the various cultural forms and media technologies that project violence, fear and spectacle.

On Being Tough

Before I conclude this chapter I need to flesh out in a little more detail what the mechanisms of social discipline and militarization have helped to create – a hardened subject population which is inured to the cost of war and the application of violence for political purposes. I have danced around this simple (and perhaps as my critics will assert simplistic) statement about the state of everyday life in advanced capitalist society. Being tough and enjoying the visual representation of violence and cruelty in our culture as represented in our daily media consumption: video streams, social media feeds and other tools for the production and consumption of images, ideas and popular culture.

Before continuing with this train of thought let me draw one of the best explications of the notion or toughness – though it is from a position of how it applies to criminal youth gangs. I still think it helps us to understand where we are now as a culture and as a society. Jack Katz writing in his classic book, *The Seductions of Crime* (1988), referred to earlier in this book, argues that in criminal gangs and certain youth sub-cultures

> [t]he person who would be tough must cultivate in others the perception that they cannot reach his sensibilities. Adolescents who would achieve a foreign and hostile presence in interactions must go further and participate in a collective project to produce an alien aesthetic. But the shaping of a tough image and the practice of an alien sensibility are

insufficient to ensure that one will be "bad". Those who would be bad are always pursued by powerful spiritual enemies who soften tough posture and upset the carefully balanced cultures of alienation, making them appear silly, puerile, and banal and thus undermining their potential for intimidation. To survive unwanted imitators, you must show that unlike the kids, you're not kidding; unlike the gays, you're not playing; unlike the fashionable middle class, you understand fully and embrace the evil of your style. You must show that you mean it.
(Katz, 1988, p. 99)

Elsewhere in his book Katz talks about how "evil" acts a seductive attractor to join and participate in the acts of violence and crime of youth gangs and criminal gangs in general. It has been the aim of this chapter and more broadly the book to try and untangle how the seductions of crime and lure of evil as a cultural and personal style statement has become a strong element in our wider society and culture. The anti-hero of the 1960s and 1970s as portrayed through the character of the "Man in Black" in *Westworld* or Darth Vader in *Star Wars* – a planet-destroying militarist – are emblematic of this shift in the dominant cultural form. The *Hero's Journey* that Joseph Campbell wrote about no longer speaks to the identarian and militarized culture that capitalism has engendered. The point that I make here is controversial: I see no difference between the "me"-first nature of identity politics and the production of a hardened militarized subject in Western society – both are the products of the dominant neo-liberal political form. One is openly contested and the other shapes and constructs the consciousness of the subject population. Both, however, flourish under the conditions of the neo-liberal political form.

Contemporary culture is littered with examples of individuals not travelling the hero's path to redemption but in fact the opposite. The role of the individual in contemporary society has in most cases come to be symbolized by a materialistic, digital nomad who seeks meaning through material possessions or meaningless posturing around food consumption and international travel – all to be captured for a "selfie" and *Instagram* likes. This is validated and rewarded both by and through the capitalist economic system, but also by and through the dominant capitalist social and political form.

Conclusion

The creation of a cultural and political form that is pre-disposed to the engagement in armed conflict in a relatively unquestioned manner is the dominant characteristic of contemporary society. Young people in particular, but the broader society as well, have been subjected to a conditioning process which builds on more than two centuries of social disciplining.

First to prepare the subject population of Western society to the demands of capitalist accumulation and now to defend a globe-spanning empire founded on a neo-liberal capitalist political form. The processes discussed in this book have the effect of producing a mentally compliant and hardened young person. The forces at work to construct the consensus and an unquestioned commitment to political violence are rarely exposed. They are not magical, nor is this the outcome of a global conspiracy – it is in fact the inescapable logic of a political form that has been constructed to project and protect economic and political power which has at its core the militarization of society in defence of the neo-liberal capitalist state. It is not possible to maintain one without the other.

References

Alford, A., & Scheibler, S. (2018). *Societal Shifts and the Horror Genre.*
Almohammad, A. (2018). ISIS child soldiers in Syria: The structural and predatory recruitment, enlistment, pre-training indoctrination, training, and deployment. *The International Centre for Counter-Terrorism*–The Hague, 8.
Anderson, D. C., & Enberg, C. (1995). Crime and the politics of hysteria: How the Willie Horton story changed American justice. *Journal of Contemporary Criminal Justice, 11*(4), 298–300.
Bani-Khair, B., Alshboul, N. M., Al-Khawaldeh, N., Al-Khawaldeh, I., & Ababneh, M. (2017). Violence patterns in Peckinpah's *The Wild Bunch* (1969): Critical reading. *International Journal of Applied Linguistics and English Literature, 6*(3), 210–214.
Barr, A., & Herfroy-Mischler, A. (2017). ISIL's execution videos: Audience segmentation and terrorist communication in the digital Age. *Studies in Conflict & Terrorism*, 1–22.
Benioff, D. W., (2011–2019). *Game of Thrones*. HBO.
Berardi, F. (2017). *Futurability: The age of impotence and the horizon of possibility*. London; Brooklyn: Verso.
Callanan, V., & Rosenberger, J. S. (2015). Media, gender, and fear of crime. *Criminal Justice Review, 40*(3), 322–339.
Danner, C. (2015). How ISIS abducts, recruits, and trains children to become Jihadists. *Intelligencer*. Retrieved from http://nymag.com/intelligencer/2015/07/how-isis-abducts-recruits-and-trains-children.html?gtm=top&gtm=top
De Avila, J. (2008, July 28, 2008). War games: Army lures civilians by letting them play soldier recruiters bring lifelike videogame to amusement parks, and kids love it. *Wall Street Journal*. Retrieved from http://online.wsj.com/news/articles/SB121721198768289035
Debord, G. (1992). *The society of the spectacle*. 1967. Paris: Les Éditions Gallimard.
Deleuze, G., Guattari, F., & Massumi, B. (1986). *Nomadology: The war machine*. New York: Semiotext(e).
Doueihi, M. (2011). *Digital cultures*. Harvard University Press.
Elwood, R. L. (2018). Frame of Thrones: Portrayals of rape in HBO's *Game of Thrones*. *Ohio St. LJ Furthermore, 79*, 113.
Featherstone, M. (2016). Chaosmic spasm: Guattari, Stiegler, Berardi, and the digital apocalypse. *Communication and Media, 11*(38), 243–268. doi:10.5937/comman12–11501
Ferreday, D. (2015). Game of Thrones, rape culture and feminist fandom. *Australian Feminist Studies, 30*(83), 21–36.

García, R. S., & Malcolm, D. (2010). Decivilizing, civilizing or informalizing? The international development of Mixed Martial Arts. *International Review for the Sociology of Sport, 45*(1), 39–58.

Gascón, L. D., & Roussell, A. (2018). An exercise in failure: Punishing "at-risk" youth and families in a South Los Angeles boot camp program. *Race and Justice, 8*(3), 270–297.

Gat, A. (2008). *War in human civilization*. OUP Oxford.

Geyer, M. (1989). The militarization of the Western world. In J. R. Gillis (Ed.), *The militarization of the Western world* (pp. 65–102). New Brunswick: Rutgers University Press.

Gierzynski A, e. a. (2015). *Game of Thrones, House of Cards* and the belief in a just world. Paper presented at the Annual Meeting of the Midwest Political Science Association.

Giroux, H. A., Di Leo, J. R., McClennen, S. A., & Saltman, K. J. (2012). *Neoliberalism, education, and terrorism: contemporary dialogues*. Boulder, CO: Paradigm Publishers.

González, A. E. (2018). *Horror without end: Narratives of fear under modern capitalism*. Oberlin College.

Gopnik, A. (2012). The caging of America. *The New Yorker* (30).

Graham, S. (2011). *Cities under siege: The new military urbanism* (Pbk. ed.). London; New York: Verso.

Graham, S. (2012). When life itself is war: On the urbanization of military and security doctrine. *International Journal of Urban and Regional Research, 36*(1), 136–155.

Green, K. (2016). Tales from the mat: Narrating men and meaning making in the mixed martial arts gym. *Journal of Contemporary Ethnography, 45*(4), 419–450.

Hall, A. L. (2013). Torture and Television in the United States. *The Muslim World, 103*(2), 267–286.

Hall, S., Critcher, C., Jefferson, T., Clarke, J., & Roberts, B. (2013). *Policing the crisis: Mugging, the state and law and order*. Palgrave Macmillan.

Hitchcock, S. J. (2016). *The veneer of fear: Understanding movie horror*. University of Southampton.

Horgan, J. G., Taylor, M., Bloom, M., & Winter, C. (2017). From cubs to lions: A six stage model of child socialization into the Islamic State. *Studies in Conflict & Terrorism, 40*(7), 645–664.

Jensen, P., Roman, J., Shaft, B., & Wrisberg, C. (2013). In the cage: MMA fighters' experience of competition. *The Sport Psychologist, 27*(1), 1–12.

Jones, S. (2018). *Sex and Horror*. London: Routledge.

Jones, D., & Smith, M. (2014). Western responsibility and response to the death cult of the Islamic state. *Quadrant, 58*(10), 10.

Karouny, M. (April 1, 2014). Apocalyptic prophecies drive both sides to Syrian battle for end of time. *Reuters*.

Katz, J. (1988). *Seductions of crime: Moral and sensual attractions in doing evil*. New York: Basic Books.

Knepper, P. (2015). Falling crime rates: What happened last time. *Theoretical Criminology, 19*(1), 59–76.

Koch, A. (2018). Jihadi beheading videos and their non-Jihadi echoes. *Perspectives on Terrorism, 12*(3), 24–34.

Kohn, R. H. (2009). The danger of militarization in an endless "war" on terrorism. *The Journal of Military History, 73*(1), 177–208.

Krotz, F. (2017). Explaining the mediatisation approach. *Javnost-The Public, 24*(2), 103–118.

Ling, G. H. T., & Ho, C. M. C. (2020). Effects of the coronavirus (COVID-19) pandemic on social behaviours: From a social dilemma perspective. *Technium Social Sciences Journal, 7*(1), 312–320.

Malhara, T. (2017). Conceptual analysis of *Game of Thrones*. *International Journal of Innovative Research and Advanced Studies, 4*(3), 263–268.

Martino, J. (2015). *War/play: Video games and the militarization of society*. New York: Peter Lang.

Mayeda, D. (2011). The sociology of MMA: Hegemonic masculinity unleashed. *Sociology In Focus*. Retrieved from http://sociologyinfocus.com/2011/12/the-sociology-of-mma-hegemonic-masculinity-unleashed/

Mills, M., & Pini, B. (2015). Punishing kids: The rise of the 'boot camp'. *International Journal of Inclusive Education, 19*(3), 270–284. doi:10.1080/13603116.2014.929748

Pearson, T. (2017). The media and teenage violence: How much is too much when it comes to adolescent aggression? Indianapolis, IN: Butler University.

Phillips, P. J. (2014). Terrorist group brutality and the emergence of the Islamic State (ISIS). Available at SSRN 2479740.

Pinker, S. (2011). *The better angels of our nature: Why violence has declined*. New York: Viking.

Pinker, S. (2018). *Enlightenment now: The case for reason, science, humanism, and progress*. Penguin.

Richard, B. (2012). Preface. In Viriolio, P., *The administration of fear* (Vol. 10). London: Semiotext(e).

Riedl, M. (2014). *Apocalyptic politics: On the permanence and transformations of a symbolic complex*. Durham, NC: Duke University.

Rødje, K. (2016). Images of blood in American cinema: The tingler to *The Wild Bunch*. Routledge.

Salter, M., & Tomsen, S. (2011). Violence and carceral masculinities in Felony Fights. *British Journal of Criminology, 52*(2), 309–323.

Schils, N., & Pauwels, L. (2014). Explaining violent extremism for subgroups by gender and immigrant background, using SAT as a framework. *Journal of Strategic Security, 7*(3), 27–47.

Schlosser, E. (1998). The prison-industrial complex. *Atlantic Monthly (10727825), 282*(6), 51–72. Retrieved from http://0-search.ebscohost.com.library.vu.edu.au/login.aspx?direct=true&db=aph&AN=1340640&site=ehost-live

Scott, J., Gibson, C., Alomaja, L., Minter, A., & Davis, L. (2017). When perceptions are deadly: Policing, given the summer in Ferguson, Missouri and other similar stories, before and since. *Ralph Bunche Journal of Public Affairs, 6*(1), 4.

Shadiack, A. (2012). The militarization of everyday life. *ABITUS*, 43.

Stern, F. (1974). *The politics of cultural despair: A study in the rise of the Germanic ideology*. Berkeley: University of California Press.

Tamborini, R., Weber, R., Bowman, N. D., Eden, A., & Skalski, P. (2013). "Violence is a many-splintered thing": The importance of realism, justification, and graphicness in understanding perceptions of and preferences for violent films and video games. *Projections, 7*(1):100–118.

Torres, N., & Gurevich, A. (2018). Introduction: Militarization of Consciousness. *Anthropology of Consciousness, 29*(2), 137–144. doi:10.1111/anoc.12101

Virilio, P. (2012). *The administration of fear* (Vol. 10). London: Semiotext(e).

Weaving, C. (2014). Cage fighting like a girl: Exploring gender constructions in the Ultimate Fighting Championship (UFC). *Journal of the Philosophy of Sport, 41*(1), 129–142.

Weil, S., & McCarthy, M. (1965). The Iliad, or the Poem of Force. *Chicago Review, 18*(2), 5–30. doi:10.2307/25294008.

Weiss, D. B., Santos, M. R., Testa, A., & Kumar, S. (2016). The 1990s homicide decline: A western world or international phenomenon? A research note. *Homicide Studies, 20*(4), 321–334.

Williams, G. T. (2016). The effectiveness of juvenile boot camps and their impact on minority youth. Chicago, IL: National Louis University.

Winter, C. (2015). Documenting the virtual 'caliphate'. *Quilliam Foundation, 33*, 1–50.

Wollen, P. (1989). The Situationist International. *New Left Review, 174*(1), 1.

Wouters, C. (1986). Formalization and informalization: Changing tension balances in civilizing processes. *Theory, Culture & Society, 3*(2), 1–18.

Chapter 6

The Corruption of Language

"Radicalization"

The Corruption of Language

Language and its use both in everyday life but also in spheres such as culture and politics often helps to construct how we see and experience the world. George Orwell, the English journalist and author of the classic novel of a dystopian political future, *1984*, was troubled by the use of language to mask political abuse or as the justification for the misuse of power. Writing not long after the end of the Second World War, Orwell eloquently laid out the argument that language is a political tool that is used to manipulate populations. During the war and the decade that led up to its outbreak, politics and language had been used to conceal almost unimaginable horrors and abuse of power. In his article entitled *Politics and the English Language* (1946) Orwell argued that "if thought corrupts language, language can also corrupt thought". The contemporary historical era may be characterized as a period in which technology has been leveraged to enable the manipulation of political and social debate in countries such as the United States and elsewhere. This has been achieved by means of social media platforms and the internet amplifying "fake" messages and imagery (memes, digitally fabricated video) (Gardner, 2018; Singer & Brooking, 2018).

Terms such as "radical" and "extremist" have been used interchangeably to describe the actions of individuals and groups that sit within Jihadist and Alt-Right movements. Language has been used to label the actions of extremist individuals and groups as being radical, or that individuals are being radicalized. Ascribing the actions of a terrorist with the term radical undermines the legitimacy of the historical tradition of radical action in the service of progressive political change. It is my assertion that this conflation negates progressive thinking and political action and that by using the term radical to describe the practices and disposition of extremist individuals and organizations, language is being used in a corrosive manner. Thus, ascribing acts of violence and extremism to a tradition steeped in political progress and change is a political tactic that sits within the broader strategy I have referred to earlier as the social war.

In this chapter I will examine the contemporary use of the term radical in both sociological and political contexts and argue that to use the term "radical" to describe current global movements such as violent forms of Jihadism and organizations such as the Islamic State (IS) as well as "radical" neo-Nazi and "White Supremacist" groups of the Alt-Right movement is to delegitimize centuries of radical thought and revolutionary action. Radical ideas originating in the Enlightenment have provided the engine for centuries of social, cultural, economic and political reform leading to the creation of global progressive movements and outcomes. It will be asserted in the pages that follow that organizations such as IS are extremist in nature and that they espouse a nihilist inspired ideology imbued with a reverence for death and the desire to usher in an apocalyptic "end of days scenario" (Fromson & Simon, 2015). This form of extremism needs to be clearly marked out from the pantheon of radical ideas, movements and individuals that have over the centuries struggled to overcome inequality, discrimination and the exploitation of women and men based on race, gender and class.

This chapter will critically assess the argument that there is no distinction between nihilistic violent extremist movements and the progressive struggles that have, since the French Revolution, helped propel western society in the direction of progress, democracy and emancipation (Israel, 2013). The example of radical movements from the 1960s – such as the May'68 radical student movement, as well as the global anti-Vietnam War struggle – will be contrasted with contemporary extremist Jihadist and Alt-Right organizations and their objectives. This is a selective set of examples and a short analysis and exposition; I could have spent the entire book simply extending my argument concerning the need to make this distinction. The chapter will attempt to blend a conceptual discussion with examples from the historical record, as well as the current fluid global political context, where terms such as "radical", "extremist", "populist" are sometimes used interchangeably. The term "revolution" or "revolutionary" has also lost much of its descriptive power – the 2019 Venezuelan opposition movement was categorized as "revolutionary" – and universally welcomed in the West as engaging in a revolution (Guardiola-Rivera, 2019). Language can be used to mask the true nature of a social or political movement – a right-wing coup can use social media to "market" itself as democratic in nature and engaged in a "social revolution" rather than as a reactionary counter-revolution movement.

Revolutionaries, Radicals and Extremists

The key argument to be considered in this chapter is the proposition that the term "radical" has been mis-applied to the actions of terrorist individuals and groups and consequently has led to the conflation of legitimate political action and revolutionary thought with contemporary forms of violent extremism. It is my assertion that acts such as the mass-murder that occurred on September 11, or the bombing of a marathon as occurred in Boston in 2013, or the New Zealand mosque mass-murder in 2019 – are neither radical nor revolutionary acts. The conscious targeting of unarmed civilians as the sole and legitimate goal of their activities, and thus the disregard for the human consequences of their actions, marks out the terrorist from the revolutionary. It is also my contention that in conflating legitimate political action and revolution with contemporary forms of violent extremism, progressive social and political movements are being undermined and demonized by conservative and right-wing power structures.

The recent renewed focus on the threat posed by environmental groups tarnished with the term "Eco-terror" is a case in point (Brown, 2019). Violence against property is equated with the murderous tactics employed by both Jihadist and Alt-Right terror groups and individuals. Much leftwing political action targets corporations and their infrastructure. Environmental activities, such as, for example, blocking the harvesting of old growth forests or the exposure of animal cruelty – are aimed at creating a media spectacle but not at killing or maiming individuals. The speed with which leftist groups have been identified as acting in a terroristic manner is in stark contrast with an almost pathological unwillingness to name Alt-Right groups as terrorist. This is despite published independent and FBI data sources that highlight the fact that the main perpetrators of violent political acts in the United States are in effect members of the Alt-Right (Corbin, 2017; Cose, 2018; Levin & Reitzel, 2018; Miller, 2017). As a recent report by the Anti-Defamation League has pointed out,

> between 2002 and 2018, 80 percent of extremist-related murders in the U.S. were carried out by people linked to rightwing movements. Only 3 percent were linked to left-wing ideologies, and 17 percent to Islamic movements. Every single extremist killing in 2018–50 in all – had a link to a right-wing movement.
> (Anti-Defamation League cited in Brown, 2019)

I will return to this point later in this chapter. For now, we need to work our way through the concepts, language and examples underpinning these distinct movements and their political actions.

Revolutionaries

It is possible to mount an argument that "radical" and "revolutionary" political figures and movements have played significant roles in the enhancement of the human condition and the dismantling of autocratic and authoritarian socio-political systems and structures for centuries. For example, radical thinkers such as the French philosopher Rousseau and his political writing on the Social Contract between the governed and their rulers have provided the fuel for profound political and social change (Blum, 1987; McDonald, 2013). His writing provided the intellectual foundations of both the American revolutionary War of Independence and the French Revolution (Blum, 1987). The struggle for human rights, social and political emancipation and a fair economic system could not have been achieved without challenging and actively undermining accepted political norms and existing power structures. The smashing of the *Ancien Régime* in France and the birth of the American nation were both the result of prolonged revolutionary struggle. Thomas Jefferson, one of the founding fathers of the American Republic, was quite explicit in his belief that liberty could only be achieved and guaranteed through the recourse to revolutionary action.

As Jefferson explains in a letter written two years before the outbreak of the French Revolution,

> what country can preserve its liberties, if its rulers are not warned from time to time, that this people preserve the spirit of resistance? Let them take arms. The remedy is to set them right as to the facts, pardon and pacify them. What signify a few lives lost in a century or two? The tree of liberty must be refreshed from time to time, with the blood of patriots and tyrants. It is its natural manure.
>
> (Jefferson, 1787)

The American example has echoed through the centuries as an illustration of how a people in chattels could engage in revolutionary struggle and war to both uplift themselves and also set an example for others. But what do I mean when I use the term revolution? Has our understanding of the idea shifted in the discourse of contemporary political language and thinking? I wish to argue that the meaning of the concept of revolution still maintains some semblance of coherence and agreement in the annals of contemporary political thinking (Beck, 2015). This is not the case when we consider the manner in which the term radical has been appropriated and applied in the contemporary discussion of extremism, but more on this later.

The meaning of the term revolution has been succinctly stated by the political scientist Theda Skocpol in a classic examination of the French, Russian and Chinese revolutions. In her book originally published in 1979 entitled *States and Social Revolutions* (Skocpol, 2015), Skocpol describes the notion of the "social revolution" as being

> rapid, basic transformations of a society's state and class structures . . . accompanied and in part carried through by class-based revolts from below. Social revolutions are set apart from other sorts of conflicts and

transformative processes above all by the combination of two coincidences: the coincidence of societal structural change with class upheaval; and the coincidence of political with social transformation.

(Skocpol, 2015)

The French, Russian and Chinese revolutions were examples of the "coincidences" that Skocpol is referring to – the social, economic and political structures of these societies were never the same. The successful completion of this revolutionary transformation was the product of prolonged struggle and intense political violence. Existing ruling classes were overthrown, violently and without mercy – the term the "Terror", first coined to describe the French transformation, vividly conjures an image of what took place (Tackett, 2015). Similar violence occurred in both the Russian and the Chinese revolutions during the 20th century. As a consequence of this dismantling of the existing order new forms of social, political and economic structures were created to replace what had been displaced. As Skocpol argues, this is a key element of what a revolution can be understood as constituting. The failed Arab Spring of 2011 and the subsequent struggles in Syria and Libya did not produce the social transformation that the French, Russian and Chinese social revolutions had (Esposito, Sonn, & Voll, 2015; Hill, 2018; Hom, 2016).

The radical individuals at the head of revolutionary groups and movements have in their minds and in their political manifestos an image of a changed society, in most cases a better one. As the history of the French, Russian and Chinese revolution illustrate, at least in the short term this has not always been the case. Nevertheless, radicals through their actions open up the potential for the creation of something new – not necessarily through violence.

Radicals

At this point it is necessary to examine the term radical. In order to place some boundaries and context for the discussion, I will limit my analysis of the concept to the domain of politics and political struggle. My starting point is the notion that being a radical is distinct from, and the antithesis of, the modern extremist. Radicals in the political domain are often part of, or the leaders of, social movements – movements which have as their key objectives the restructuring of society, and/or the ending of some form of exploitation, discrimination or inequality. Radicals position themselves in opposition to aspects of everyday life; issues and practices that at particular points in history are regarded as normal or unexceptional. Problems such as gender or class inequality or institutionalized discrimination directed towards specific ethnic or racial groups have been the focus of political action by radicals and social movements at one time or another. Radicals and the social movements that they often lead or participate in are not intrinsically oriented towards using violence and non-legitimate political activities to attain their goals.

The term "radical", as Raymond Williams (2013) pointed out in his classic book on language, culture and politics – *Keywords: A Vocabulary of Culture and Society*, has had a "curious . . . history". It was for many years used in the English language to denote the commitment to "vigorous" change within the tradition of Liberalism. During the 20th century the term became synonymous with the Left – it was used as short-hand for the concepts of socialism or communism. In this context it was closely aligned with the idea of revolutionary change and the abolition of political and economic oppression and exploitation under capitalist social relations. It was in this context that the term radical began to take on its contemporary negative connotations.

Radicals engaged in political activism are not initially motivated to engage in political violence – though as in the case of the African National Congress (ANC) and the struggle led by Nelson Mandela for political emancipation and the end of Apartheid – violence might become the only option in the face of State violence (McKinley, 2018). Activists – (here I am also referring to "radical" political actors such as the worker and green movements who might be blocked in some way from getting their message across to the general population) – do not then routinely drift into violent and extremist action. As a 2009 piece of research pointed out, there is

> little systematic evidence linking peaceful political action to political violence. Indeed a . . . survey study that included members of U.S. activist groups found that intentions for legal activism were little related to intentions for illegal and violent political action.
> (Moskalenko & McCauley, 2009)

It is my contention that this continues to be the case and that groups that are currently active in political violence such as the neo-Nazi movements of the Alt-Right see violence as a legitimate first step, not as a last resort. The Alt-Right, as well as the Jihadist movements, clearly position themselves as extremist and as agents of chaos and not simply as radical political actors, in the sense that they see violence and upheaval as not only legitimate, but as something to celebrate, as well as an end in itself (Ali & Post, 2008; Worley & Copsey, 2016). For example, members of the global Jihadist movement (groups such as the Islamic State) see their actions as part of a larger apocalyptic struggle which will culminate in the destruction of the West and the emergence of a global caliphate (Aldrovandi, 2014; Berger, 2015).

The neo-Nazis who marched in a 1930s-style night-time torch parade in Charlottesville in 2017 were clear about their message: it was one filled with hate, veiled threats of violence and, as the vehicular homicide that occurred at the time demonstrates, murderous in intent (Cose, 2018). Their chants of "Jews will not replace us" harkens back to a place and a time in history that we had thought was a thing of the past, instead we all witnessed the echoes of a brutal, violent and murderous period (Cose, 2018). The neo-Nazis and their Alt-Right allies also see their actions as ushering a new era and share similar apocalyptic visions of the political landscape.

"Engine of Change": Politically Radical Students, Paris '68 and the Anti-Vietnam War Movement

I would like the reader to consider the following propositions – first, it is indefensible to assert that the struggle for radical change, the desire to dismantle existing power structures in order to emancipate segments of the population, or in the name of a broader notion such as equality, or the mobilization of segments of the population to end an illegal war, is equivalent to the actions of a terror bomber. Second, linking the term radical to violent action has for decades been successfully used to diminish the ideas at the center of progressive political struggles for change or the ability to mobilize support (Beck, 2015; Sedgwick, 2010). This is despite the reality that much radical political action in for example the United States in the 20th century led to progressive political reform such as: the Civil Rights movement; the end to an illegal war in Vietnam; and reproductive rights for women and environmental reform. Radical political action has in effect acted as an "engine of change" (Hayden, 2005). In the section below I will tease this idea out a little more through the exploration of a series of events during a key period in the latter half of the 20th century and its political impact at a global level.

The example that I wish to draw upon is the political struggles that shook Western societies in the 1960s and early 1970s. Struggles that initially saw demands for educational reform, the end to imperialist war and the dismantling of capitalism. Struggles that helped enable Civil Rights in the United States, a new environmental movement and the quest for gender equality. This success should also be placed into the context of both the disillusionment and nihilism that emerged following the split in the radical student and youth movements and the emergence of violent political cells such as the American Weather Underground and in Europe, "Red" political factions that emerged in the post-1960s period (Harcourt, 2017; Totton, 2018). These groups differed from the larger movements that they splintered from in that they saw violence as the only solution to contemporary political conditions.

The war in Vietnam and the May '68 movement both in Paris and beyond are examples of political events where radicals and radical action played pivotal roles. Paris in 1968 became the center of an emerging global radical youth movement – part of a broader struggle against the war in Vietnam and the constraints of capitalist culture and society. The iconic symbol of youthful global revolt became the Argentinian-born co-leader of the Cuban revolution, Ernesto "Che" Guevara. His political ideas would become foundational concepts in the broad demands of the violent wings of the student movement and the revolutionary cells that emerged out of those same movements.

By the time student activists began to mobilize in and occupy their universities in France the anti-war movement had been active in the United States and beyond (for example in Australia) for some years (Marks, 2018). The formation of the New Left movement, the production of the Port Huron statement in 1962 and the establishment of the activist Students for a Democratic Society (SDS) three years earlier was a turning point in the political life of America and the West in general (Flacks & Lichtenstein, 2015). The Port Huron statement was a clear articulation of the case for radical change, and a call for American youth to take up the cause of social, political and economic reform. These sentiments are captured in this extract from the statement:

> We are people of this generation, bred in at least modest comfort, housed now in universities, looking uncomfortably to the world we inherit . . . Some would have us believe that Americans feel contentment amidst prosperity—but might it not better be called a glaze above deeply felt anxieties about their role in the new world? And if these anxieties produce a developed indifference to human affairs, do they not as well produce a yearning to believe there is an alternative to the present, that something can be done to change circumstances in the school, the workplaces, the bureaucracies, the government? It is to this latter yearning, at once the spark and engine of change, that we direct our present appeal. The search for truly democratic alternatives to the present, and a commitment to social experimentation with them, is a worthy and fulfilling human enterprise, one which moves us and, we hope, others today.
>
> (Hayden, 2005)

In the years following this statement American students actively engaged in political action in support of issues such as the struggle for African American civil rights and the opposition to the war in Vietnam (Andrews, 2018). The establishment of political groups across America's university campuses enabled activists to project their demand for change onto the national stage. The heightening of the conflict in Vietnam in the mid-1960s with the expanded program of drafting young men into military service helped to politicize a whole generation of young people (Abney, 2019; Erikson & Stoker, 2011).

As a 2011 paper by Erikson and Stoker, examining data derived from a study conducted in 1965 of high school seniors, shows,

> political attitudes of this cohort's members changed in divergent ways as a function of their draft number. Whether they had a low (vulnerable) or high (safe) draft number not only affected their degree of support for the war, but also their basic partisan and ideological attitudes. The effects were enduring, lasting years and- in some instances- for decades, if not a lifetime. The depth and breadth of these changes reveal how powerfully citizens can react when government policy directly affects their lives. The government randomly reshuffled the self-interests among men in the targeted cohort, and the men shifted their politics accordingly.
>
> (Erikson & Stoker, 2011)

That the draft helped propel many students in the direction of radical politics and the nascent anti-Vietnam War movement is clear. It is also evident that the war in Vietnam acted as a funnel for a range of social and political issues and helped distil the underlying social conflicts based on class and race that had been bubbling under the surface for decades.

The American radicals were able through their activism to effect popular perceptions concerning these issues. In particular, the war in Vietnam became increasingly unpopular at home and through the concerted actions of the student movement and its supporters in civil society the United States government was effectively pressured to end the war. Public support for American institutions, in particular for the Government, and the de-militarization both of the nation and of American foreign policy, were outcomes of the defeat in Vietnam (Nef, 2018; Notaker, Scott-Smith, & Snyder, 2016).

The war in Vietnam and the mass movement to oppose it had a profound impact on young people internationally. In Europe, particularly in France, the activist actions of the youth radicals in America acted as an example for them (Mohandesi, 2018). But what was different in Paris was the support given to the activists by the organized working class – through factory occupations and mass mobilization against the State.

The war in Vietnam also opened up spaces in which political activists could engage in actions directed at eroding the American will to continue with or escalate its involvement in the war in Vietnam. For example, elements within the French Left clearly identified the role radical action could play in confronting American interests by creating a series of "home fronts" in Western Europe (Mohandesi, 2018). A similar position on the strategy of bringing the war to the domestic political context was adopted by student activists in the United States and Australia (Irving, 2016; Vítek, 2016). It was not possible to physically disrupt the massive war machine now focused on the people of Vietnam, but it was possible to confront elements of the apparatus of war at home. For example the French radicals concluded that "the best way to support the Vietnamese revolution would be to 'create a Vietnam' in France" (Mohandesi, 2018). As a consequence of this position gaining traction in the pre-'68 period it was concluded that

> [t]he best form of solidarity, therefore, was one that could reproduce the distant struggle they sought to support. To do so, they translated that struggle into their own particular contexts. In France, young radicals' efforts to bring home the anti-imperialist revolution in Vietnam triggered a series of events that would set off May '68. Internationally, just as Vietnamese revolutionaries inspired the French, the events of May '68 inspired radicals elsewhere, who in turn tried to translate May '68 into their own domestic vernaculars.
> (Mohandesi, 2018)

It can be argued that the May '68 movement in France was both a sequence of revolutionary actions and also a domestic political intervention directed at an external power engaged in an unjust war. The May '68 movement was the outcome of the revolutionary fervor of the emergent French radical youth movement – but it also took on a larger internationalist stance as part of a broad front focusing on helping to end the war in Vietnam, and also helped distil a critique of the society around them (Alper, 2016; Beck, 2015; Keenan, 2009).

The French radicals were supported by workers who occupied factories, marched in support of the students and stood in the streets confronting the repressive forces of the State (Gregoire & Perlman, 1970). Student grievances and anti-Vietnam War sentiments morphed into a broader critique of contemporary capitalist society and created a euphoric pro-revolutionary atmosphere. The factory occupations in support of the students were acts that reflected a broader perception amongst elements of the French working-class that this was an epochal moment – that things really could change (Gregoire & Perlman, 1970; Vigna, 2011). This sense of hope and the possibility of change did not last. Nor was this emergent student/worker alliance successful in its broader demands for societal change (Totton, 2018).

A degree of melancholia set in after May '68, a mental state that led many former student activists to believe that the methods that they had used up to that point had failed and that instead it would be necessary to take extreme action (Totton, 2018). Extremist Left political groups such as the Red Army factions emerged in Europe in the decade after 1968. Similar groups developed in America, for example the Weather Underground and Symbionese Liberation Army (a splinter group of the Weather Underground) (Chard, 2017; Malkki, 2018). These groups differed in their objectives and methods from the broader Left movement – in particular their methods were quite distinct from both the American Students for a Democratic Society and the French youth radicals of the May'68 movement, as well as from the broader International radical youth movement (Hendrickson, 2012; Marks, 2018).

Small political groups within the Left (here I am referring to the splinter groups that emerged out of the SDS such as the Weather Underground and Symbionese Liberation Army in the US), as well as the revolutionary organizations – Red factions (Maoist and vanguardist) in Europe – that had grown out of the youth and anti-war movements, had become extremist in both their demands and in their methods. The adoption of guerrilla warfare as the leitmotif of the politically violent wings of the Left was the outcome of a growing attraction to the notion of the "Urban guerrilla". They would become the Che Guevaras of the urban centers of the advanced economies. In Europe and Japan extremists of the Left began adopting the *"foco"* theory of action that advocated violence regardless of a lack of a revolutionary or mass movement to embed it within. *Foco* was an idea drawn from the successful revolutions in China and Cuba and promulgated by Che Guevara (Childs, 1995; Falciola, 2016; Malkki, 2018).

Foco theory drew on the experiences of Fidel Castro and Che Guevara in the Cuban struggle where their "Rebel Army" engaged in guerilla war in the Cuban *Sierra* (the mountains and the countryside). This approach was rooted in the notion that a small "Vanguard" group could create the conditions necessary for the overthrow of the State. As Guevara stated in his classic revolutionary handbook *Guerrilla Warfare* the

> minimum number with which it is possible to initiate a guerrilla war can be mentioned. In my opinion, considering the normal desertions and weakness in spite of the rigorous process of selection, there should be a nucleus of 30 to 50 men; this figure is sufficient to initiate an armed fight in any country of the Americas with their conditions of favourable territory for operations, hunger for land, repeated attacks upon justice, etc.
>
> (Che Guevara cited in Childs, 1995)

In Europe splinter groups from the larger Left and the anti- Vietnam War movement coalesced around this idea of forcing revolution through spectacularly violent actions. The absence of a mass movement agitating for revolutionary change was irrelevant. Groups such as *Baader-Meinhof* in West Germany, the Red Brigades in Italy and the Red Army faction in Japan privileged direct terror attacks on civilians (Beck, 2015).

In contrast to this, the dominant elements within the American Left veered away from the indiscriminate targeting of humans in their conduct of political action. This does not mean that people were not killed and injured by these groups – but this was not the aim (Falciola, 2016). They did not seek to create through violent spectacle a body of revolutionary followers or to achieve their political goals. Falciola (2016), writing about the turn away from human targeted acts, argues that from the early 1970s Left groups in America such as the

> Weatherman, together with all white leftist vanguards, engaged in low-intensity armed propaganda that avoided violence against people. Attacks targeting property, preceded by warning calls to clear the buildings, became their favorite repertoire of action.
>
> (Falciola, 2016)

According to a study examining the number of people killed in acts of political violence by American leftist groups in the period from 1968 to 1982, only one person was killed intentionally (Hewitt, 2005). Drawing on this work, Luca Falciola states in his paper, *A Bloodless Guerrilla Warfare: Why US White Leftists Renounced Violence Against People During the 1970s*, that

> [a]ccording to estimates, between 1968 and 1982 U.S. leftist militants carried out 670 bombings and arsons, 30 robberies, and 26 shootings. These actions resulted in 66 people injured. But in only a few cases did leftists plan to hit them. Out of 8 confirmed fatalities, only one was a premeditated murder; the others were either unintentional victims of bombings (1) or people shot during robberies or at police stops (6).
>
> (Falciola, 2016)

This historical data marks out a clear point of distinction between the "radical action" and "radical politics" of the 1960s in the United States and the extremist political violence of revolutionary vanguard groups in Europe and Japan. This legacy of engaging in "low-intensity armed propaganda" by elements within the American radical Left continues today. Radical ecological groups such as Animal Liberation and the Earth Liberation Front have been engaged in these forms of activism for decades (Brown, 2019). Their actions are in stark contrast to the violence perpetrated by violent political extremism, both religious and non-religious in nature, which targets humans as a propaganda tool.

The extremists of the Alt-Right and the Jihadist movements have this in common – they advocate violent action and foster a nihilistic wish to usher in an "End of Days" conflict (Aldrovandi, 2014; Lyons, 2017). Whilst in the United States the radical movement of the 1960s and 1970s shifted away from violence and the ultimately impotent "foco" strategy adopted by its European allies, the Alt-Right and the Jihadist movements of the 21st century in contrast have adopted murder and mayhem as their dominant modus operandi. The targeting of property, whilst part of their tactics, is secondary to the creation of spectacular assaults on persons. We could go through a checklist of attacks that, whilst damaging property, were in conception about killing and maiming as many people as possible: from the 1995 Oklahoma City bombing (Mallonee et al., 1996), the attacks on 9/11 (Mitchell, 2011) to the mosque assaults in New Zealand (Lee, 2019) in 2019 – the spectacle of mass murder is both the end product and the primary motivator for their actions.

The next section of this chapter will explore the popular perception of who or what constitutes an ongoing threat, this perspective will then be contrasted with the reality of political violence over the past decade or more and its characteristics. Following on from this discussion I will then make some concluding remarks.

Existential Threats

Looking back over the past decade of political violence it could be argued that the threat posed by groups sitting under the umbrella term Jihadist have dominated both the public discourse and policy direction in the West. The post-9/11 political landscape consisted of a series of legislative reforms, social, political and military initiatives and actions all directed at the perception of an emergence of an existential threat to the citizens of the Western democracies. A 2017 report by the *Cost of War* project at the Watson Institute at Brown University documents the $5.6 trillion expended by the United States on the "War on Terror" from the events of 9/11 up to the beginning of the 2018 financial year. This figure covers domestic expenditure, as well as the wars and military actions in Afghanistan, Iraq, Pakistan and Syria (Crawford, 2017). The same level of fear, policy development or economic expenditure in the cause of prevention was not directed at the ongoing threat posed by elements within the broad Alt-Right movement (Corbin, 2017; Lyons, 2017).

As I pointed out earlier in this chapter, the violence inflicted upon the citizens of America by the Alt-Right in the post-9/11 era dwarfs all other forms of politically motivated acts of violence. The "Unite the Right" rally held in 2017 in the Southern city of Charlottesville, Virginia, and the subsequent murder of a peaceful counter protestor – Heather Heyer – is representative of where the extremist Alt-Right has positioned itself. The Alt-Right is no longer a basement-dwelling underground movement – similarly to the Jihadists – they now see open acts of political violence as both necessary and viable tools in their propaganda strategy. The social media technologies discussed throughout this book have amplified their messages and enabled them to project their ideology onto the global stage far more effectively and with a greater reach than their numbers would warrant.

In 2019, Alt-Right ultra-nationalist sympathizers in the United States and in New Zealand embarked on an apparent contest – to kill as many people as they could. Both the New Zealand shooter and the El Paso killer stated in their online manifestos the desire to use violence to halt the "Great Replacement" of the White race by Black and Brown populations (Arango, Bogel-Burrougha, & Benner, 2019; Davey & Ebner, 2019; Deem, 2019). As the authors of a 2019 report on the impact of these xenophobic ideas point out, the

> [p]roponents of the so-called 'Great Replacement' theory argue that white European populations are being deliberately replaced at an ethnic and cultural level through migration and the growth of minority communities. This propagation often relies on demographic projections to point to population changes in the West and the possibility that ethnically white populations are becoming minority groups. Certain ethnic and religious groups – primarily Muslims – are typically singled out as being culturally incompatible with the lives of majority groups in Western countries and thus a particular threat.
>
> (Davey, & Ebner, 2019)

In some ways these groups have until recently slipped under the radar. They have not been at the forefront of public concern around issues of political violence. This is highly problematic at many levels. The violent elements within the Alt-Right have been able to conduct their acts of violence without being identified as "terror" groups. Meaning that the vast apparatus of counterterrorism applied to external threats has not been utilized in the United States or elsewhere to counter these groups. They have in effect been operating under the cover of the "mainstreaming" of many of their ideas by populist and nativist politicians and media commentators (Davey & Ebner, 2019).

Unlike the Jihadist terror organizations the Alt-Right is also closely aligned with mainstream political groups and they have been successful in having their ideas canvassed by traditional political structures as a result of the Trump ascendancy and the co-opting of the Republican party. This has not been restricted to the United States. "Populist" extreme right-oriented movements in Europe and Australia have been able to insert their ideas into, and have them debated in, the mainstream media and political structures. The ideas promulgated by the extremists of the Alt-Right are described as "nationalist", "nativist" or simply as an expression of "populist" discontent with intersectional, multicultural societies and more broadly the dominant "elites" of the West. Here it is important to point out that the "elite" that the Alt-Right are concerned with are the usual suspects: Jews, "Wall Street" and the pro-Globalist 1% perhaps best represented in the person of George Soros.

The Alt-Right has been able to galvanize a dispirited grouping of individuals, political movements, groups and parties around a range of issues in a way that was not previously possible. Until the rise of Trump and the populist movements of Europe, critics of the movement have dismissed it as simply being

> a code term for white nationalism, a much-maligned movement associated with neo-Nazis and Klansmen. The movement, however, is more nuanced, as it encompasses a much broader spectrum of rightist activists and intellectuals besides white nationalists, including those who believe in libertarianism, men's rights, cultural conservatism, isolationism, and populism. Nonetheless, its origins can be traced to various American white nationalist movements that have endured for decades.
> (Michael, 2017)

Race and identity play an important part in the thinking underpinning the Alt-Right (Michael, 2017), whilst in the case of the Jihadist movement identity and the perception of religious slight or insult are also present. What distinguishes these groups the Jihadist from the Alt-Right is the mainstreaming of their ideas. The acceptance in normal political circles in Europe and the United States as well as elsewhere of some of the underpinning thoughts and ideological constructs is a sobering aspect of the contemporary political environment.

The ongoing process of marginalizing progressive groups by and through the coopting of the term radical by dominant political groups to use as a catch-all phrase for their opponents has gained traction. As recently as 2020 and "Covid-19 Uprising", legitimate Anti-Fascist groups such as "ANTIFA" and peaceful protestors were described as terrorist formations by President Trump. In contemporary political discourse "radical" and "terrorist" are now inter-changeable as descriptors.

Conclusion

The mainstreaming of extremist Alt-Right ideas, at the same time as the re-working of the notion of what being "radical" means, cannot be separated. Language is political – as is who we regard as mainstream and who we regard as on the margins of political and social life. Where once "White nationalism" was easily dismissed as a fringe movement destined for the dustbin of history, as were their precursors – the Nazi/Fascist movements of the last century — we cannot be so smug. Language in the 21st century has been perverted. The racist fears and rhetoric of the Alt-Right are amplified by powerful political and social forces. Today, political language, as Orwell once put it so eloquently and in such a timeless manner,

> is designed to make lies sound truthful and murder respectable, and to give an appearance of solidity to pure wind. One cannot change this all in a moment, but one can at least change one's own habits, and from time to time one can even, if one jeers loudly enough, send some worn-out and useless phrase — some jackboot, Achilles' heel, hotbed, melting pot, acid test, veritable inferno, or other lump of verbal refuse — into the dustbin where it belongs.
>
> (Orwell, 1946)

In 2017 a neo-Nazi murdered a peaceful protestor who had been opposing a fascist torch march in Charlottesville — a made-for-social media event that reproduced images torn from the dark days of the Third Reich. In a press conference following the murder President Trump stated that at both events, "you also had people that were very fine people, on both sides" (Holan, 2019).

References

Abney, W. (2019). *Random destiny: How the Vietnam War draft lottery shaped a generation*. Vernon Press.

Aldrovandi, C. (2014). Millenarianism, messianism and absolute politics. In *Apocalyptic movements in contemporary politics* (pp. 36–61). Springer.

Ali, F., & Post, J. (2008). The history and evolution of martyrdom in the service of defensive Jihad: An analysis of suicide bombers in current conflicts. *Social Research, 75*(2), 615–654.

Alper, E. (2016). Protest diffusion and rising political violence in the Turkish '68 movement: The Arab-Israeli War, "Paris May" and the hot summer of 1968. In *Dynamics of political violence* (pp. 255–274). Routledge.

Andrews, K. T. (2018). *Freedom is a constant struggle: The Mississippi civil rights movement and its legacy*. University of Chicago Press.

Arango, T., Bogel-Burrougha, N., & Benner, K. (2019). Minutes before El Paso killing, hate-filled manifesto appears online. *The New York Times*.

Beck, C. J. (2015). *Radicals, revolutionaries, and terrorists*. Cambridge, UK: Polity.

Berger, J. M. (2015). The metronome of apocalyptic time. *Perspectives on Terrorism*.

Blum, C. (1987). *Rousseau and the republic of virtue: The language of politics in the French Revolution*. Ithaca, NY: Cornell University Press.

Brown, A. (2019). The green scare: How a movement that never killed anyone became the FBI's No. 1 domestic terrorism threat. *The Intercept*. Retrieved from https://theintercept.com/2019/03/23/ecoterrorism-fbi-animal-rights/

Chard, D. S. (2017). *Bad moon rising: How the weather underground beat the FBI and lost the revolution*. Oxford: Oxford University Press.

Childs, M. D. (1995). An historical critique of the emergence and evolution of Ernesto Che Guevara's foco theory. *Journal of Latin American Studies, 27*(3), 593–624.

Corbin, C. M. (2017). Terrorists are always Muslim but never white: At the intersection of critical race theory and propaganda. *Fordham Law Review, 86*, 455.

Cose, E. (2018). One year after Charlottesville, Trump has normalized racism in America. *USA Today*. Retrieved from https://www.usatoday.com/story/opinion/2018/08/10/white-supremacists-neo-nazis-charlottesville-unite-right-rally-trump-column/935708002/

Crawford, N. C. (2017). United States budgetary costs of Post-9/11 wars through FY2018.

Davey, J., & Ebner, J. (2019). *The 'Great Replacement': The violent consequences of mainstreamed extremism*. London.

Deem, A. (2019). Extreme speech: The digital traces of #whitegenocide and Alt-Right affective economies of transgression. *International Journal of Communication, 13*, 20.

Erikson, R. S., & Stoker, L. (2011). Caught in the draft: The effects of Vietnam draft lottery status on political attitudes. *American Political Science Review, 105*(2), 221–237.

Esposito, J. L., Sonn, T., & Voll, J. O. (2015). *Islam and democracy after the Arab Spring*. Oxford University Press.

Falciola, L. (2016). A bloodless guerrilla warfare: Why US white leftists renounced violence against people during the 1970s. *Terrorism and Political Violence, 28*(5), 928–949.

Flacks, R., & Lichtenstein, N. (2015). *The Port Huron statement: Sources and legacies of the new left's founding manifesto*. University of Pennsylvania Press.

Fromson, J., & Simon, S. (2015). ISIS: the dubious paradise of apocalypse now. *Survival, 57*(3), 7–56.

Gardner, B. (2018). Social engineering in non-linear warfare. *Journal of Applied Digital Evidence, 1*(1), 1.

Gregoire, R., & Perlman, F. (1970). *Worker-student action committees, France, May '68*. Detroit: Black & Red.

Guardiola-Rivera, O. (2019). Guaido's coup-by-media shows his Venezuelan revolution to be little more than a PR campaign. *The Independent*. Retrieved from https://www.independent.co.uk/voices/venezuela-coup-juan-guaido-leopoldo-lopez-nicolas-maduro-chavez-media-a8894891.html

Harcourt, B. E. (2017). *Waking up from May '68 and the repressive hangover: Stages of critique past Althusser and Foucault*. Kyoto: Kyoto University.

Hayden, T. (2005). *The Port Huron statement*. New York: Thunder's Mouth.

Hendrickson, B. (2012). March 1968: practicing transnational activism from Tunis to Paris. *International Journal of Middle East Studies, 44*(4), 755–774.

Hewitt, C. (2005). *Political violence and terrorism in modern America: A chronology*. Greenwood Publishing Group.

Hill, J. (2018). Authoritarian resilience in Morocco after the Arab spring: A critical assessment of educational exchanges in soft power. *The Journal of North African Studies, 23*(3), 399–417.

Holan, A. D. (2019). In Context: Donald Trump's 'very fine people on both sides' remarks (transcript). *Politifact*. Retrieved from https://www.politifact.com/article/2019/apr/26/context-trumps-very-fine-people-both-sides-remarks/

Hom, A. R. (2016). Angst springs eternal: Dangerous times and the dangers of timing the 'Arab Spring'. *Security Dialogue, 47*(2), 165–183.

Irving, N. (2016). Answering the "international call": Contextualising Sydney anti-nuclear and anti-war activism in the 1960s. *Journal of Australian Studies, 40*(3), 291–301.

Israel, J. (2013). *Democratic enlightenment: Philosophy, revolution, and human rights 1750–1790*. Oxford University Press.

Jefferson, T. (1787, November 13). [Letter to William Stephens Smith].

Keenan, B. S. (2009). *"Vietnam is fighting for us": French identities and the US–Vietnam War, 1965–1973*. The University of North Carolina at Chapel Hill.

Lee, T. (2019). Social media sites struggle to contain video of New Zealand shooting. Retrieved from https://arstechnica.com/tech-policy/2019/03/social-media-sites-struggle-to-contain-video-of-new-zealand-shooting/

Levin, B., & Reitzel, J. D. (2018). *Report to the nation: Hate crimes rise in US cities and counties in time of division and foreign interference*. Washington, DC: Center for Victim Research.

Lyons, M. N. (January 20, 2017). Ctrl-alt-delete: The origins and ideology of the alternative right. Somerville, MA: Political Research Associates, *January, 20*.

Malkki, L. (2018). Left-wing terrorism. In *Routledge Handbook of Terrorism and Counterterrorism* (pp. 113–123). Routledge.

Mallonee, S., Shariat, S., Stennies, G., Waxweiler, R., Hogan, D., & Jordan, F. (1996). Physical injuries and fatalities resulting from the Oklahoma City bombing. *Jama, 276*(5), 382–387.

Marks, R. (2018). "1968" in Australia: The student movement and the New Left. In *The Far Left in Australia since 1945* (pp. 148–164). Routledge.

McDonald, J. (2013). *Rousseau and the French Revolution 1762–1791*. Bloomsbury Publishing.

McKinley, D. T. (2018). Umkhonto We Sizwe: A critical analysis of the armed struggle of the African National Congress. *South African Historical Journal, 70*(1), 27–41.

Michael, G. (2017). The rise of the alt-right and the politics of polarization in America. *Skeptic (Altadena, CA), 22*(2), 9–18.

Miller, E. (2017). *Ideological Motivations of Terrorism in the United States, 1970–2016*. Maryland: College Park.

Mitchell, W. J. T. (2011). *Cloning terror: The war of images, 9/11 to the present*. University of Chicago Press.

Mohandesi, S. (2018). Bringing Vietnam home: The Vietnam War, internationalism, and May '68.

Moskalenko, S., & McCauley, C. (2009). Measuring political mobilization: The distinction between activism and radicalism. *Terrorism and Political Violence, 21*(2), 239–260. doi:10.1080/09546550902765508

Nef, J. (2018). Demilitarization and democratic transition in Latin America. In *Capital, power, and inequality in Latin America* (pp. 81–108). Routledge.

Notaker, H., Scott-Smith, G., & Snyder, D. J. (2016). *Reasserting America in the 1970s: US public diplomacy and the rebuilding of America's image abroad*. Oxford University Press.

Orwell, G. (1946). Politics and the English Language. *Horizon*.

Sedgwick, M. (2010). The concept of radicalization as a source of confusion. *Terrorism and Political Violence, 22*(4), 479–494. doi:10.1080/09546553.2010.491009

Singer, P. W., & Brooking, E. T. (2018). *LikeWar: The Weaponization of social media*. Eamon Dolan Books.

Skocpol, T. (2015). *States and social revolutions : A comparative analysis of France, Russia, and China*. Cambridge : Cambridge University Press.

Tackett, T. (2015). *The coming of the terror in the French Revolution*. Harvard University Press.

Totton, N. (2018). May—"The Strangest Disease": May'68 and its consequences. *Psychotherapy and Politics International, 16*(2), e1450.

Vigna, X. (2011). Beyond tradition: The strikes of May–June 1968. In *May 68* (pp. 47–57). Springer.

Vítek, T. (2016). *The failure of the New Left in the US: The case of SDS*. (Phd). Charles University, Prague, Czech Republic.

Williams, R. (2013). *Keywords (Routledge revivals): A vocabulary of culture and society*. Routledge.

Worley, M., & Copsey, N. (2016). White youth: The far right, punk and British youth culture. *JOMEC Journal, 9*, 27–47.

Chapter 7

"Hell Is Empty. And All the Devils Are Here."

Apocalyptic Thinking and the Emergence of "Death Cults"

> "Hell is empty. And all the devils are here."
> —Ariel, Act 1, Scene 2. William Shakespeare, *The Tempest*.

Apocalyptic Thinking

In the early decades of the 21st century "extremist" movements and organizations began to effectively marshal the tools of social media and the ubiquity of the internet to attract young people, particularly the disaffected and the alienated, to their causes. Movements such as the Islamic State (IS) operating in Syria, Iraq and globally through small cells and single (Lone Wolf) attackers have been able over the past decade to draw individuals, families and young people into their religious-inspired campaign of terror and open warfare (Brooking & Singer, 2016; Glenn, 2016). The use of these technologies to promote the goals of violent political movements is not restricted to religious groupings. Extremist groups on the right-wing of the political spectrum have also been active, and successful in harnessing these technologies to promote, recruit and control followers. These movements, the IS and the Alt-Right, share a common apocalyptic-infused world-view of a coming conflict that will destroy the corrupt and "morally bankrupt" secular "liberal" societies of the West (Barkun, 2002; Belew, 2018; Berger, 2015).

In the chapter which follows I will briefly examine the significance of "apocalyptic thinking" and the notion of a future apocalyptic conflict or war, as a core belief in the ideological framework of extremist groups such as IS and the Alt-Right movement. For these groups apocalyptic thinking is pivotal to the way they prosecute their political agenda and how they fashion the propaganda and ideological messages used to attract new followers. By projecting an end of days message wrapped up in a call to action, these groups are appealing to a deep sense of "cultural despair" and alienation in segments of Western society (Barkun, 2002; Hedges, 2008; Karouny, 2014; Khalaji, 2008). Each of these movements has tailored a message that resonates with particular segments of society. Their adeptness at crafting propaganda messages enables them to present themselves as embodying a solution to the problems of cultural despair and alienation. In effect they are calling on young people to engage in war, a war that will bring on the ultimate battle. The shadow of war hovers over the actions of both IS and the Alt-Right. As Hedges has argued, "[w]ar gives purpose, meaning [and] a reason for living" (Hedges, 2003).

It is not an overstatement to assert that despite fundamental differences in both the origins of these movements and their major ideological beliefs – they have many similarities. As I have argued, these movements use a comparable "apocalyptic" vision of a coming "End of Days" conflagration to attract, motivate and cohere their followers to their political agenda and goals. The importance of examining the role of apocalyptic thinking in contemporary political culture – globally and within the various current theatres of low-intensity and terroristic conflict such as in Afghanistan, Iraq, Syria and Sub-Saharan Africa (this is not an exhaustive list) as well as amongst the political actors within the Alt-Right (neo-Nazi/nativist groups) cannot be ignored. As Marega (2017) has pointed out in her important study, *Apocalyptic Trends in Contemporary Politics*, the

> worldwide occurrence of terroristic attacks, wars of religion, the intensification of fundamentalisms, the new rise of nationalism and xenophobia, [has emphasized] the need to investigate the revival of religious beliefs as a phenomenon of deep urgency and topicality. Among the various aspects worthy of being analyzed, it is legitimate to focus deeply on the role of apocalyptic symbolism and its exploitation by political actors: the hypothesis is that it has a persisting - and mostly underestimated - influence on the contemporary political conjuncture.
>
> (Marega, 2017)

Political and religious movements have over the past decade been particularly adept at identifying and attracting young people looking for meaning and a sense of belonging in their lives through the dissemination of apocalyptic discourse (Bott, 2009; Marega, 2017). During the mid-2010s the Islamic State (IS) organization was able to appeal to and, in some cases, recruit followers within the Islamic diaspora found in the West using sophisticated media tools and techniques (Barr & Herfroy-Mischler, 2017; Roversi, 2017). Similarly during the same period, the Alt-Right has projected its message using new media and sophisticated propaganda techniques to appeal to segments of the old working-class and the economically and culturally disenfranchised within the United States, Europe and Australia (Barnett, 2016; Morris, 2016; Roversi, 2017).

Islamic State: An Apocalyptic Death Cult

When the Islamic State emerged out of the collapse of al-Qaeda in Iraq (AQI) in 2004 its adherents were energized by and imbued with a sense of divine purpose (Karouny, 2014; Berger, 2015). They would over the coming years insert themselves into the chaos of the conflict in Syria, before their assault on the Iraqi cities of Mosul and Tikrit in 2014 and the subsequent declaration of a new Caliphate (Glenn, 2016). IS, like a number of terror-oriented political movements with religious pretensions and origins – as well as others such as the science fiction inspired *Aum Shinrikyō* – saw their violence as the gateway to a utopian future. The apocalyptic and "End of Days" thinking underpinning movements such as IS is not an end to the Caliphate or its subjects, it is in fact an end to the world inhabited by non-believers and those they describe as "apostates".

Whilst not exclusively targeting young people with their messages both IS and the Alt-Right movements have been successful in adapting to the current new media landscape to attract young people to their causes (Goracy, 2016; Roversi, 2017). IS in its initial emergence as an insurgent group (Kalyvas, 2018) sweeping through Iraq and Syria, adopted a media intensive "shock & awe" campaign. Mass executions, beheadings, extreme acts of violence in general were captured on smartphones and uploaded to the internet, then to be circulated through social media platforms, both as recruitment tools and as propaganda in an information war (Barr and Herfroy-Mischler, 2017; Gambhir, 2016; Winter, 2015).

Before examining modern manifestations of political death cults and their attraction for the disaffected and those seeking some locus of meaning for their existence in modern capitalist society, it is important to clarify several key points. First, it is necessary to discuss some of the key words or terms that I will use in this chapter. In the first section of the chapter I will deal with notions of millenarianism and the apocalypse. These are the key ideas that will help us to understand the position we find ourselves in, in the first half of the 21st century. A position where conflicting ideologies, some in the garb of religious movements, others espousing "nativist" ideology, are engaged in both open and subterranean conflict with existing nation states and societies. In this context the use of concepts summed up as an "End of World" discourse is able to attract and motivate segments of both Western and non-Western societies to act. Here, let me emphasize I am not using these ideas to present or defend Huntington's "Clash of Civilization" (Huntington, 1993) argument. In my view there is only one dominant global civilization that we inhabit – advanced capitalism. Let me also emphasize that whilst the groups I will examine in this chapter, and the entire book, share many elements, their ideologies are quite distinct. What is not distinct or unique is the love of and joy for inflicting and celebrating violence that the groups I will discuss share.

Second, I need to give the reader a rationale for why I will make some of the claims that follow. I am cognizant of the reaction that some will have to the parallels I intend to draw between modern political cults and movements and particular cult-like political organizations and structures from the last century. The political death cult that I am going to discuss as a comparative starting point to the current global formations will be the Nazi Party's *Schutzstaffel* (*SS*, "Protective Squadron"). Whilst the *SS* was the product of a unique set of historical and political circumstances, nevertheless it presents a model for how violent political formations operating outside of, and then within, a state structure are able to attract otherwise intelligent individuals to a nihilistic and violent cause. Understanding how they were to both attract and harness young people to their warped quasi-religious cult will help create a data point or angle from which we can view later manifestations. That said we can now proceed.

Cults

The appeal of extremist political movements for individuals seeking a sense of belonging or a means to become part of something larger than themselves as a mechanism with which to dull the pain of the alienation caused by advanced capitalist society (Jaeggi, 2014) has been facilitated by new forms of technology such as the internet and social media (Schwartz, 2007; Von Behr, Reding, Edwards, & Gribbon, 2013). At the core of how these movements function in contemporary society we find a new form of digitally enabled and augmented connectedness. This connectedness has enabled the promotion of an "End of Days" strand of thinking – though distinct in its make-up and reasoning, both the Alt-Right and the Jihadi IS movement share a willingness to bring on the apocalypse (Aldrovandi, 2014; Berger, 2015; David, 2018; Riedl, 2014; Simi & Futrell, 2015).

Both the Islamic State and groups within the Alt-Right (neo-Nazi/ nativist) movement have found new and innovative methods and technologically amplified forms of propaganda to incite political violence and project an apocalyptic vision for contemporary cultural politics (Morris, 2014, 2016). Modern forms of new media and technology, specifically the internet with its "Deep Web" and the "Dark Web" (Weimann, 2016) – where hackers, criminals and extremist political groups loiter – as well as Facebook, YouTube and communications tools such as the encrypted email service *Telegram* (Hume, 2016), provide contemporary organizations and movements such as Islamic State and the groups within the broad Alt-Right with powerful propaganda and logistical tools. These mechanisms enable non-State actors to project their message in ways that had previously been the domain of advanced State formations.

In our contemporary political and cultural landscape technology has enabled cult-like behavior to transcend distance, location and culture.

Before exploring what I mean by this in detail, it is important to define the terrain to explore how cult-like ideas have emerged within both the extremist movements such as IS and the Alt-Right. It is important to map out why I am using the term "cult" in the context of contemporary terror and political violence. The term cult is not associated with contemporary political terror and violence in popular discourse in much of the academic literature which focuses on these matters. In Australia, for example, the notion of the Islamic State as a "Death Cult" was both ridiculed and deemed to be too offensive to use (Olding, 2015). This is despite the explicit statements made by key thinkers within the broader Jihadi movement, as described in the important work of Raffaello Pantucci (2015), " *We Love Death as You Love Life": Britain's Suburban Terrorists*. As Pantucci points out, the London 2005 bomber Siddique Khan announced in his video message to the world that his act of terror was a celebration of death and martyrdom. He asserted that: "We love death as you love life" (Pantucci, 2015). According to Pantucci this statement reflects a strain of Islamicist ideology that can be traced back to al-Qaeda and its "cult of death" (Pantucci, 2015).

Individuals such as Khan are drawn to an ideology which has at its core the notion that the end of the world is near – or that through armed conflict it can be brought about. Elements within the broad Alt-Right share the view that the end is near and that through conflict "race war" its arrival can be accelerated. Although, as I have argued, these groups approach this way of thinking from quite distinct perspectives and with quite different contexts, they share a hatred for Western society and the permissive liberal culture that has evolved since the mid-20th century. It is in this context that I introduce the argument that extremist groups such as IS and its various progenitors (al-Qaeda) and off-shoots (Boko Haram), as well as elements within the broad Alt-Right and its extremist "White Power", conspiracy and neo-Nazi elements, are modern "Death Cults" or share elements which can be described in such a manner.

I am aware that it is problematic to use the term "cult" to analyze the specific movements that I have singled out for discussion in this book. It will require a clear explanation of how these movements have taken on some of the aspects of cults. IS and elements within the Alt-Right share the idea that death is a useful political tool – as did other modern cults such as the Branch Davidians or *Aum Shinrikyō* (Barkun, 2002; Lifton, 2000, 2003; Neocleous, 2005; Tourish & Wohlforth, 2015; Whitsel, 1998).

It is important to restate the argument that these movements, specifically IS and its "franchises" – Boko Haram and others – share a form of ideology that has at its core the celebration of death and the construction of a death cult as an organizing and recruiting mechanism. Not recognizing that these organizations function in this manner – removing the concept from our discourse – robs us of the power to fully engage with and counter such political formations. If we are not cognizant of the underlying thought processes and organizational principles at work in these formations we will be unable to fully grasp the existential threat that such ideas pose but also, we will lack the willingness to confront these nihilistic political movements and their ideologies.

As Lifton (2000) has argued, the term *cult* has become a pejorative term in popular discourse; it is often used to describe what might better be referred to as "new religious" movements. According to Lifton (2000), a cult is a group that displays three key characteristics: "totalistic or thought-reform-like practices, a shift from worship of spiritual principles to worship of the person of the guru or leader, and a combination of spiritual quest from below and exploitation, usually economic or sexual, from above" (2000). This is the standard understanding of what cults are and how they function to control and exploit their members.

According to Tourish and Wohlforth, writing in their study of right-wing and left-wing political cults *On the Edge* (2015), our understanding of cults and cult-like behavior is still evolving. In their book, Tourish and Wohlforth use a definition of cult behavior promulgated by the American Family Foundation, in a special edition of the *Cultic Studies Journal* (West & Langone, 1986). In that special edition it asserted that a cult can be described as a

> group or movement exhibiting great or excessive devotion or dedication to some person, idea, or thing, and employing unethical manipulative or coercive techniques of persuasion and control (e.g. isolation from former friends and family, debilitation, use of special methods to heighten suggestibility and subservience, powerful group pressures, information management, suspension of individuality or critical judgement, promotion of total dependency on the group and fear of leaving it), designed to advance the goals of the group's leaders, to the actual or possible detriment of members, their families or the community.
>
> (West & Langone, 1986)

Movements such as the Islamic State, as well as the various groups that embrace the ideology of the Alt-Right (or the Christian Right as it was referred to up until the emergence of the Trump phenomenon) have used religion or religious-based ideology as a justification for their actions (Hedges, 2008). Religion is used to both legitimize their overall strategy, but also to give meaning and justification for violent actions. The Alt-Right groups such as the American "Aryan nation" have also adopted religious ideology and thinking, in particular the imagery and trappings of a form of "Whites only" variant of Christianity to attract new recruits, but also to justify the movement's race-based ideology, political actions and violence (Barnett, 2016; Belew, 2018; Jackson, 2014).

These groups share a form of "millenarianism" – which in its modern form has been with us since the turn of the century but which has its antecedents in both Judeo/Christian and Islamic religious doctrine. In this section of the book, I will examine how the following ideas: "millenarianism", apocalyptic thinking, and an "End of Days" discourse, have become embedded in the ideology of terror organizations, both secular and religious (Berger, 2015; Sullivan, 2015). In the pages which follow I will argue that this type of thinking ("End of World"-ism and the yearning for an apocalyptic final confrontation) represents the emergence of a form of "political death cult" (Lalich, 1992; West & Langone, 1986). The notion that radical movements such as Islamic State and other politically oriented violent and extremist groups are a form of "death cult" will be critically discussed and analyzed.

Modern political "death cults" and the movements that have given birth to them are the outcome of more than half a century of permanent war and the application of militarization both to organize capitalist economies and to maintain control over subject populations. The emergence of permanent war and the social, political and economic structures needed to maintain such an effort have opened spaces for the emergence of new forms of cultural politics and the renovation of old ones. In the early decades of the 21st century these new movements and the cultural and political transformations that they embody have only just begun to fully emerge.

Cults and cult-like movements have in the form of the Islamic State filled the vacuum created by the disruption and destabilization of nation states such as Afghanistan, Iraq, Syria and Libya in the Middle East. Beyond the Middle East and the "War on Terror", the wreckage created in the lives of particular segments within the societies of the West by the application of extremist neo-liberalist economics have similarly opened up spaces where social cohesion has been weakened – into which extremist groups have been able to emerge. Both radical groups from religious orientations and radical groups with secular agendas have tapped into a growing cultural malaise, amplified by economic and social policies which undermine community solidarity – here I am referring specifically to the dismantling of working-class communities and their sense of cohesion and solidarity (Duina, 2017; Hedges, 2012).

The decline in social cohesion and the rise of extremist movements both religious and political is occurring at a time when in the societies of the West there is an emerging sense of exhaustion. A sense in the West that we have reached a *fin de siècle*, and that the West is culturally and politically bankrupt, unable to solve the problems of disease, population, the environment, inequality and the maintenance of social and political harmony. Extremist and populist movements have been able to tap into the sense of cultural dread that permeates contemporary culture. The emergence of right-wing and left-wing populist movements such as Five Star in

Italy, Alt-Right in the United States and One Nation in Australia are all examples of this.

In the past century there have been many examples of the emergence within Western society of forms of quasi-religious groups operating under the guise of formal religions but functioning in effect as tightly controlled cultic ideological formations. Examples of this are groups such as the Branch Davidians, who were part of a mass suicide in Waco, Texas (Barkun, 2002), or the Japanese religious terror group *Aum Shinrikyō* (Lifton, 2000). A similar statement could be made about Scientology, which shares many of these characteristics, though not the celebration of violence or an explicit end of days ideology. The vast array of conspiracy groups who emerged in the wake of the Covid-19 pandemic in 2020 also sit within this broad category of cultic ideological formations – though they are not tightly controlled.

Cultural Despair and Crisis Cults

What links these specific forms of cult to older incarnations (the Nazi State and its internal political cult – the "*SS*") is the idea of crisis. The emergence of crisis cults and their impact on a range of non-European societies has been a focus of study in the anthropological literature for many decades (Connor, 1989). In the literature, the idea of a crisis cult has been identified as a characteristic of non-Western societies and their failures or collapse. There has been a reluctance to apply the notion to advanced societies such as the United States or the nations of Europe. This is changing, as the recent work of writers such as Chris Hedges (2014) has highlighted – Western society, and Western civilization is being analyzed in terms of potential "collapse" of a complex system (Bardi, 2017; Diamond, 2005).

As Hedges (2014) has argued, the existentialist crisis generated by the planetary-wide exploitation and environmental destruction underpinning the advance of capitalism over the past 500 years has provided many opportunities for notions of crisis to emerge. Our society has grown increasingly complex – there appear to be no simple solutions to the myriad of problems which confront the modern state and its populace: homelessness, poverty, gendered violence, inequality, racism, sexism, environmental degradation, political violence, disease – the list goes on. As Hedges has eloquently stated,

> Complex civilizations have a bad habit of ultimately destroying themselves. Anthropologists including Joseph Tainter in "The Collapse of Complex Societies," Charles L. Redman in "Human Impact on Ancient Environments" and Ronald Wright in "A Short History of Progress" have laid out the familiar patterns that lead to systems breakdown. The difference this time is that when we go down the whole planet

will go with us. There will, with this final collapse, be no new lands left to exploit, no new civilizations to conquer, no new peoples to subjugate. The long struggle between the human species and the earth will conclude with the remnants of the human species learning a painful lesson about unrestrained greed, hubris and idolatry.

(Hedges, 2014)

What lurks in the shadows is a sense that things are ending, or that there is a real possibility that that is what could happen. The horrors of popular culture – the end of the world, post-apocalyptic visions of the *Walking Dead* or *Mad Max* – have cultural resonance. As Hedges goes on to say,

as the collapse becomes palpable, if human history is any guide, we, like past societies in distress, will retreat into what anthropologists call "crisis cults." The powerlessness we will feel in the face of ecological and economic chaos will unleash further collective delusions, such as fundamentalist beliefs in a god or gods who will come back to earth and save us. The Christian right provides a haven for this escapism. These cults perform absurd rituals to make it all go away, giving rise to a religiosity that peddles collective self-delusion and magical thinking. Crisis cults spread rapidly among Native American societies in the later part of the 19th century as the buffalo herds and the last remaining tribes were slaughtered. The Ghost Dance held out the hope that all the horrors of white civilization – the railroads, the murderous cavalry units, the timber merchants, the mine speculators, the hated tribal agencies, the barbed wire, the machine guns, even the white man himself – would disappear. And our psychological hard wiring is no different.

(Hedges, 2014)

The pull of crisis cults has played a significant part in the history of Western society – at least it did in the early to mid-20th century. Looking back to the period before the outbreak of the Second World War and to the turmoil that gripped Germany, we can see what crisis and fear of societal collapse can produce. Fear of societal collapse opens spaces within which extremist movements can emerge and flourish. The economic, political and social crises that undermined the legitimacy of the fledgling Weimar Republic in Germany provided fertile ground for the popular appeal of a messianic leader with a simple solution to the vagaries and complexity faced by the people of Germany. Here I am not equating Weimar Germany with contemporary Western society – at least not directly. But as during that historical period – the inter-war era – when cultural consensus, identity, progress and a sense of belonging are undermined, then space is opened up for the emergence of anomie and the search for meaning. We in effect have a template for how crisis appears, how the fear of societal collapse can occur and what horrors it can lead to. We currently inhabit just such a vacuum and, in that vacuum, brought on by fear of societal collapse and a diminution of a sense of the future, extremist groups have flourished.

In working through an understanding of the significance of the emergence of crisis cults for our current discussion, it is important to highlight the role of culture in creating the conditions upon which this phenomenon emerges. Culture is central to this discussion in the following ways. We have experienced an unparalleled disruption to both contemporary social relations, economics and the weakening of social and political institutions. At the center of this shift has been the unchecked application of neo-liberalism through, and in the name of, the market. Political reform – the decline of the State and state regulation of the economy – has been facilitated and abetted by the disruptive and transformative capacity of advances in information technology. The combination of a triumphant neo-liberal political formation and rapid advances and affordances made possible through new forms of digital technology have accomplished profound structural renovations of contemporary society, and transformed the lives of individuals, as well as the nature of societies and cultures.

The emergence of populist political movements, the distrust of institutions (the media, education, the police and science) and the disenchantment with economic and social progress that we can see at play in the United States and elsewhere have weakened the liberal/progressive ideology that underpinned the post-war consensus in most developed societies. This has led to the emergence of a sense of "cultural despair" or pessimism. Fritz Stern (1974), in his classic discussion of the decline of German liberalism in the 19th and 20th centuries, *The Politics of Cultural Despair: A Study in the Rise of Germanic Ideology*, argued that emergence of a sense of cultural and political despair helped to produce the foundations upon which the rise of the Nazis occurred. Stern argues that the Germans experienced this cultural despair throughout the late 19th and early 20th centuries and it became emblematic of their culture and society. It was reflected in art and literature and was a center of the literary criticism that helped sway the thinking of the German elites and directed their negativity at ideas of liberal progress and democratic thinking, as well as ethnic and religious minorities (Stern, 1974). It is my assertion that in our century, the nations of the West have experienced the rise of a similar shift towards a sense of cultural despair. This shift has been enabled through the embedding of a form of "permanent war" and the militarization of society (a point I will expand upon later in this book in detail).

In the last century, the devastation and mass murder of the First World War coupled with the unwillingness by segments of society (the Conservative establishment – economic, social and political) to accept the liberalism of the Weimar Republic and its culture, created the conditions necessary for the emergence of a violent political movement – the ascendant National Socialist movement. This is not to equate the current period with the political conditions of Europe in the early to mid-20th century. I am simply arguing that the conditions of cultural pessimism that created the circumstances conducive to the emergence of extremist political movements – on the Left and the Right – has echoes in our current century.

The sense of cultural despair that Stern talks about – a sense of powerlessness, cultural displacement, economic disruption, and its concomitant amplification of alienation – already inherent in capitalist society, is once again with us. When faced with such traumatic conditions Germany looked for simple solutions to their complex social, economic and political problems. The early period of this century has also led to a similar quest for simple solutions and a sense of belonging. The rise of populism, both in Europe and the United States, is just one example of the tendency to look for simple solutions. The attraction of extremist thinking, whether religious in origin as in the case of IS and its supporters, or in the form of the nationalist and exclusionary cultural politics of the Alt-Right, have sought to attract and salve the alienation and despair of segments of various societies.

Connor, writing about the idea that Nazi Germany and its institutions became in effect a crisis cult, argues that culture has both "symbolic" and "emotional" meaning (Connor, 1989). According to Connor,

> culture [is] a way of life, it is a symbolic, emotional construct by means of which humans derive meaning out of life and are able to transcend themselves and their mortality; there can be no simple separation of a culture and its people.
>
> (Connor, 1989)

When culture is impacted by changes in society and in human relations, a type of dissonance emerges. The cultural despair that Stern (Stern, 1974) wrote about and the fear of collapse that Hedges (2014) and others are pointing to are both the flip of the same trend. The extremist groups such as Islamic State and the Alt-Right have been able to promulgate their messages in a way that resonates with young people who feel this dissonance keenly – more keenly than older generations. It is the young who seek out meaning and connectedness as a way of rooting their sense of self and their place within society.

In times of crisis or the fear of impending collapse and cultural despair, cults offer a haven – a sense of meaning, a plan for action and a solution to complex issues. When we examine contemporary forms of apocalyptic political thinking, as embodied in organizations such as the Islamic State, it can be argued that they share much with an earlier violent political cult and the movement that helped birth it. Here I am referring to the Nazi Party's *Schutzstaffel* (*SS*, "Protective Squadron").

The SS: A Political Death Cult

The SS and the broader Nazi party and the emergent Nazi State offered the people of Germany a safe harbor – a new political cultural form, in the face of collapse and the dominant sense of cultural despair that enveloped the nation in the first part of the 20th century (Gellately et al., 1992; Lambert, 2007; Ponzio, 2015; Stern, 1974). It is my assertion that a celebration of death, violence and cruelty has been shared by both the Islamic State and the Nazi political military formation the SS. Let me caution the reader, I am not making the claim that Islamic political movements are in fact modern incarnations of the German National Socialist movement. Though they do share many similarities in their views towards the Jewish religion, the role and status of women and the importance of self-sacrifice for a political/cultural end. Here I am describing their similarities whilst recognizing their differences. Intellectually both movements are motivated by a similar form of counter enlightenment as a central element within their political ideology.

From its creation in 1923 as a protective organization within the Nazi party charged with the safety of the Party leader Adolf Hitler, the *Schutzstaffel* (*SS*) was steeped in both the celebration of violence and in its application for political ends. The SS was a distinct organizational unit within the structure of the broader National Socialist movement and would in time grow to rival and then replace the more proletarian *Sturmabteilung* ("Assault Division"), colloquially referred to as the *SA* grouping or the "Brown Shirts" (*Braunhemden*). The SA, whilst sharing a love of violence with the emergent SS, was a broad-based and "proletarian" movement (Blum & Bromhead, 2017). The SA did not have the same obsession with purity, race and the distinct "blood" based racially charged ideology. The SA was established as a tool with which the Nazi Party was able to engage in street violence – attacking their opponents on the left and singling out individuals for special treatment. This was particularly the case in the lead up to and the events of *"Kristallnacht"* on November 9, 1938 – the manufactured "spontaneous" night of targeted anti-Jewish violence and arson chaos (Fitzgerald, 2017; Lutjens, 2017).

The chaos generated through the violence and arson inflicted on the Jewish population of Germany on that day highlighted the extent to which the unsophisticated nature of the *SA* – its street fighting heritage – made it too much of a blunt object in the political and ideological work of the Nazi party and the emergent Nazi state. As Timothy Snyder points out in his masterful book *Black Earth: The Holocaust as History and Warning* (Snyder, 2015), the reaction of the German population to the open violence of the SA during *Kristallnacht* was not what its architect, Goering, had envisioned. According to Snyder, *Kristallnacht* demonstrated that such disorderly

> violence within the Reich itself was [in effect] revealed to be a dead end. Most of German public opinion was opposed to the chaos. Visible

despair led to expressions of sympathy with Jews, rather than the spiritual distancing that the Nazis expected. Of course, it was possible for Germans not to wish to see violence inflicted upon Jews while at the same time not wishing to see Jews at all.

(Snyder, 2015)

The type of political and social engineering that the Nazis envisaged would require a more nuanced approach, one that the *SA* as a mass movement was not capable of delivering. The Nazi leadership would replace the *SA* with the *SS* as both the mechanism with which to apply the perverted racial ideology of the Nazis, but also to create through the application of extreme violence a future pure Aryan state that was the end point of their racial fantasies. The *SS* was conceived as being both the model for the future political leadership of the global Third Reich – but also as a quasi-religious order. It had strict membership requirements but as the war progressed the SS took on the shape of a mass organization when it reached a total size of some 80,000 in both its Police units and the *Waffen SS* (*Armed SS*) (Weale, 2012).

The *SS* created a state within a state, with its own schools, hospitals, police and military formations. It also constructed a system of breeding centers for the promulgation of the pure Aryan race through racial discrimination and eugenic practices (Conroy, 2017; Lipnick, 2018). It was a militarized hardened political cult with an obsession with blood, purity and an absolute belief that their movement would transform the planet and remake it so that it would conform to Nazi ideals as expressed by their movement and its leader (Mineau, 2013; Snyder, 2015).

"Blutkitt" (Blood Cement)

The foundation upon which the *SS* constructed its organizational structure and its political work can be found in the Nazi obsession with blood and race. The *SS* were political soldiers engaged in both a physical struggle, as well as an ideological war. In their *"Weltanschauung"* (world view), blood and the purity of race was a pivotal aspect of what the Nazi globe spanning new order would be built on.

The following is an extract from an *SS* publication *"Ewig ist das Blut"* which translates as "The blood is eternal", in which an *SS* author expands on the significance of blood for the *SS* ontology. According to the *SS* author,

> Blood is immortal. We live in a community the borders of which are made of blood. And that community is where our soul survives, in our children and in our works. We exist through time, today, as we existed yesterday and will exist tomorrow. What flows inside of you is the

blood of free Germanic peasants, who have always been the pillars of higher culture, due to the outstanding creativity of that blood. This is the blood of the *Ostlandfahrer,* who have conquered by the sword and brought the ploughshare to foreign lands. Fight for the future of that blood! In this way, you were, you are, and you will be, from eternity to eternity. You are immortal in your Volk.

(Mineau, 2013)

The SS was imbued with a racially based ideological construct – a construct which placed them at the center of the struggle to bring about an emergent National Socialist Aryan nation and which necessitated a form of commitment and praxis. It is in this context that the idea of the SS as an early form of political death cult begins to take form. The SS was engaged in the construction of a new society – one in which those who did not fit their idea of what it meant to be human had no place (Mineau, 2013). Constructing this new society would demand a commitment and a specific willingness to take extreme measures to bring into being what would be in their view a perfect future society. The concentration camps, the death camps and the brutal and murderous practices of the *Einsatzgruppen* (Tenenbaum, 1955) in the occupied countries of Eastern Europe were part of the cleansing process the SS ideology called for (Matthäus, Böhler, & Mallmann, 2014). In order to achieve the insane political and ideological objectives of the Nazi leadership an armed force was needed, one with unflinching commitment to these objectives. Here the SS as the political army of the Reich had been constructed in order to do just that, with their training, structure and fanaticism ensuring Hitler could rely upon them – absolutely.

One of the earliest studies of the origins and function of the SS highlighted the extent to which the organization was a closed structure operating with a distinct set of rules. Rules which were inspired by the techniques used to enforce discipline in organized criminal gangs and conquering armies. Alexander, writing not long after the end of the Second World War in a paper entitled "The Socio-Psychological Structure of the SS", argued that

[t]he SS was a criminal organization not only because its members committed crimes, but also because the essential mode of its thinking and its group behavior were those of all criminal organizations. If a member did anything which put his loyalty to the organization in a questionable light, either he was liquidated—killed—or he had to undertake a criminal act which definitely and irrevocably tied him to the organization. According to the age-old custom of criminal gangs, this act had to include murder. In the SS this process of reinforcement of group cohesion was called *Blutkitt* (blood cement), a term which

Hitler himself is said to have obtained from a book on Genghis Khan in which this technique of obtaining group cohesion was emphasized.
(Alexander, 1948)

Political movements such as the Islamic State and earlier political structures such as the German *SS* share many of the characteristics of a cult. Cults operate as closed social and cultural containers where adherents to the cult are surveilled, indoctrinated, rewarded and punished, and their beliefs are constantly reinforced. Religious and non-religious cults share those key aspects. IS, whilst ostensibly a religious movement, also operates as a political cult. A cult that was and is infatuated with death and the subjugation, removal and murder of others, of non-adherents and the unworthy. Here it is possible to see parallels between Islamic State and the *SS*, both in how the two organizations functioned when in power and in how both organizations justified their existence and why their members were driven to commit the gross acts of inhumanity that they did in both historical situations on a daily basis.

At the core of political cults such as Islamic State and the Nazi party's *SS* is a fundamental belief in the rightness of their beliefs and the need to use violence and murder to accomplish their political goals. If we look closely at the Nazi movement and its vanguard organization, the desire to make every sacrifice necessary for victory in the service of the National Socialist state and its leader was embedded in the psychology of the Nazi movement (Alexander, 1948; Reichel, 2016; Sax, 1997; Snyder, 2015).

White Power and the "End of Times"

The existence of extremist political movements on the political right has been a fact of modern life since the middle of the last century. Whilst never dominant in the West – except for the period leading up to the Second World War where for example fascist movements gained power in Italy in the 1920s to 1943, Germany from the early 1930s till 1945 and in Spain from the late 1930s until the early 1980s – nationalist and xenophobic ideas never disappeared completely from Western political culture. Extremist nationalist and xenophobic organizations, drawing inspiration from the Fascist movements of the mid-20th century, have been an ever-present factor in the political life of advanced societies such as the United States, the nations of Europe and settler societies such as Australia and South Africa. These groups have historically been small, but they have at times been quite vocal and have had both cultural and political impact beyond what the size of their following would warrant. In Europe and Australia their re-insertion into the public discourse, after their retreat in the post-war period, has been facilitated through debate and open hostility shown towards the issue of North African and Middle Eastern refugees and other forms of irregular migration.

In the United States there has been a long tradition of racially based White nationalist groupings with cultural and historical links that have their roots in the American Civil War and its aftermath. The election of the nationalist government of President Donald Trump reinvigorated these movements in America. The torchlight march through Charlottesville in 2017 in which participants changed racially charged statements on the importance of blood and their struggle against the Jews had frightening echoes of an earlier era.

The Alt-Right has for decades used technology to project its message, to recruit and to engage in harassment of its enemies (Morris, 2014, 2016). Neo-Nazi and nativist (groups advocating the need to privilege locals, their interests and wellbeing above all else) Alt-Right groups have had a sustained web presence and have been highly successful in both projecting their message through new forms of technology and in recruiting and organizing online (O'Callaghan et al., 2014; Roversi, 2017; Simi & Futrell, 2015). These groups, as in the case of IS, have been adept at mediatizing their message in order to project an image of themselves that amplifies both their impact and their potency. The torchlight procession in Charlottesville, North Carolina in 2017 mentioned above was reminiscent of fascist Italy in the 1920s and Germany in the 1930s, when similar events were organized to demonstrate the power of the fascist/Nazi movements and to intimidate their opponents (Reichel, 2016). Images and video of this procession were captured and disseminated through new media technology (see below for a more detailed discussion) – projecting a chilling reminder of the "dark times", as Arendt once described the mid-20th century (Atkinson, 2018).

These groups share a common approach in that they have created political spaces, both in the real world and online, in which their ideas are circulated, amplified and their ideological messages are consumed (Braddock, 2012). It is my assertion that in this context a form of cult (or cult-like) behavior has emerged as both a useful organizing tool and a recruitment mechanism, but also as a means for operating in the contemporary political landscape.

The Islamic State and the Alt-Right share a great deal ideologically (their belief that they are chosen ones engaged in a death struggle with their enemies), in how they operate in the shadows, attracting individuals using a combination of tried and true propaganda strategies, and in tapping into the affordances created by new forms of technology. They share a love of death in the name of their cause and are willing to sacrifice themselves, either by dying for their cause as in the suicide killers of IS or by committing "lone wolf" attacks and immediately surrendering and being taken captive (Anders Breivik in Norway or the New Zealand mass murderer are examples), in what they see as a war against and within the dominant society and its culture (Martino, 2012). Their acts of violence are a kind of subverted Nietzschean "Will to Power" – they kill and maim in order to bring into existence their religious or racial Utopias.

They also share a highly sophisticated understanding of the application of information in a weaponized form. In many ways the technology of social media and the internet have created a "poor man's" capacity to inflict "Shock and Awe". State and non-State actors are both capable of inflicting what I have called elsewhere in this book "perceptual damage" – extremists of IS and the Alt-Right are able to draw on these technologies to inflict harm on their adversaries in the hope that they can bring about a collapse of the societies that they despise.

Making Sense of Apocalyptic Thinking in the Islamic and Alt-Right Political Movements

One would assume that because of the racist roots and nature of the Alt-Right movement, they would have little in common with the Islamic extremists of IS or al-Qaeda. To restate what I have argued earlier, these movements share a commitment to violence and the idea that through their violent acts they will, in a sense, will into existence the cleansing Apocalypse. The relationship between religion and terrorism has been explored extensively since the September 11 (9/11) attacks on New York and the Pentagon and the subsequent now near-decades-long global conflict that these attacks signaled (Jenkins, 2017; Jones, 2008; Juergensmeyer, 2008). Since 9/11, scholars have been grappling with the question of why religious-inspired violence has emerged as a global phenomenon (Juergensmeyer, 2008; McDonald, 2013; Pantucci, 2015).

As McDonald (2013), in a study of historical apocalyptic movements, has argued,- what we have witnessed over the past few decades has been

> the transformation of the originally determinist apocalyptic visions into modern ideologies suggesting violent action. The ulterior motive of many religious terrorists is to bring about Armageddon, the final battle which will put an end to the old world and open up the future for a new world conforming to their ideas of order. Yet . . . no ancient or medieval apocalyptic author believed that humans could achieve this; the apocalyptic cataclysm was believed to be the sole work of God.
> (McDonald, 2013)

This is a key element in understanding current political and cultural conditions – the extremists of the IS and the Alt-Right believe that they have within their grasp the Armageddon that, in the case of IS, only God had hitherto the capacity to bring forth, and in the case of the Alt-Right the correct political conditions – alienation, growing economic division, racial, cultural and religious discord.

In both cases these groups have embraced a form of "millenarianism" and a sense that we are in fact at the "End of Times". Driving them on is a shared concept of history, one which "envisions a final condition of ultimate perfection, harmony or happiness, either on this earth or in heaven" (Aldrovandi, 2014). It is a sobering thought to consider that one of the salient elements of life in the 21st century is an awareness that there are highly motivated individuals and groups working towards killing, maiming and creating as much disruption in our societies as possible.

Alienation in the 21st Century as an Explanation for the Attraction to Death Cults

One of the prevailing explanations of why young people and others sign up for the kinds of organizations we are examining in this chapter and the rest of the book is the concept of "alienation". These individuals are attracted to IS and the Alt-Right because they are estranged from their society and seek to lash out at the world around them both to punish it for their perceived grievances or mark out their true uniqueness. Alienation has also been a dominant explanation for why young people join gangs or engage in violent anti-social criminal activities. Sociologists, criminologists and psychologists have grappled for many years with the question: why do these people sign up for the kinds of death cults we have thus far examined? As Pantucci has argued it takes a lot,

> for a person to be persuaded that he ought to attack the society in which he lives, he must convincingly believe that the latter is already against him.
>
> (Pantucci, 2015)

The quote from Pantucci above is quite telling. It is no small feat to turn on the society that you have been part of perhaps since birth and take violent action. It requires a mental stance where one's neighbors are transformed into mortal enemies. In order to try to understand how these movements have been able to encourage such a view amongst groups and individuals it is necessary to look at the way groups and individuals have come to be attracted to these movements. The concept of alienation, whilst out of fashion in much contemporary sociological and psychological discourses in the past 1980s neo-liberal context, does offer a way into the minds of these individuals. In the psychological literature much work has been conducted tracing the trajectory of disaffected young people in the West in the direction of radical political movements. My argument does not draw upon this literature.

I wish to focus on the political and cultural roots of contemporary alienation. The concept of alienation is a term that has had a long tradition in the sociological and psychological literature. It has even entered everyday public discourse. Its origins can be found in the writings of Karl Marx (Marx and Engels, 2009), where it was first used to describe the sense of separation or distance that workers have had historically from the products that they create through their labor (Archibald, 2009; Jaeggi, 2014; Marx, 2015). In common parlance the term alienation is often used to account for a sense of distance or estrangement of an individual from his or her surroundings. There is no agreed-upon definition or understanding of the concept.

It is my contention that the alienated individual – someone who feels a sense of distance, estrangement and a diminished sense of sociality – has been and continues to be a prime focus of groups such as IS. It is from here that individuals become capable of acting in the way that domestic terrorists – the al-Qaeda and IS-inspired, as well as the Alt-Right adherents, such as the Oklahoma bomber – are able to kill and maim in the places that they once called home. Starting from this point we might begin to discern patterns and identify the processes that enable these individuals to act in such violent and destructive ways. Alienation has, I will assert, provided the glue which bonds individuals young and mature to destructive apocalyptic political movements and death cults.

Unlike the progressive and anti-war movements of the 1960s and 1970s who marched peacefully in the United States and elsewhere for civil rights and an end to the war in Indochina, contemporary extremist organizations such as IS base their political agenda and appeal on violence. They also differ profoundly from the mass mobilizations which followed the death of George Floyd in 2020. These groupings and individuals, unlike IS and the Alt-Right, were inspired by a simple idea – people should be treated equally by the State regardless of color. They should not be murdered indiscriminately.

As Pantucci (Pantucci, 2015) has argued, IS and other Islamist extremists celebrate violence and look to death as a vehicle to gain access to the bounties of the afterlife. Groups within the Alt-Right movement also exhibit a deep attraction to the use of violence both to achieve their ends – provoking a race war and the final "End of Days" conflagration – and as the embodiment of their struggle for racial purity. The Charlottesville Nazi-inspired torch march was both an act of provocation and blow against the dominance of non-White multiculturalist agenda, and was an embodiment of symbolic violence (Atkinson, 2018; Guilford, 2017).

Looking back at what happened in Syria and Iraq under the rule of IS, terror and violence was not simply a means to an end but was in fact the key organizing principle of life under their rule. It attracted the disaffected, the alienated youth of many nations, to a space and time that lifted them out of their humdrum existence. By engaging in a range of murderous acts they are able to fulfil the political agenda of their leadership to create the blood cement that would bind them to a new more powerful community, free from their previous alienated existence.

Conclusion

In this chapter I have attempted to map out some of the mechanisms used by political groups such as IS and the Alt-Right and progenitors to attract followers and build a sense of community which uses concepts such as blood bonding to create a shared sense of community, in order to accomplish their political agendas. The use of violence to both intimidate their adversaries as well as to create a form of "Shock and Awe" has been a dominant feature of all of these movements and their sub-groupings and imitators. Their application of violence and their promotion of it as a solution to the sense of alienation felt by many young people within Western society has been a salient feature of the past few decades.

Often in political debates the term "culture wars" is applied to the traditional conflict between Left and Right political movements and elites. We are in fact amid a social war which has as its goal the sowing of discord and the dismantling and defeat of democratic states. It is an active campaign shared by extremist political groupings (as well as by nation-states). The ideological underpinnings of these groups seem on the surface to be quite distinct – however, they share a perception that Western society is at a tipping point and in one way or another, through mass civil unrest, attacks by alienated but newly energized blood soldiers, or health crises, they have the capacity to bring on their "End of Days" phantasmagoria.

The similarity in both the operation and organizing principles between terror groupings such as the *SS* and the Islamic State is quite striking. They share cult-like characteristics and are, I have argued, a variant of what has been described as a "death cult". The celebration of violence, cruelty and murder as an organizing principle but also as a ticket to membership is a common characteristic. It provides what has been referred to as a form of "blood cement" which binds the individual to the ideological and political agenda of the group. Death and the destruction of one's opponents is a cause for celebration and the means with which to validate their actions and to attract new followers.

At the core of this conflict is the array of social media now easily accessible through the internet and capable of amplifying a specific idea or message in a way that is simple to construct, disseminate and deny. The social war is a war without boundaries and a war that embraces apocalyptic thinking and the celebration of conflict, blood and violence. It is also enveloped in a sense of impending doom and fear of social collapse.

References

Aldrovandi, C. (2014). Millenarianism, messianism and absolute politics. In *Apocalyptic movements in contemporary politics* (pp. 36–61). Springer.

Alexander, L. (1948). The socio-psychological structure of the SS. *Folia Psychiatrica, 2*, 2–14.

Archibald, W. P. (2009). Marx, globalization and alienation: Received and underappreciated wisdoms. *Critical Sociology, 35*(2), 151–174. doi:10.1177/0896920508099190

Atkinson, D. C. (2018). Charlottesville and the alt-right: A turning point? *Politics, Groups, and Identities, 6*(2), 309–315.

Bardi, U. (2017). *The Seneca Effect: Why growth is slow but collapse is rapid*. Springer.

Barkun, M. (2002). Project Megiddo, the FBI and the Academic Community. *Terrorism and Political Violence, 14*(1), 95–108.

Barnett, B. A. (2016). League of the South's internet rhetoric: Neo-confederate community-building online. *Director's Advisory Board, Chair Molly Pepper, Ph.D., 13*, 151.

Barr, A., & Herfroy-Mischler, A. (2017). ISIL's execution videos: Audience segmentation and terrorist communication in the digital age. *Studies in Conflict & Terrorism*, 1–22.

Belew, K. (2018). *Bring the war home: The white power movement and paramilitary America*. Harvard University Press.

Berger, J. M. (2015). The metronome of apocalyptic time: Social media as carrier wave for millenarian contagion. *Perspectives on Terrorism*. Retrieved from http://terrorismanalysts.com/pt/index.php/pot/article/view/444

Blum, M., & Bromhead, A. d. (April, 2017). *Rise and fall in the Third Reich: Social mobility and Nazi membership*. Retrieved from Ris database.

Bott, C. (2009). *Recruitment and radicalization of school-aged youth by international terrorist groups: Final report*. Homeland Security Institute. Arlington, Virginia.

Braddock, K. (2012). *Fighting words*. (Doctor of Philosophy). The Pennsylvania State University.

Brooking, E., & Singer, P. (2016). War goes viral. Retrieved from x-devonthink-item:// D188258 3-9A5B-4F2C-BCE 0-2498D59581E5

Connor, J. W. (1989). From ghost dance to death camps: Nazi Germany as a crisis cult. *Ethos, 17*(3), 259–288.

Conroy, M. (2017). *Nazi eugenics: Precursors, policy, aftermath*. Columbia University Press.

David, M. D. (2018). Confronting Charlottesville: Using interdisciplinary research as critical engagement praxis. *Politics, Groups, and Identities, 6*(2), 303–308. doi:10.1080/2156 5503.2018.1454331

Diamond, J. (2005). *Collapse: How societies choose to fail or succeed*: Penguin.

Duina, F. G. (2017). *Broke and patriotic: Why poor Americans love their country*. Stanford California: Stanford University Press.

Fitzgerald, S. (2017). *Kristallnacht*. Capstone.

Gambhir, H. (2016). *The Virtual Caliphate: ISIS's Information Warfare*. Institute for the Study of War.

Gellately, R., Browder, G. C., Lessman, P., Best, W., Ziegler, H. F., Weyrauch, W. O., . . . Werle, G. (1992). Situating the "SS-State" in a social-historical context: Recent histories of the SS, the police, and the courts in the Third Reich. *The Journal of Modern History, 64*(2), 338–365.

Glenn, C. (December 20, 2016). Timeline: Rise and spread of the Islamic State. Retrieved from https://www.wilsoncenter.org/article/timeline-the-rise-spread-and-fall-the-islamic-state.

Goracy, N. (2016). *Lone wolf, the young lion, and the impressionable American: The impact of social media platforms on homegrown Islamic extremism*. (Bachelor of American Studies). Washington, DC : George Washington University.

Guilford, G. (2017). The complete story of what happened in Charlottesville, according to the Alt-Right. Retrieved from https://qz.com/1053220/charlottesville-attack-how-the-violence-unfolded-through-the-eyes-of-the-alt-right/

Hedges, C. (2003). *War is a force that gives us meaning*. Anchor.

Hedges, C. (2008). *American fascists: The Christian right and the war on America*. Simon and Schuster.

Hedges, C. (2012). *Days of destruction, days of revolt*. Nation Books.

Hedges, C. (2014). The myth of human progress and the collapse of complex societies. Truthdig.

Hume, T. (August 1, 2016). Priest's killers met on messaging app 4 days before attack, source says. *CNN*.

Huntington, S. P. (1993). The clash of civilizations? *Foreign affairs*, 22–49.

Jackson, P. (2014). Accumulative extremism: The post-war tradition of Anglo-American Neo-Nazi activism. In *The Post-War Anglo-American Far Right: A Special Relationship of Hate* (pp. 2–37). Springer.

Jaeggi, R. (2014). Alienation. In *New directions in critical theory* (pp. xxv, 274). New York: Columbia University Press.

Jenkins, B. M. (2017). *The Origins of America's Jihadists*. Rand Corporation.

Jones, J. W. (2008). *Converting to terrorism: What the psychology of religion tells us about religiously motivated terrorism*. Paper presented at the Annual Meeting of the American Psychological Association.

Juergensmeyer, M. (2008). Martyrdom and sacrifice in a time of terror. *Social Research*, 75(2), 417–434.

Kalyvas, S. N. (2018). Jihadi Rebels in Civil War. *Daedalus*, 147(1), 36–47.

Karouny, M. (2014). *Apocalyptic prophecies drive both sides to Syrian battle for end of time*. Reuters.

Khalaji, M. (2008). Apocalyptic politics. *Washington Institute for Near East Policy (WINEP), Policy Focus, 79*, 20.

Lalich, J. (1992). The cadre ideal: Origins and development of a political cult. *Cultic Studies Journal*, 9(1), 1–77.

Lambert, P. (2007). Heroisation and demonisation in the Third Reich: The Consensus-building value of a Nazi pantheon of heroes. *Totalitarian Movements and Political Religions*, 8(3), 523–546. doi:10.1080/14690760701571155

Lifton, R. J. (2000). *Destroying the world to save it: Aum Shinrikyō, apocalyptic violence, and the the new global terrorism*. New York: Henry Holt and Co.

Lifton, R. J. (2003). " In the Lord's Hands": America's apocalyptic mindset. *World Policy Journal*, 20(3), 59–69.

Lipnick, C. J. (2018). *Victims of the past: Walter Groß, the RPA and the Nazi propaganda war against the disabled*. Drew University, EndNote Tagged Import Format database.

Lutjens, R. N. (2017). Ordinary crime and the persecution of Jewish Germans in deportation-era Berlin. *Holocaust and Genocide Studies*, 31(3), 433–456.

Marega, S. (2017). Apocalyptic trends in contemporary politics. *Estudios* (35), 41 1–431.

Martino, J. (March 29, 2012). Anders Breivik, video games and the militarisation of society. *The Conversation*. Retrieved from http://theconversation.edu.au/anders-breivik-videogames-and-the-militarisation-of-society-6670

Marx, K. (2015). Alienated labour. In *Working in America* (pp. 21–28). Routledge.
Marx, K., & Engels, F. (2009). *The economic and philosophic manuscripts of 1844 and the Communist manifesto*: Prometheus Books.
Matthäus, J., Böhler, J., & Mallmann, K.-M. (2014). *War, pacification, and mass murder, 1939: The Einsatzgruppen in Poland*. Rowman & Littlefield.
McDonald, K. (2013). *Our violent world: Terrorism in society*. Palgrave Macmillan.
Mineau, A. (2013). *SS thinking and the Holocaust*. Amsterdam; New York: Rodopi.
Morris, T. (2014). Networking vehement frames: Neo-Nazi and violent Jihadi demagoguery. *Behavioral Sciences of Terrorism and Political Aggression, 6*(3), 163–182.
Morris, T. (2016). *Dark ideas: How Neo-Nazi and Violent Jihadi ideologues shaped modern terrorism*. Lexington Books.
Neocleous, M. (2005). Long live death! Fascism, resurrection, immortality. *Journal of Political Ideologies, 10*(1), 31–49. doi:10.1080/1356931052000310272
O'Callaghan, D., Prucha, N., Greene, D., Conway, M., Carthy, J., & Cunningham, P. (2014). Online social media in the Syria conflict: Encompassing the extremes and the in-betweens. *arXiv preprint arXiv:1401.7535*.
Olding, R. (May 12, 2015). Counter-terrorism adviser: Abbott's IS 'death cult' label is counter-productive. *Sydney Morning Herald*.
Pantucci, R. (2015). *"We love death as you love life": Britain's suburban terrorists*. Oxford University Press.
Ponzio, A. (2015). *Shaping the new man: Youth training regimes in Fascist Italy and Nazi Germany*. University of Wisconsin Press.
Reichel, P. (2016). *Nazi Germany*. Springer.
Riedl, M. (2014). *Apocalyptic politics: On the permanence and transformations of a symbolic complex*. Durham, NC: Duke University.
Roversi, A. (2017). *Hate on the net: Extremist sites, neo-fascism on-line, electronic Jihad*. Routledge.
Sax, B. (1997). What is a" Jewish Dog"? Konrad Lorenz and the Cult of Wildness. *Society & Animals, 5*(1), 3–21.
Schwartz, D. C. (2007). *Political alienation and political behavior {electronic resource}*. New Brunswick, NJ: AldineTransaction.
Simi, P., & Futrell, R. (2015). *American Swastika: Inside the white power movement's hidden spaces of hate*. Rowman & Littlefield.
Snyder, T. (2015). *Black earth: The Holocaust as history and warning*. London: Vintage Digital.
Stern, F. (1974). *The politics of cultural despair: A study in the rise of the Germanic ideology*. Berkeley: University of California Press.
Sullivan, E. R. (2015). *The Islamic State: Terrorists or millenarian mass movement?* US Army War College.
Tenenbaum, J. (1955). The Einsatzgruppen. *Jewish Social Studies, 17*(1), 43–64.
Tourish, D., & Wohlforth, T. (2015). *On the edge: Political cults right and left*. Armonk: Routledge.
Von Behr, I., Reding, A., Edwards, C., & Gribbon, L. (2013). *Radicalisation in the digital era: The use of the internet in 15 cases of terrorism and extremism*. RAND Corportion. Rand Europe.
Weale, A. (2012). *Army of evil: A history of the SS*: Penguin.
Weimann, G. (2016). Terrorist migration to the dark web. *Perspectives on Terrorism, 10*(3).
West, L., & Langone, M. (1986). Cultism: A conference for scholars and policy makers. *Cultic Studies Journal*.
Whitsel, B. (1998). The Turner diaries and cosmotheism: William Pierce's theology. *Nova Religio, 1*(2), 183–197. doi:10.1525/nr.1998.1.2.183
Winter, C. (2015). Documenting the virtual 'caliphate'. *Quilliam Foundation, 33*, 1–50.

Chapter 8

Habitus and the Mechanics of Militarization

Habitus and Militarization

The concept of a "social war" that I have been discussing in this book has been prosecuted using a range of media technologies, technologies that have matured over the past three decades. New media and digital technology in the form of social media and video games – as well as the internet – have provided the mechanisms and platforms through which political warfare and propaganda have been able to achieve unparalleled levels of success in shaping our thinking. The social war has evolved within the context of an ongoing process that has been described as militarization (Geyer, 1989; Torres & Gurevich, 2018). A societal process that first emerged during the Second World War, and which has been amplified by the advent of digital technology and the digital culture that it has engendered.

"Militarization" is an ongoing process which has at its core the structuring of society in ways that facilitate and normalize the application of violence for political purposes – as well as constructing the political consensus necessary for the maintenance of a "military-industrial complex" – which provides the logistical basis for this societal process. Militarization has maintained its ability to shape neo-liberal societies through a range of technological affordances and social, political and cultural institutions, practices and a cultural predisposition to see violence as both normal and useful. One of the ways we can understand how this political form has been both maintained and facilitated is to examine the sociological concept of "habitus".

There are many conflicting and contested definitions and explanations of the function of this socio-cultural process. For the purpose of this book I argue that the definition and application of habitus as understood by the French sociologist Pierre Bourdieu (P. Bourdieu, 1977) is both an acceptable and powerful conceptualization. Habitus as Bourdieu has argued refers to

> systems of durable, transposable dispositions, structured structures predisposed to function as structuring structures' that is, as principles of the generation . . . and structuring of practices and representations

which can be objectively 'regulated' and 'regular' without any way being the product of obedience to rules, objectively adapted to their goals without presupposing a conscious aiming at ends or an express mastery of the operations necessary to attain them.

(P. Bourdieu, 1977)

In this chapter Bourdieu's notion of habitus will be utilized as a starting point for our understanding of the means through which militarization functions at the level of the individual and of society. It will weave together a picture of both the affordances made for this process by new forms of technology as well as the way society has been more generally re-configured to enhance and promulgate militarization. Before I do that let us examine the nature of the militarization of society.

Militarization

To restate what I have been describing elsewhere in this book, the concept of militarization as I understand it refers to "the contradictory and tense social process in which civil society organizes itself for the production of violence" (Geyer, 1989). It is a process which is distinct from historical models of "militarism" with their open and often flamboyant embracing of militaristic modes of leadership, government and conflict. Here I am referring to Fascist Italy, Nazi Germany, Imperial Japan and the range of African and Latin American dictatorships of the last century. Militarization as a process and as a political form is quite different. As Lutz has pointed out,

> [m]ilitarization is intimately connected not only to the obvious increase in the size of armies and resurgence of militant nationalisms and militant fundamentalisms but also to the less visible deformation of human potentials into the hierarchies of race, class, gender, and sexuality, and to the shaping of national histories in ways that glorify and legitimate military action.
>
> (Lutz, 2002)

This is a process that has emerged and matured over many decades and has in effect led to the "deformation of human potentials". Vast amounts of resources, human ingenuity as well as human lives have been applied to the preparation for war and the systematic reframing of what is normal has led to the normalization of war.

This did not just happen. The drift towards a militarized society can be traced directly to the mid-20th century and the establishment of a vast apparatus to engage in conflict on a global scale. Militarization as a political form was the product of the need to create a bulwark against the existential threat faced by the democratic societies posed by Nazi Germany, Fascist Italy and Imperial Japan at the height of the Second World War. There was a need to build up the military and to create the social, political and economic means to engage in a "Total War" (Horne, 2019; Neumann, 2009). The "Total War" stance adopted by the warring political Blocs, the Allies and the Axis, developed into a structure which did not end with the defeat of the aggressor.

Despite the victory of the liberal-democracies and their Soviet ally, the war would continue – not in the globe spanning "hot" war of the previous decade but as an ideological and small-scale series of "brush fire" wars – under the rubric of the "Cold War" (Betts, 2012; Robin, 2009). The Military-Industrial Complex established during the Second World War did not dissolve once the enemy was defeated (Eisenhower, 1960; Robin, 2009; Wright Mills, 1956). It cemented its place within the fabric of the evolving capitalist state and was sustained throughout the subsequent decades by small and large brushfire wars, such as Korea and Vietnam and the plethora of engagements by proxy in Africa and Latin America. It provided the social, political, cultural and economic foundations upon which militarization was constructed and sustained.

Its expanding demand for resources – human, technological and logistical – required a new economic base upon which to draw. Its demand for resources helped to create the economic turmoil that engulfed the Western nations in the 1970s – the so-called "Oil shock" and the rising levels of mass unemployment. The Keynesian accord that had ensured a strong and interventionist state in the post-war years was no longer conducive to the demands of the process of capitalist accumulation and the Military-Industrial Complex.

A new economic and political form was needed to both sustain the Military-Industrial Complex and re-force the process of militarization – neo-liberal capitalism. This economic and political form became a central element in post-1970s. Writing about the rise of neo-liberalism and its impact on democracy, Simon Reid-Henry (2019) in *Empire of Democracy: The Remaking of the West Since the Cold War, 1971–2017* argues that

> [n]eoliberalism was two things: as a set of economic ideas it was a reaction to the Keynesian consensus that dominated mid-twentieth-century politics and an effort to secure the conditions for a return to laissez-faire capitalism in the modern world; as a political movement, it was focused on bringing about a reinvention of the state – a new 'constitution of liberty', as Hayek had put it in 1960 – which would oversee the free operation of the market without the interference of special interests as democracy enabled. It was, put bluntly, a solution to the challenge posed by democracy to the market; and for this reason

it reappeared – at this point – as a potentially useful roadmap for the transformation in challenging times.

(Reid-Henry, 2019)

Without the emergence of the Military-Industrial Complex, the re-configuring of modern society in order to facilitate its militarization would not have been feasible. It helped to establish the socio-political, economic and cultural foundations for the ongoing process of militarization. In the next section of the book I will examine the notion of the Military-Industrial Complex in more detail.

The "Military-Industrial Complex"

In his farewell speech on leaving office President Eisenhower popularized the concept of the Military-Industrial Complex at the height of the Cold War when he cautioned the American people to be vigilant against its growth. The Military-Industrial Complex is a configuration of government, academic and industrial networks and policy settings which first emerged during the Second World War. Critics from both the center and the left of American politics have argued that the emergence of the Military-Industrial Complex has had a negative impact on the well-being of society. It was seen both by Eisenhower and academic critics as representing a profoundly un-democratic turn in the body politic (Wright Mills, 1956).

The Military-Industrial Complex does not function in the same way as did the military states of the 20th century. The State and military institutions such as the Army have not been used to take control of government and other political and social institutions as they were under the Axis (Germany, Italy and Japan) nations in the mid-20th century. Nor is the Military-Industrial Complex anything like the late-20th-century post-colonial military governments of Africa and Latin America.

The term was first coined in the mid-1950s by the sociologist C. Wright-Mills who pointed to the way the Military-Industrial Complex that had emerged during the Second World War had not dissolved following the end of the war. In fact, it was argued that the Military-Industrial Complex had begun to transform American society. The war effort necessary to defeat the Axis powers during the Second World War had led to the emergence of close connections between industrial enterprises, the military, the scientific establishment and the government. The wartime alignment between these powerful institutions did not dissolve in the post-war period. According to Wright-Mills, a pattern was established after the war in which corporations seeking lucrative contracts began to employ ex-military officers, particularly generals, to manage corporations.

Wright-Mills argued that the traffic between corporations, academia and the military represented far more than simply a means to gain military contracts. The establishment of the networks and power flows upon which the Military-Industrial Complex rests represents a profound shift in American society. With the emergence of the Military-Industrial Complex in the post-war era, America became not only the leading industrial power but also the leading military state.

The positioning of America as a leading military state was an outcome of the tremendous effort required to conduct a global war – and to win. What began as a series of special arrangements and strategic decisions in order to ensure the flow of military innovations, men and material had in fact led to the establishment of a permanent "war state" with a "war economy". The harnessing of the American economy and its technical capacity to the task of waging war both "hot" and "cold" on a planetary scale has been one of the most profound outcomes of the emergence of the Military-Industrial Complex.

The emergence of the Military-Industrial Complex was publicly confirmed by President Dwight D. Eisenhower in his farewell speech to the American people on January 17, 1961. In his fireside chat, President Eisenhower described the growth of the Military-Industrial Complex, which he argued was a product of the totalizing forces of a vast military establishment and an ever-expanding arms industry. Eisenhower cautioned that this trend was exerting its influence in every level of American life and was in danger of corroding the American polity. He warned the American people that the creation of this new structure had the potential to undermine democracy and to imperil the American Republic.

Eisenhower argued that whilst he understood the need for this development – the Cold War was at its height – the Nazi threat had morphed into the Totalitarian enemy embodied in Joseph Stalin and his successors. He cautioned Americans not to

> fail to comprehend its grave implications. Our toil, resources and livelihood are all involved; so is the very structure of our society. In the councils of government, we must guard against the acquisition of unwarranted influence, whether sought or unsought, by the military-industrial complex. The potential for the disastrous rise of misplaced power exists and will persist.
>
> (Eisenhower, 1960)

Both Eisenhower and Wright-Mills cautioned that the emergence of this structure would have the potential to re-shape America. The Cold War (1947–91), the Korean War (1950–53) and the conflicts in South East Asia in Vietnam, Laos and Cambodia (1955–75) provided the rationale for the maintenance of a permanent state of war. The Military-Industrial Complex cemented its hold over the conduct of American politics and even after the collapse of the Soviet Union in 1991 maintained its influence.

The post-9/11 military incursions into Afghanistan (2001) and Iraq (2003) further extended the power and influence of the Military-Industrial Complex through the global "War on Terror" waged against Islamic extremists. The invasions of Afghanistan and Iraq by the United States under then-President George W. Bush were sustained by the Military-Industrial Complex and opened entirely new avenues for military and commercial cooperation. This was not a new phenomenon, nor was it one that emerged out the desire to seek vengeance for the attacks of 9/11. The mechanisms set in motion had a direct connection to the vast military apparatus that emerged in the mid-20th century – however, they were dependent upon the existence of militarization as a cultural and political form.

Militarization as a Cultural and Political Form

Militarization is a cultural and political form that enables society to in essence feel comfortable with the application of military force. It exists as a consequence of both societal and individual predispositions. Militarization exists both within the everyday life of ordinary people and as an integral component of the political structures within contemporary liberal-capitalist society. It inhabits a space made possible by both economic and cultural forces and structures. The United States has become both its best example and lead protagonist. The *"Empire"* that the United States now controls – global in scope and hugely costly for its own population – exists as a product of the penetration of "militarized" modes of thought and action into the fabric of society. The creation of a global "Garrison" and the "militarized" policing of its own population has enabled the US to participate in armed conflict, in one form or another, continuously since 1941.

Militarization, as Boggs and Pollard have argued, has created

> a rationality that deeply influences the structures and practices of the general society through storytelling, mythology, media images, political messages, academic discourses, and simple patriotic indoctrination.
> (Boggs & Pollard, 2007)

This is a powerful set of tools and practices that have embedded the notion that the "military", in the form of a vast planetary machine, is both necessary but also fundamentally just – it has been the guarantor of global peace and stability. The period of the Trump administration, whilst rhetorically objecting to this position, has in effect done little to shift the role or reach of the military apparatus in any meaningful way from this stance.

The current stage in the process of militarization draws heavily upon the tools and affordances embedded within and made possible by new forms of digital technologies through communication, information harvesting and algorithmic manipulation. These technologies have enabled the growth and increasing sophistication of new forms of media and digital culture such as video games, social media and streaming media. These technologies build on existing highly effective mechanisms – those structures and practices that Boggs and Pollard (2007) referred to as social, cultural and political forms, practices and processes which facilitated the militarization of everyday life in the 20th century. The form of militarization that emerged out of the Second World War has been augmented by powerful digital tools, aimed at society in general but impacting young people in particular (Anderson & Jiang, 2018). If we accept the definition of militarization promulgated by Geyer (1989) and others (Beier, 2011; Enloe, 2000), it is a highly nuanced process that does not need to openly display military forms such we would see in a military dictatorship – but instead helps to position society for the frictionless application of military violence and the acceptance of the need for military preparedness and action.

"Habitus"

The concept of habitus describes a complex process that extends into the domains of institutions such as the family and the school in order to reproduce and thus perpetuate the existing dominant social order. In the context of this book I am using the concept of habitus to help explain how militarization is both enhanced and extended through something as innocuous as playing a video game. The creation of a militarized form of habitus sits within the broader process of militarization as a pedagogy – a point I will return to shortly.

The entry of the concept of habitus as we now understand it into the English-speaking academic world was through the work of French sociologist Pierre Bourdieu in the late 1960s and 1970s. The term habitus has been used extensively in the critique of capitalism and how families and other institutions have helped to reproduce the existing system of class relations. Habitus operates at an almost subterranean level in the development of human consciousness – it helps us to understand how our mental framework is constructed. How we internalize the rules which govern how we experience and interact with the world and how to understand what acceptable patterns of behavior are. What will be rewarded and what will be sanctioned. Habitus constructs our consciousness and helps to ensure that capitalism can function in a manner which is as frictionless as possible.

Habitus, according to Pierre Bourdieu (1977), creates,

> systems of durable, transposable *dispositions*, structured structures predisposed to function as structuring structures' that is, as principles of the generation . . . and structuring of practices and representations

which can be objectively "regulated" and "regular" without any way being the product of obedience to rules, objectively adapted to their goals without presupposing a conscious aiming at ends or an express mastery of the operations necessary to attain them.

(Bourdieu, 1977)

These internal structures help construct a mental architecture which can be relied upon at a system level to more or less ensure that the society functions in knowable and predictable ways. Habitus both reinforces the social and cultural capital upon which capitalism depends and thus helps to create what Bourdieu refers to as "individual and collective practices" that in turn help to create what we can refer to as our lived experience (Bourdieu, 1977). According to Pierre Bourdieu, habitus constructs "history" which in turn happens

in accordance with the schemata engendered by history. It ensures the active presence of past experiences which, deposited in each organism in the form of schemata of thought and action, tend, more surely than all formal rules and all explicit norms, to guarantee the conformity of practices and their constancy across time.

(Bourdieu, 1990)

The schemata of thought to which Bourdieu refers is imbedded in the mental architecture of subjects in a range of settings and in a range of ways. The concept of habitus has been deployed to help comprehend how individuals' function within a range of settings or fields. His work has been highly significant in the development of an understanding of how capitalism reproduces itself through institutions such as the family and schooling. However, this concept is not restricted to these sites, habitus can be extended to help understand a diverse array of activities, settings and cultural formations.

Loïc Wacquant, a student of Bourdieu, has helped to extend his ideas by examining how habitus is developed in settings outside of the family or the school. Wacquant studied the habitus and the lived experience embodied in a Chicago boxing gym. In his analysis of the gym, Wacquant was able to identify at a molecular level how habitus is constructed. In his book Wacquant asserts that

the notion of habitus proposes that human agents are historical animals who carry within their bodies acquired sensibilities and categories that are the sedimented products of their past social experiences.

(Wacquant, 2011)

This idea that habitus is a process of "sedimentation" is crucial to understanding how it works at the level of the individual, but also at the level of the capitalist system and the society it has created. Habitus is layered, it builds up over a lifetime and is constantly renewed and added to, layer upon layer. In conducting his research Wacquant identified a specific form of habitus: the "pugilistic habitus" (Wacquant, 2004).

Sports and sports training have been the focus of significant work conducted on how forms of habitus are constituted and inscribed on both the mental schema and the body of individuals (Noble & Watkins, 2003). Wacquant's study highlights the manner with which habitus helps us to understand how a specific set of skills, disposition and culture become embodied. According to Wacquant (Wacquant, 2004), this process is dependent on a complex interplay of physical and socio-cultural processes which enable the development of the boxer. Wacquant observed that this process involves observing other fighters in the ring and in the cultural milieu that the boxing club had created. Wacquant (Wacquant, 2004) argues that in acquiring the skills of the boxer

> [t]raining teaches the movements – that is the most obvious part – but it also inculcates in a practical manner the schemata that allows one to better differentiate, distinguish, evaluate, and eventually reproduce these movements. It sets into motion a *dialectic of corporeal mastery and visual mastery*: to understand what you have to do, you watch the others box, but you do not truly see what they are doing unless you have already understood a little with your eyes, that is to say, with your body. Every new gesture thus apprehended - comprehended becomes in turn the support, the materials, the tool that makes possible the discovery and thence the assimilation of the next.
> (Wacquant, 2004)

Thus the boxer, in learning how to fight, engages in a process that builds on the tension between actual ring time, which encompasses the physical components of becoming a boxer – corporeal mastery and observation – the visual mastery of the fighter and the fight. The acquisition of the identity of the boxer is attained by becoming inured to the culture of the ring, to the pedagogy of boxing – a pugilistic pedagogy. This is attained over a period of time through box direct instruction through the development of conative and cognitive structures (Wacquant, 2011). These structures are constituent of habitus and

> are malleable and transmissible because they result from pedagogical work. If you want to pry into habitus, then study the organized practices of inculcation through which it is layered.
> (Wacquant, 2011)

The boxing club that Wacquant (2004, 2011) observed was a pedagogic space within which pedagogic work occurred and a process of inculcation took hold. Wacquant (2004, 2011) wrote about a closed world in which the code of the gym – language, physicality, sociability across color and ethnic lines – and the promotion of manly values and a particular way of conducting oneself emerges through vigorous training and the inculcation of the habitus of the boxer through what he describes as a habitus constructed by and through a pugilistic pedagogy (Wacquant, 2004).

At this point I want to consider how habitus and the notion of pedagogy help us to better understand how militarization has re-written modern society at a granular level. It is my assertion that a militarized form of habitus is embedded in the everyday life of the inhabitants of neo-liberal capitalist society.

Pedagogies

In working through our analysis of these processes we need to further elaborate on the underpinning concepts which help to construct our militarized form of society: here I am referring specifically to the idea of pedagogy. Pedagogy is a complex process and has taken specific form within the educational domain. Here though, I am thinking of pedagogy in a broader and more expansive sense than how the educationalists usually deploy the term. Pedagogy can take more than one shape. For the purpose of this analysis it is important to make

> a distinction between two senses of pedagogy: the familiar and the specialized sense of pedagogy as a philosophy (or ideology) of teaching, including classroom practices and instructional methods; and the broad sense of pedagogy as education in general, or what the Greeks called paideia.
>
> (Worsham, 1992)

Forms of pedagogy exist at both the concrete and symbolic levels. Schooling is the most visible locus of pedagogy in advanced society, but it is not the only one. The everyday is drenched with pedagogic practices, messages and constructs. Everyday pedagogies reinforce the initial forms of habitus that have been constructed within the key socialization structures: the family and the school.

Other institutions reinforce the work of schools and schooling and help to transmit the values, morals, culture, social and political relations that form various types of habitus as part of what Elias (2000) described as a "civilizing process". This occurs in every component of life, as Lutz (2018) argues,

> the capillaries of militarization have fed and molded social institutions seemingly little connected to battle. In other words, the process of

militarization has been not simply a matter of weaponry wielded and bodies buried. It has also created what is taken as knowledge, with just two examples being the fields of physics and psychology, both significantly shaped by military funding and goals.

(Lutz, 2018)

As argued elsewhere in this book, militarization has helped construct both the culture and economy of liberal-capitalist societies and has re-configured what we understand to be normal both at the individual and social level. For example, Cynthia Enloe's (2000) work on militarization and masculinity has highlighted the extent to which this process has re-configured crucial aspects of what it means to be human. Militarization has in effect redefined what we think of when considering notions such as masculinity by "marginalizing anyone but the male heterosexual – the only category of person seen as fit for the full citizenship conferred by combat" (Lutz, 2018).

In these contexts, as in others, there are both visible and invisible forms of pedagogy at work (Bernstein, 1975, 2004). The form of pedagogy that I will discuss in the next section of this chapter has been described by Beier (2011) as a set of "militarized pedagogies". Militarized pedagogies

> operate through aspects of everyday life in ways both visible and unseen . . . Together with other pedagogies of the everyday, they contribute to the development of logical competencies and conceptual literacies according to which militarism is naturalized.
>
> (Beier, 2011)

The embedding of militarization in our everyday lives is dependent upon a type of pedagogy which functions as a form of symbolic violence and helps to shape the culture and society of advanced capitalism (Bourdieu, 1977). The preparation for war through the dominance of militarization as a socio-economic, political and cultural force has become part of the everyday experience of life in neo-liberal society and thus constructs the foundations upon which the wars of *Empire* (Hardt & Negri, 2001) are conducted. Media in general and playable media such as the militarized variants of video games and videogaming technologies (First-Person Shooters, *Xbox* and *PlayStation* control pads), are examples of the extension of militarized forms of pedagogy into everyday life.

When I use the term pedagogy I am applying it in the sense that Worsham (1992), Bourdieu and Passeron (1990) and Giroux (1981, 1983, 2005) have developed. In their writing pedagogy is not simply something that happens in schools or other educational institutions. As Worsham has argued we can make

> a distinction between two senses of pedagogy: the familiar and the specialized sense of pedagogy as a philosophy (or ideology) of teaching,

including classroom practices and instructional methods; and the broad sense of pedagogy as education in general, or what the Greeks called *paideia*.

(Worsham, 1992)

It is the Greek notion of *paideia* that helps us to build a picture of how militarization has constructed forms of habitus that ensure the capacity to engage in war and violent conflict.

In this context the detailed examination of the relationship between pedagogy and militarization by the American sociologist Henry Giroux helps us to understand this process. Henry Giroux has written a number of studies focusing on the extent to which a form of "public pedagogy" saturated with forms of militarized culture and militarization has taken root in American society. According to Giroux, under contemporary capitalism public pedagogy instills "the values and the aesthetic of militarization through a variety of pedagogical sites and cultural venues" (Giroux, 2004b).

It is in these sites that the pedagogical work of advanced capitalism takes place and it is within these sites that the militarization of culture has taken hold. Whilst other forms of domination and exploitation such as gender, class and ethnicity are also manifested and reinforced by and through public pedagogy, both Bier (2011) and Giroux (2005) point to the emergence of "militarized pedagogy" as a dominant aspect of public pedagogy one which has facilitated the extension of militarization.

Militarized pedagogies include advertising, both to recruit new soldiers but also to link militarized consumer objects with virility and adventure. Giroux (2004b) talks about advertisements for the Humvee vehicle in particular, but there are many other examples. Butterworth and Moskal (2009) have pointed to the annual Bell Helicopter Armed Forces bowl football game as an example of the extension of militarization into the domain of everyday life. Butterworth and Moskal (2009) argue that

> [b]y expanding the familiar conflation of sport and war, the Armed Forces Bowl simultaneously trivializes the seriousness of war as it emphasizes the seriousness of supporting the American military. This rhetorical division offers a delimited conception of appropriate American identity, thereby normalizing war in general and endorsing the "war on terror" specifically.
>
> (Butterworth & Moskal, 2009)

Within the societal patterning that occurs through the various forms of pedagogy the human subject undergoes a structuring of their mental framework. Specifically, a form of habitus permeates the various facets of contemporary life through the family, institutions and relations of and to production. Habitus predispose people to accept their social position and the structure of contemporary society as normal. Habitus is fed by both seen and unseen forms of pedagogy. It is the kind of pedagogic work that institutions such as schools were created for, but its function is not restricted to such institutions. Pedagogic work takes place in the media, in the family, in the workplace and in the culture of video games, social media and the internet (Martino, 2012, 2015). Before extending our understanding of habitus in the context of militarization and the hardening of youth it is important to analyze the outcome of the process of habitus – the constructing through various pedagogies of a form of social disciple.

"Social Discipline" and Habitus

One of the key elements which has helped to ensure the maintenance and longevity of capitalist society both in its industrial and neo-liberal political form has been the continued application of the pre-industrial practices referred to as "social discipline" (Oestreich, Oestreich, & Koenigsberger, 1982; Regilme, 2012). Habitus constructs the mental frame through which social discipline is instilled and takes form.

Prisoners and slaves make ineffective workers and cannot be citizens. The constant resort to violence which marked life in pre-capitalist societies was unworkable. Violence would always be there as a last resort. However other mechanisms were required in order to maintain power and provide a psychological, political, social and cultural climate conducive to the process initially of capitalist accumulation and later the process of militarization. Universal and compulsory State-supported, or regulated, schooling came to be seen as one of a number of new and useful mechanisms to be utilized in the shift from physical to "symbolic violence" as the basis for the social order in Europe and the European settler societies of North America and Australia.

Social discipline was carried over from the pre-capitalist era, into the age of industrial capitalism; it provided the cement which bound all classes to the process of capitalist accumulation. Where the social reproduction theory asserts that the hierarchical division of labor inherent in the capitalist system of production determined the shape of mass schooling, I argued that industrial capitalism was the beneficiary of a cultural process begun well before the advent of this social formation – social discipline. Writing about the formation of the early modern State, Oestreich (Oestreich et al., 1982) summed up the reality of what the process of social discipline meant for the majority of the people living in the 19th century.

According to Oestreich, they were subjected for the first time in history to an "effective" form of government, which had as its aim the social disciplining of the masses. People living in Western Europe came to understand that

> [b]eing governed means being under police supervision, being inspected, spied upon, directed, buried under laws, regulated, hemmed

in, indoctrinated, preached at, controlled, assessed, censored, commanded, noted, registered, captured, appraised, stamped, surveyed, evaluated, taxed, patented, licensed, authorized, recommended, admonished, prevented, reformed, aligned, and punished in every action, every transaction, every movement.

(Oestreich et al., 1982)

In the historical evolution of the nation-state its agencies became the mechanisms through which on the one hand, notions such as the work ethic, "timed labor", sobriety, and a general acceptance of regimen of factory work (in sum, social discipline became firmly implanted in the consciousness of working people); and on the other hand, the modernization of the economy and capitalist accumulation, was accelerated through the creation of a territorially bounded national capitalist state.

The quest for social discipline was carried over from the pre-capitalist era, into the age of industrial capitalism; it provided the cement which bound all classes to the process of capitalist accumulation. Where the social reproduction theory (Bourdieu & Passeron, 1990) asserts that the hierarchical division of labor inherent in the capitalist system of production determined the shape of mass schooling, I have argued that industrial capitalism was the beneficiary of a cultural process begun well before the advent of this social formation.

Whilst in the period of industrialization social discipline helped establish both the vast armies of industrial workers attuned to the needs and demands of the mill and the factory, over time the processes and institutions created to accomplish this helped create other enduring social mechanisms. In the 20th century (and beyond) social discipline has enabled the production of both a dedicated and in many ways pliant labor force, it has also helped with the establishment of vast military structures and organizations, as well as the ability to engage in globe spanning military conflicts.

The process of militarization has drawn upon the complex socio-cultural lattice which was established through the embedding of social discipline in the fabric of capitalist societies. Where in the era of industrialization social discipline focused on basic literacy, time management and rigid adherence to authority structures and routinization through schooling, the 20th and 21st centuries demanded other skills and patterns of behavior. As described elsewhere in this book, during the 20th century and into the 21st, capitalist societies of the West evolved to accommodate the privileging of war, militaristic thought, and apocalyptic cultural messages, all delivered and enhanced through a range of digital technological affordances. By this I mean that the normalization of war and violence, as well as the construction of militarized approaches to the social and political world, have become the new core of the centuries-old process of social disciplining of the subject populations of the West.

Militarization utilizes social discipline in the 21st century in both overt and covert ways. Militarization depends on the maintenance of war-oriented military structures and practices such as reserve and standing armies but its function and effectiveness is contingent on more than this. It depends on the embedding of an acceptance of hierarchies, strict codes of discipline, punishment and the routinization of war and killing both virtually, as a form of play and entertainment and, in the real world as the cost of Empire and a normal and hidden element of contemporary society.

The work of Giroux (2012), Enloe (2000), Lutz (2002, 2018) and Geyer have illuminated a process that has reconfigured society in the post-Second World War period and has embedded itself within the fabric of contemporary society. In the next chapter I will examine a set of specific practices which have helped build upon this process – the colonization of play by and through military themed and oriented new forms of media. Before I do this, I will briefly set up a framework through which we can comprehend how this function.

Ludic Military Habitus

The term "ludic military habitus" refers to the process through which the playing of military themed video games (such as the First-Person Shooter genre) – but also more broadly the interplay between new media and digital technology (images, narratives and content) and significant elements in popular culture – shapes and sets in place a mental schema that contains a predisposition to the normalization of war and violence. Let me caution the reader here, I am not asserting that it is only First-Person Shooter video games that have helped to foster the acceptance of violence, guns and the normalization of conflict in the everyday lives of Americans (Jenkins, 2006; Mantello, 2017; Martino, 2015). The culture of cruelty I have written about elsewhere in this book, such as in streaming videos (YouTube) and episodic programming (*Netflix*) depicting realistic unrestrained acts of violence and the various horror genres in media, have contributed to the success of this socio/cultural project (Alford & Scheibler, 2018; Elwood, 2018; Evans, 2019; González, 2018; Joy, 2019).

There are many more processes both media based and socio-cultural that have worked in tangent to help create the dominant militarized political form. How in particular does gaming and specifically war-themed video games contribute to the maintenance and strengthening of militarization? This technology in particular creates a pedagogic space within which the player can observe, learn and rehearse military ideas, practices and predispositions. It does not create directly transferrable military skills, but it does help construct a mental schema that predisposes citizens to the existence of a large offense-oriented military structure and application of military solutions to geopolitical problems.

There was recognition by the military in the early years of the 21st century that play (or the *"ludic"*), using video and computer games technology, could strengthen the Military-Industrial Complex that they relied upon. Coupled with this was the need to enhance the process of recruitment, as well as the promotion of the US Army as a "brand". Gaming, media and the representation of the military in popular culture were seen as tools with which to engage with these issues. Gaming in particular was identified as a domain in which issues such as recruitment and the strengthening of military values and culture within popular culture and by extension the broader society could be addressed. In this context digital technology and a focus on the use of "play" could assist with finding solutions to these issues (Allen, 2017; Davis, 2004; DiRomualdo, 2007).

In the later part of the 20th century and more fully in the 21st the idea that new media technologies could be utilized to project a positive image of the military, as well as enhancing recruitment, became an important aspect of US military thinking (Delwiche, 2007; Macedonia, 2005). In this context using video games to train and also to recruit candidates into all ranks of the military was happening in tandem with an effort to mitigate the historic aversion shown by soldiers to killing the enemy (Chambers, 2003; Field, 2012; Spiller, 1988).

Killing inside a simulation, or a First-Person Shooter, whilst not the real thing, does loosen societal constraints and the taboo around killing. It also adds a competitive edge, at least in the case of First-Person Shooter games with league tables, kill/death ratios and head shot bonuses. This enculturation into the culture of war and the construction of war as entertainment is facilitated through a ludic military habitus embedded within these games and simulators. First-Person Shooter video games and the culture surrounding them – online forums, webpages, leader boards and the closed world of the gaming clan and the Twitch feed – generate an environment similar to that of the gym that Wacquant (2004, 2011) has described. Gaming creates a pedagogic space where killing and military themes are celebrated, rehearsed and fully embraced.

Video game technology, in particular the First-Person Shooter, creates a pedagogic space where pedagogic work takes place. In the military itself, by using virtual battlespace simulators, the young recruit and, in the outside world increasingly gamers, are immersed in simulated war experiences, and through this play they are inured into the culture of war and the culture of the soldier. Technology has progressed to the point where it offers these affordances – the capacity to think like a soldier, to solve a military problem and to engage in virtual combat in a safe and secure environment. These opportunities are not restricted to the domain of actual military training; the *Xbox* for example is a potent military simulator when loaded with the right kind of software.

In Chapter 6 of this book I examine the relationship between play and war themed digital artifacts such as video games and as well as video gaming technologies and their pedagogic use in greater detail.

Conclusion: The Ludic Military Habitus as the Pedagogy of Militarization

A theme that I have been working through in this book has been the extent to which State and non-State actors are able to draw young people into their war-fighting and political agendas. In Chapter 2 I analyzed the notion of the social war in order to understand the manner in which State and non-State actors have utilized new forms of media and digital technologies to extend their reach in order to narrow cast their message directly to individuals through the algorithmic technologies underpinning social media applications and the search engines that are used to navigate the internet. The social war refers to new media (internet, social media, video games, and streaming media) as technological affordances that enable State and non-State actors to engage in algorithmic-based perceptual warfare. These forms of technology and the media that they deliver have been integral in the expansion of the more than half-century long process of militarization – the social war has in effect augmented and amplified this trend. In this chapter I have barely scratched the surface of the complexity of the intertwining of these processes and their internal mechanisms.

The central argument of this chapter has been that militarization has been facilitated by and through its integration into a broader process of pedagogy – Giroux has described it as a form of "public pedagogy" (2004a), which is at the service of the neo-liberal capitalist political form. Through a range of social, cultural, political and economic structures and practices a specific militarized form of habitus has been constructed. It draws on the everyday embedding of military ideas, images and relations (economic and social) which underpin the process. New forms of media and digital technologies have amplified the effectiveness of militarization as a pedagogic process as well as providing the basis for the legitimization for the application of violence for political ends. Militarization has drawn on these technologies and practices to construct a particular militarized form of habitus.

Video games, streaming media, social media and the internet have in effect become pedagogic tools that have enhanced the effectiveness of this process. The process of militarization begun in the shadow of the fascist onslaught in the mid-20th century is now the dominant organizing principle with the neo-liberal societies.

References

Alford, A., & Scheibler, S. (2018). *Societal Shifts and the Horror Genre*. Los Angeles: Loyola Marymount University.

Allen, R. (2017). *America's digital army: Games at work and war*. Lincoln: University of Nebraska Press.

Anderson, M., & Jiang, J. (2018). Teens, social media and technology. *Pew Research Center, 31*, 2018.

Beier, J. M. (2011). *The militarization of childhood: Thinking beyond the global south*. New York, NY: Palgrave Macmillan.

Bernstein, B. (1975). Class and pedagogies: Visible and invisible. *Educational studies, 1*(1), 23–41.

Bernstein, B. (2004). Social class and pedagogic practice. *The RoutledgeFalmer Reader in Sociology of Education*, 196–217.

Betts, R. K. (2012). From cold war to hot peace: The habit of American force. *Political Science Quarterly, 127*(3), 353–368.

Boggs, C., & Pollard, L. T. (2007). *The Hollywood war machine: US militarism and popular culture*: Paradigm Pub.

Bourdieu, P. (1977). *Outline of a theory of practice (Esquisse d'une theorie de la pratique)*. Translated by Richard Nice. (Repr.) (Vol. 16). New York: Cambridge University Press.

Bourdieu, P. (1990). *The logic of practice*. Stanford University Press.

Bourdieu, P., & Passeron, J.-C. (1990). *Reproduction in education, society and culture* (Vol. 4). Sage.

Butterworth, M. L., & Moskal, S. D. (2009). American football, flags, and "fun": The Bell Helicopter Armed Forces Bowl and the rhetorical production of militarism. *Communication, Culture & Critique, 2*(4), 411–433.

Chambers, J. W. (2003). SLA Marshall's men against fire: New Evidence regarding fire ratios. *Parameters, 33*(3), 113–121.

Davis, M. (2004). *America's Army PC game vision and realization*. San Francisco: US Army and the Moves Institute.

Delwiche, A. (2007). From The Green Berets to America's Army: Video games as a vehicle for political propaganda. *The Player's Realm: Studies on the culture of video games and gaming*. Jefferson, NC: McFarland and Company, Inc, 91–109.

DiRomualdo, T. (2007). *US Army playing the recruiting game: How the U.S. Army has pioneered the use of game technology to recruit the Digital Generation*. Retrieved from Oxford: www.careerinnovation.com

Eisenhower, D. D. (1960). Military-industrial complex speech, 1961. *Public papers of the presidents, Dwight D. Eisenhower*.

Elias, N. (2000). *The civilizing process: Sociogenetic and psychogenetic investigations*: Oxford, UK & Malden, MA: Blackwell Publishers.

Elwood, R. L. (2018). Frame of Thrones: Portrayals of rape in HBO's *Game of Thrones*. *Ohio St. LJ Furthermore, 79*, 113.

Enloe, C. H. (2000). *Maneuvers: The international politics of militarizing women's lives*. University of California Press.

Evans, T. (2019). Some knights are dark and full of terror: The queer monstrous feminine, masculinity, and violence in the Martinverse. *Journal of Language, Literature and Culture, 66*(3), 134–156.

Field, A. (2012). Prosocial behavior: Lessons from the military. *Available at SSRN 2085076*.

Geyer, M. (1989). The militarization of Europe, 1914–1945. In J. R. Gillis (Ed.), *The militarization of the Western world* (pp. 65–102). New Brunswick: Rutgers University Press.

Giroux, H. A. (1981). *Ideology, culture and the process of schooling*. Philadelphia: Temple University Press.

Giroux, H. A. (1983). *Theory and resistance in education: A pedagogy for the opposition*. South Hadley, MA: Bergin & Garvey.

Giroux, H. A. (2004a). Public pedagogy and the politics of neo-liberalism: Making the political more pedagogical. *Policy Futures in Education, 2*(3–4), 494–503.

Giroux, H. A. (2004b). *The terror of neoliberalism*. Boulder Aurora, Ontario: Paradigm Garamond Press.

Giroux, H. A. (2005). *Border crossings: Cultural workers and the politics of education* (2nd ed.). New York: Routledge.

Giroux, H. A. (2012). The Post-9/11 militarization of higher education and the popular culture of depravity: Threats to the future of American democracy. *International Journal of Sociology of Education, 1*(1), 27–53.

González, A. E. (2018). *Horror Without End: Narratives of fear under modern capitalism*. Oberlin College,

Hardt, M., & Negri, A. (2001). *Empire*. Harvard University Press.

Horne, J. (2019). A world at war: 1911–1949 – Conclusion. In *A world at war, 1911–1949* (pp. 279–305). Brill.

Jenkins, H. (2006). The war between effects and meaning: Rethinking the video game violence debate. In D. Buckingham & R. Willett (Eds.), *Digital generations: Children, young people, and new media* (pp. 19–31). Lawrence Erlbaum Associates Publishers.

Joy, S. (2019). Sexual violence in serial form: Breaking Bad habits on TV. *Feminist Media Studies, 19*(1), 118–129.

Lutz, C. (2002). Making war at home in the United States: Militarization and the current crisis. *American Anthropologist, 104*(3), 723–735.

Lutz, C. (2018). Militarization. *The International Encyclopedia of Anthropology*, 1–4.

Macedonia, M. (2005). Ender's game redux [computer games]. *Computer, 38*(2), 95–97.

Mantello, P. (2017). Military shooter video games and the ontopolitics of derivative wars and arms culture. *American Journal of Economics and Sociology, 76*(2), 483–521. doi:10.1111/ajes.12184

Martino, J. (2012). Video games and the militarisation of society: Towards a theoretical and conceptual framework. In *ICT Critical Infrastructures and Society* (pp. 264–273). Springer.

Martino, J. (2015). *War/play: Video games and the militarization of society*. New York: Peter Lang.

Neumann, F. (2009). *Behemoth: The Structure and practice of National Socialism, 1933–1944*: Rowman & Littlefield.

Noble, G., & Watkins, M. (2003). So, how did Bourdieu learn to play tennis? Habitus, consciousness and habituation. *Cultural Studies, 17*(3–4), 520–539.

Oestreich, G., Oestreich, B., & Koenigsberger, H. G. (1982). *Neostoicism and the early modern state*. Cambridge, UK; New York: Cambridge University Press.

Regilme, S. S. F. (2012). Social discipline, democracy, and modernity: Are they all uniquely 'European'? *Hamburg Review of Social Sciecnes, 6*(3), 94–117.

Reid-Henry, S. (2019). *Empire of democracy: The remaking of the West since the Cold War, 1971–2017*. (First Simon & Schuster hardcover edition. ed., pp. 1 online resource).

Robin, R. T. (2009). *The making of the Cold War enemy: Culture and politics in the military-intellectual complex*. Princeton University Press.

Spiller, R. J. (1988). SLA Marshall and the ratio of fire. *The RUSI Journal, 133*(4), 63–71.

Torres, N., & Gurevich, A. (2018). Introduction: Militarization of consciousness. *Anthropology of Consciousness, 29*(2), 137–144. doi:10.1111/anoc.12101

Wacquant, L. (2004). *Body and soul*. New York: Oxford University Press.

Wacquant, L. (2011). Habitus as topic and tool: Reflections on becoming a prizefighter. *Qualitative Research in Psychology, 8*(1), 81–92.

Worsham, L. (1992). Emotion and pedagogic violence. *Discourse, 15*(2), 119–148.

Wright Mills, C. (1956). *The power elite*. New York: Oxford University Press.

Chapter 9

Militarization

The New "Civilizing Process"

Militarization and the "Civilizing Process"

The long process of pacification in Europe and its colonies that began centuries ago that Elias (2000) described as the "civilizing" process has been re-fashioned to instill a form of militarized consciousness (Orr, 2004). Militarization has embedded itself in almost every facet of the daily conduct of life in the West (Enloe, 2000, 2016). Militarization, as Geyer (1989) and others have argued, functions to position society in a manner in which the application of violence and the conduct of war is perpetual (Lutz, 2018; Orr, 2004). In this context new media provides the conduits through which political violence is legitimized, celebrated and promulgated. In this book I will examine and document the emergence of militarization as a form of public pedagogy. I will also expand on the proposition that the "civilizing process" at work in Western society as theorized by Norbert Elias (2000) has been supplanted by militarization. The implications for society of the emergence of two socio/political processes this century, on the one hand the lure of violent extremism and on the other militarization, is profound.

The "Civilizing Process": Life in "Late Barbarian Society"

The major work of Elias rests on the notion that society has evolved away from the unbridled use of violence between and within states and as an undercurrent within society – at least in the West. Elias wrote about the transformation of feudal society into the network of nation-states that constitute modern Europe. He was particularly interested in the shift in attitudes in relation to sex, nudity, hygiene and violence. Elias was also interested in the emergence of a more specialized division of labor, the expansion of urbanization, the creation of monetary systems and the emergence of markets. He was also concerned with the manner in which the nature of personalities changed as people became more closely connected to each other (Turner, 2004).

An understanding of the concept of the "civilizing process" helps us to comprehend the way social practices are internalized through socialization (habitus) and how in the history of Western society this trend has been appropriated and harnessed in the process of state-formation. Central to Elias's thesis is the repudiation of the concept as advocated by his critics that human characteristics such as "morality" as well as the propensity to live harmoniously with others is "natural" or "innate" (Dunning & Mennell, 1998). Elias believed that a gradual process of socialization at the individual level through the auspices of the family and schools has over time produced a distinct "habitus" – (a term that was well worn before its popularization in English by Bourdieu) which has formed the kernel upon which modern Western society has evolved.

The shift in the "habitus" of the population of Europe occurred as part of a

> long-term process in parallel with the monopolization of violence by the State. This, in turn, is held to have occurred interdependently with the monopolization of taxation. Expressed simply, Elias contends that monopolies of violence and taxation are the major means of ruling and that, in their development in Western Europe since the Middle Ages, they have been mutually reinforcing.
> (Dunning & Mennell, 1998)

The monopoly on the use of violence as well as the ability to tax were fundamental to the process of state-formation. The internalization of "self-constraint" was essential to the emergence and growing prosperity of the European political form as it negated the need to inflict regular doses of violence on the subject population. The use of violence by the State in response to uprisings and attempted revolutions gradually diminished as a consequence of this change. Self-restraint and a willingness to work with and for other individuals and with representatives of the State was an outcome of this long process. The emergent habitus to which Elias refers had at its core the "pacification" (Braun, 2019) of the subject population of Western Europe. Its long-term effect was to transform the various societies of Europe into relatively peaceful and massively productive territorially bounded power containers.

At this point it is necessary to make a brief aside – it is clear from the historical record that the European nation-states that explored the "New World" and elsewhere transported their propensity to inflict violence with them. So, whilst the European nations were busy creating the conditions where a form of pacified habitus became the dominant element in European socialization, elsewhere this was not the case. Whether it was in Ireland, or the American colonies, Australia or in India, the State felt no constraints on its application of violence, nor did the colonists or administrators. It could be argued that without colonialism the European story might look somewhat different to Europeans.

As Braun (2019) has argued, "Elias's research interest [was] in social processes and the process-related development of typical Western civilized 'modes of behavior'" (Braun, 2019). In particular Elias pointed to the emergence of a specifically Western mode of habitus which had at its center the application of both individual and societal "self-constraint" (Elias, 2000). At this point it is necessary to state that Elias wrote about Western society and was not attempting to present an argument which could be applied universally. I wish to follow this line of argument and state that this discussion is about Western society – a concept that I think still applies.

Elias argues that over the centuries that followed, the emergence of feudal society and then its collapse, there evolved a gradual movement away from the unrestrained application of violence to solve personal grievances or intra-familiar or clan conflict, as a consequence of the centralization of the legitimate use of violence by the State. The subsumption of baser passions through codes of behavior – "chivalry" for example, and later through sport, the process of civilizing society gained traction. The practice of restraint was internalized – it became unquestioned and unquestionable. This did not occur overnight. In the centuries that followed, European society normalized the acceptance of this habitus – what once needed to be justified and explained in time became internalized.

Over the same period socialization spread from the family into the emergent institutions such as schools and public or civil services – the army, the police and the various State bureaucracies that were established in European societies. These bureaucracies were the product of the nation-state political form that emerged out of the collapse of ideology of the divine rule of kings. The destruction of the *Ancien Régime* as a consequence of the French Revolution enabled the formation of institutions and processes which had at their core the reproduction of a pacified civil population. The State, its agents and the population which they governed were imbued with this mode of thought.

The pacification of society was not a simple or straightforward process – it also required mechanisms through which people could dissipate aggressive instincts inherent in humans. There was a need to permit people to experience violence by witnessing it, or mimicking it, rather than actually physically engaging in it at an individual level. Organizations, institutions and rituals established to enable the experiencing of "mimetic" acts of violence – in this context the creation of codified and regulated forms sport – particularly in the 19th century, did just that (Braun, 2019; Elias, 2000). Violence was constrained, codified and presented for mass consumption. But it would never again be sanctioned as an act that an individual could engage in without severe consequences. Violence was now the preserve of what Lenin called "special bodies of armed men". The protean states of Europe in the centuries following the French Revolution constructed mechanisms that ensured that their citizens had internalized the view that only the State could engage in acts of direct violence. By the end of the 19th century, the European populations and their settler society colonies had been, on the whole, pacified. As the 20th century petered out, Western society had to come to terms with a new scenario – the need to be prepared for violence and war, but in a manner which did not upturn the many centuries of pacification that Elias has spoken about (Elias, 2000).

The wars of the early- to mid-20th century were devastating in human terms and profoundly shook the foundations of Western society and, in the case of the First World War, created revolutionary conditions across Europe culminating in the Russian Revolution of 1917. Intra-state conflict was a reality despite the effectiveness of the civilizing process and the pacification of the European subject population. War between the nation-states of the West became an unimaginable proposition following the end of the Second World War. Instead this prospect was replaced by the potential of war between rival ideological and economic blocs and alliances. Intra-state conflict in Europe was replaced with the prospect of global "thermonuclear" war. This period was known as the Cold War era and was marked by the "low intensity conflicts" or "brush-fire" wars of Korea, Vietnam and the various Third-World flashpoints. One way of interpreting these conflicts is that they were arenas in which the rivalry between the competing ideological blocs could take place without the direct military confrontation that would lead to a nuclear conflagration – they acted as a safety valve.

With the end of the Cold War the supposed "peace dividend" did not appear. The collapse of the Soviet Union was followed by a resurgence in tribalism, religious extremism and ethnocentrism, leading to outbreaks of terrorism and genocide (Betts, 2012). It became apparent that the perpetual state of war that the West found itself embroiled in required a reliable pool of human materiel (Betts, 2012; Danner, 2005; Gregory, 2011; Horne, 2019; Leitenberg, 2006).

From a military perspective the mass mobilizations of the early and mid-century conflicts were no longer necessary and in fact proved, as the century wore on, difficult to sustain. As I have argued previously in this book, in the late 20th century the draft ceased to be effective and led to mass civil disorder. The war in Vietnam and the draft created huge political and social problems for the United States and its Western allies such as Australia (Abney, 2019; Fielding, 2012). The ongoing process of pacification in Western society had perhaps worked too well. In America and Australia young men resisted being forced to go to war in Vietnam and as a consequence the conscript army of the First and Second World Wars became an all-volunteer force. This trend was soon adopted by the various nations of the West (Choulis, Bakaki, & Böhmelt, 2019; Poutvaara & Wagener, 2007).

At the same time technological advances meant that fewer soldiers were needed to engage in armed conflict. The development of advanced digitally controlled technology such as armed drone aircraft now meant that killing could occur at a distance (Martino, 2015). It also became apparent that when the United States engaged in conventional warfare – as seen in Gulf War I – its opponents were easily and quickly defeated. This was the consequence of both the size and capability of the United States armed forces, as well the relative weakness and incompetence of its opponent. Gulf War II on the other hand, and the subsequent state of perpetual war, was an altogether different prospect. Modern asymmetrical warfare has meant that war in Afghanistan, Iraq and Syria requires a constant stream of fresh recruits. The commitment to these conflicts has been open-ended and they all share a common characteristic: the US and its allies have had no clear military objective or exit strategy. Unlike the invasion of Kuwait in Gulf War I, where the removal of Iraq's army of occupation was a clear goal and a measurable outcome, the current state of perpetual war seems aimless. Civil wars rarely have a decisive end and in fact continue to produce animosity and conflict for decades.

After the turn of the century the need to engage in sustained conflict in the post-9/11 period demanded a steady stream of potential military recruits. As I pointed out earlier, this need led many in the military establishment to look for opportunities short of conscription to meet their needs. The process of militarization which had been operating at a societal level was given a cultural boost through the addition of entertainment to the mechanisms being harnessed to achieve its goals. What had been driven by the engine of the military-industrial complex was now augmented by entertainment – a shift that has been given the descriptive term "the military-industrial-entertainment complex" (Beauchamp, 2018; Eisenhower, 1960; Gagnon, 2010; Lenoir & Lowood, 2005; Leonard, 2004; Spigel, 2004). The American journalist Nick Turse (2008) has coined the shortened term "the Complex" to refer to this set of arrangements and affordances.

I wish to re-state the underlying argument of this book – that the process of militarization which had been at work for much of the 20th century was not simply augmented by the growth in entertainment as a cultural and economic force – the expansion of entertainment through new digital technologies positioned it as the dominant characteristic of Western society (Enloe, 2016; Lutz, 2018; Orr, 2004). Militarization has become the mechanism which constructs both individual habitus as well as manufacturing the societal disposition conducive to the prosecution of armed conflict – it positions the whole of society for the application of violence and the conduct of the current perpetual war. It has replaced the "civilizing process" – the pacification of subject populations and the instilling of a particular habitus that integrated a series of rules and schema that constrained the use of violence and made the adherence to acting in a particular way as normal – as the only way to live within Western societies.

In the 21st century the nature of habitus has been modified in Western societies. It now has at its core on the one hand the maintenance of the sublimation and containment of violence – here I recognize that at the micro-level violence between individuals still occurs, but it is at least in the West rigorously constrained and sanctioned through legal structures. On the other hand, the needs of the perpetual war that the United States and its allies find themselves in requires the modification of the habitus in order to inculcate military ideas and thinking within the subject population. Throughout this book I have argued that this process is enacted through the affordances presented by digital technology. New media, video games, the internet and other technologies help to disseminate and construct the militarized form of habitus. In the following sections of this chapter I will draw together how militarization has morphed out of the civilizing process and helped to reconstitute the foundations of Western society. Contemporary nation-states are functioning within the context of global garrison at the service of the first truly global Empire (Bernazzoli & Flint, 2010; Lasswell & Stanley, 2018).

Militarization and the Lifeworld

Looking even more closely at the process of militarization it is important to consider what this means for the future of American society and more broadly for the liberal democracies of the West. The current decade is marked not merely by the continuation of existing conflicts, despite the rhetoric of the Trump Presidency – the reality of the global reach of the militarized United States and its allies has not diminished. His authoritarian approach fits snugly with the existing structural alignment of American society, culture and economy to the extension and maintenance of militarization. Perhaps what is most significant in the second decade of the 21st century is the manner in which America under Trump came to apply a "market" mechanism to the continuation of the military-industrial-entertainment complex. Trump has openly spoken of the US military as a kind of mercenary force – guns and drones for hire (Mandelbaum, 2017). There was and is no discussion of a reduction in the size or capacity of the military as Figure 9.1 clearly demonstrates. The size reach and capacity of the American military dwarfs its rivals and allies combined. In order to maintain the vast global apparatus for war-making, the entire culture of the United States has been reconfigured and reoriented.

Militarization is the leitmotif of contemporary American and Western society and culture. As I pointed out earlier, it operates at a level which in contemporary society is almost imperceptible. It is both a cultural as well as a social and political force. As Enloe has argued, militarization inhabits the everyday life of ordinary citizens and is present in elements as innocuous

The share of world military expenditure of the 15 states with the highest spending in 2018

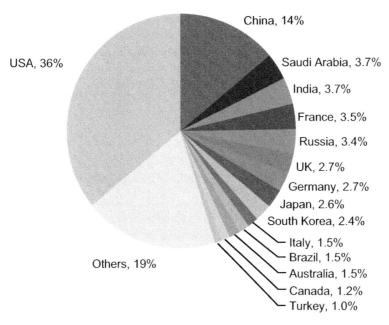

Figure 9.1 World Military Expenditure

Source: SIPRI Military Expenditure Database (29 Apr. 2019)

as a can of Campbell's Soup. In fact, in her ground-breaking account of the process Enloe wrote about the production of a *Star Wars* themed can of soup. According to Enloe,

> [i]n the Star Wars soup scenario a lot of people have become militarized – corporate marketers, dieticians, mothers, and children. They may not run out to enlist in the army as soon as they have finished their lunch, but militarization is progressing nonetheless. Militarization is never simply about joining a military. It is a far more subtle process. And it sprawls over far more of the gendered social landscape.
>
> (Enloe, 2000)

Even though Enloe was writing two decades ago, the process has not diminished, nor has it become an historical anachronism. The process of militarization shapes the way people think and perceive the world. It has, in retrospect, achieved this through a variety of mechanisms – through institutions such as schools; through mechanisms of policing and surveillance; through fashion and media (films, print and TV). More recently it has extended its influence through new forms of media such as video games, social media and the internet. The social, cultural, economic and political consequences of this assemblage of technology and processes has been the projection of military thinking and the ideology of militarization. As Enloe and others (Enloe, 2000; Giroux, 2012; Kim, 2009; Torres & Gurevich, 2018) have pointed out, the process of militarization could not succeed in its penetration of the lifeworld without a complex lattice of factors working together to create the tools with which to configure peoples' consciousness or mental framework.

As Mariscal has argued,

> [i]n liberal democracies in particular, the values of . . . (militarization) . . . do not reside in a single group but are diffused across a wide variety of cultural locations. In twenty first-century America, no one is exempt from militaristic values because the processes of militarization allow those values to permeate the fabric of everyday life.
>
> (Mariscal, 2003)

The successful penetration of everyday life (the lifeworld) by militarization has meant that the, "the contradictory and tense social process" to which Geyer (1989) referred has become far less contradictory or tense. In the 21st century the process has enabled the creation of what I and others have described as a state of "permanent war" (Bacevich, 2010; Martino, 2015). When Geyer (1989) was writing, militarization was at work but it was yet to fully engage American and Western society in the process of the reconstruction of society in a manner where the application of violence was a non-issue in the broader political context. The process that emerged out of the "Total War" (Baumann & Hellmann, 2001) configuration of the mid-20th century did not fully extend its reach nor its potential for the creation of militarized mental framework until the past three decades. As I have pointed to earlier, technology – digital technology in particular – has amplified and enabled the creation of a particular form of consciousness. Imperceptible to most of us but nevertheless effective in creating the conditions necessary for a permanent war state (Martino, 2015).

Militarization has been able to invade the social and cultural context of American and Western society through a process of boundary weakening "between military and civilian institutions, activities and aims" (Orr, 2004). The position of the military within American society and in most Western societies is firmly entrenched and positively looked upon. American culture – which is the dominant cultural force in the West – has spent decades renovating and rehabilitating the reputation of the military in the post-Vietnam era. The American military as portrayed in literature, films, television, comics and the press and other news media for many decades has been essential to this process of boundary weakening.

It is my assertion that militarization has been successful in positioning Western society in general but the United States in particular for the ready application of violence to solve political and diplomatic issues. This has created a new variant of the "civilizing process" that Elias so eloquently described last century. The pacification process at the core of the civilizing process is now able in Western society to function with little need for State intervention. People have internalized the norms of peaceable co-existence and an acceptance – except in the minds of extremists – of the undisputed monopoly of the application of force and violence by the State.

Civilizing and Militarizing

The civilizing process that Elias argued for constrains the destructive elements of human relations, such as our propensity to engage in conflict (Elias, 2000; Pinker, 2011). It softens human interactions and creates boundaries within which humans can work cohesively in complex social contexts and within which the State and economy can rely on its citizens and workers. The emergent territorially bounded power container, the nation-state, could now rely on relatively stable social and political contexts – the Industrial Revolution could not have occurred without the pacification of the European and American subject populations. The course of pacification that lay at the core of the civilizing process has been subsumed by the multifaceted and highly complex process of militarization. Militarization is an ongoing process. Rather than completely displacing the civilizing process, it is my view that the civilization process has "morphed" into a new political form which has created the culture and consciousness which binds the modern – territorially bounded power container – the "neo-liberal nation-state".

Within this political form – the territorially-bounded power container – militarization has enabled violence and war to be normalized, though unlike in other historical periods in contemporary society, violence and war have been placed at a distance and/or simulated. Here I am not talking about the micro-level of interpersonal and/or gendered violence which is still highly problematic. Militarization has been able to construct a culture and a particular form of consciousness through its penetration into the everyday – and through in particular the power and reach of media, old and new (Beier, 2011; Lutz, 2018; Orr, 2004). It is not necessary to create mass armies to have "boots on the ground" to facilitate war – war and violence are now simulated, live streamed, pay-per-view and on-demand.

One of the core ideas in Elias's thinking was the relationship between pacification and sport. The creation of codified forms of combat which gradually prohibited actually killing one's opponents was essential for the success of the pacification project. Violence needed to be constrained in order to harden the boundaries between who could legitimately engage in violence – the State – and those who would be violently sanctioned if they acted violently – the subject population. Widespread engagement in team and individual sports helped cement the development of a pacificated subject population. Violence could be channeled into non-destructive competition and participants could engage in a mimetic form of combat (Braun, 2019; Dunning, 1994; Van Gestel, 2018). The boxer inflicts violence without needing to kill their opponent – winning the match on points is celebrated as a victory, a "KO" is a simulated kill.

In contemporary society there are multiple examples of this form of sanitized individual and team sporting conflict. New media and digital technology have added another level to this sanitization of violence by allowing individuals and teams to simulate actual combat and warfare. Where the creation of codes of conduct and sporting rules and regulations has acted as a brake on actual violence, a simulation does not need such constraint. Embedded in militarization is the opportunity to experience a mimetic form of combat through the affordances offered by new forms of technology – video games and the First-Person Shooter. Players are now able – with increasing levels of realism – to engage in acts of simulated violence.

It is now possible to experience war at a visceral level as part of a highly sophisticated simulation such as the First-Person Shooter, where terms such as "headshot", or enjoying a "killgasm" are part of the everyday gameplay being consumed (Bittanti, 2006).

As Bittanti eloquently stated,

> [v]ideo games – and first-person shooters in particular – are the quintessential thrill machine. The first-person shooter is a direct evolution of New Hollywood cinema as it offers spectacularly realistic simulations – not mere depictions – of gunplay. These games literally transform the viewers into techno-visual weapons, allowing them to orchestrate – rather than simply witness – an imaginary carnage in a geometrically constructed space.
>
> (Bittanti, 2006)

This is one of the core elements of militarization – through the use of techno-tools such as the First-Person Shooter, the player is in effect transported directly into a thrilling simulation – not a simple representation, but a place where they can act out their carnal thoughts through digital action. In many cases there is no need for constraint, or the player is given the option of playing the game in a somewhat restrained manner or committing slaughter. In the game *Call of Duty: Modern Warfare 2* (*CoD*), players are engaged in a counter terror operation and at one point in Moscow Airport the player is given the choice to follow orders and massacre the civilians or continue on another path in the gameplay (ACTIVISION, 2009; Allen & Stroken, 2012; Campbell, 2013; Grizzard et al., 2015). This is a moral dilemma faced by the player but it also signifies the underlying brutality and celebration of violence present in the game. But it is more than simply choosing between one set of moving images and another. It is simulated carnage.

When one is playing the game, the distinction between the real world and the immersive combat zone diminishes or in effect dissolves (Gooskens, 2011).

> In Call of Duty 2 . . . situated in World War II, the player incarnates the character of Corporal Taylor. While playing, I become Corporal Taylor in a way; I respond to artificial teammates shouting "Taylor, get your ass over here" by coming their way. Whereas the actual I sits in front of the screen using the controller, the image-world-I (Corporal Taylor) is in France around 1944, firing at German soldiers. The actual I and the image-world-I are separated by an abyss.
>
> (Gooskens, 2011)

You, the player, are "in the zone" – you have been militarized, you inhabit the battle space, you are part of a digital army engaged in a digital war. As Bittani (2006) asserted you are in a "thrill machine". In Elias's terms we could describe this as the "quest for excitement" (Elias & Dunning, 2008). Where sport once presented the opportunity to experience violence in a mimetic way, now video games such as *Call of Duty*, streaming video such as presented through *Netflix* and the hand-to-hand combat of blood sports such as in Mixed Martial Arts create the ultimate thrill.

When earlier in this book I wrote about new media and other digital tools facilitating the process of militarization it is this type of activity that I was referring to. Let me state the obvious, when one is playing a video game such as a First-Person Shooter, you are not in a real war zone, nor are you an actual soldier. For many people the thought that playing a game where you are encouraged to kill or in the case of the *Call of Duty: Modern Warfare 2* game, to choose how immoral your actions could be is, simply put, a game. But the notion that players enjoy the killing or learn to think and act in military terms in order to progress or to win the game is part of the process of being militarized. It is not necessary that you gain actual military skills – that can come later. What happens is – just as Wacquant (Wacquant, 2004, 2011) argues that the boxer learns to be a boxer by watching people train and spar – the military habitus at the core of militarization enables the embodiment of military thinking and dispositions.

This application of new forms of digital technology and media to the process of militarization has enhanced the "toughening up" to which I referred earlier in this book. The combination of video game play, streaming video, live blood sports, such as Mixed Martial Arts and the UFC tournament, act to instil a more aggressive mode of thinking. This does not need to be as open or blatant as the propaganda films of the Second World War, such as *Why We Fight* by Frank Capra, which set out the case for why America was at war with the fascist Axis states of Nazi Germany, Fascist Italy and militarist Japan. However, the new digital tools, as well as normalizing violence and military-themed forms of entertainment, do share a similar objective – the establishment of a militarized and pro-war mode of thinking and consciousness (Susca, 2012).

Conclusion

In this chapter I have sought to flesh out my argument that militarization has supplanted or perhaps subsumed what Elias had referred to as the civilizing process. The discussion here has not been exhaustive. To do justice to the argument I will need to take it up at another point. The chapter has been a brief argument based on a range of examples but perhaps for me the best example I can give to support the view that we have been militarized as a society is this: despite a short lived campaign opposing Gulf War II, we have been at war in the Middle-East since the last part of 2001. Nations such as Australia have joined with the United States and a range of others, as members of the "coalition of the willing", have expended blood and resources to achieve very little. In addition, there has been little cost to ruling elites by spending these decades in a fruitless and counter-productive endeavor. In fact, it could be argued that what has happened is that potential for the post-Cold War peace has transitioned into a state of perpetual war and the perception of an enduring threat both at home and abroad. In a sense we have created an "architecture of fear" where there is little questioning of military solutions to social and political problems.

Perhaps the decades ahead of us might be a time where this incredible waste of resources, lives and human potential is critiqued and ended. Perhaps the looming shadow of global environmental and health collapse might be the final straw that convinces populations that war and destruction have had their day – I am always hopeful.

References

Abney, W. (2019). *Random destiny: How the Vietnam War draft lottery shaped a generation.* Vernon Press.
ACTIVISION. (2009). *Call of Duty: Modern Warfare 2*. USA.
Allen, R., & Stroken, K. (2012). Games without tears, wars without frontiers. *War, Technology, Anthropology,* 83–93.
Bacevich, A. J. (2010). *Washington rules: America's path to permanent war.* Macmillan.

Baumann, R., & Hellmann, G. (2001). Germany and the use of military force: "Total war", the "Culture of restraint", and the quest for normality. *German Politics, 10*(1), 61–82.

Beauchamp, S. (2018). War Games: The cozy relationship between perpetual war and total entertainment. *The Baffler*(39), 6–11.

Beier, J. M. (2011). *The militarization of childhood: Thinking beyond the Global South*. New York: Palgrave Macmillan.

Bernazzoli, R. M., & Flint, C. (2010). Embodying the garrison state?: Everyday geographies of militarization in American society. *Political Geography, 29*(3), 157–166.

Betts, R. K. (2012). From cold war to hot peace: The habit of American force. *Political Science Quarterly, 127*(3), 353–368.

Bittanti, M. (2006). From GunPlay to GunPorn. A techno-visual history of the first-person shooter. URL: http://www.mattscape.com/images/GunPlayGunPorn.pdf Accessed September 12, 2006.

Braun, A. (2019). Interpersonal violence as an intrinsic part of the civilizing process: A neurosociological approach. *European Journal of Sociology, 60*(2), 283–312. doi:10.1017/S0003975619000122

Campbell, V. (2013). Playing with controversial images in videogames: The terrorist mission controversy in *Call of Duty: Modern Warfare 2*. In *Controversial images* (pp. 254–268). Springer.

Choulis, I., Bakaki, Z.., & Böhmelt, T. (2019). Public support for the armed forces: The role of conscription. *Defence and Peace Economics*, 1–12.

Danner, M. (2005). Taking stock of the forever war. *The New York Times Magazine, 11*, 44–53.

Dunning, E. (1994). Sport in space and time: "civilizing processes", trajectories of state-formation and the development of modern sport. *International Review for the Sociology of Sport, 29*(4), 331–345.

Dunning, E., & Mennell, S. (1998). Elias on Germany, Nazism and the Holocaust: On the balance between 'civilizing' and 'decivilizing' trends in the social development of Western Europe. *The British Journal of Sociology, 49*(3), 339–357. doi:10.2307/591387

Eisenhower, D. D. (1960). Military-industrial complex speech, 1961. *Public papers of the presidents, Dwight D. Eisenhower*.

Elias, N. (2000). *The civilizing process: Sociogenetic and psychogenetic investigations*. Oxford, UK & Malden, MA: Blackwell Publishers.

Elias, N., & Dunning, E. (2008). *Quest for excitement: Sport and leisure in the civilising process*. University College Dublin Press.

Enloe, C. (2000). *Maneuvers: The international politics of militarizing women's lives*. University of California Press.

Enloe, C. (2016). *Globalization and militarism: Feminists make the link*. Rowman & Littlefield.

Fielding, L. (2012). How did media coverage affect the American involvement in and attitudes towards the Vietnam War? Munich: GRIN Verlag.

Gagnon, F. (2010). "Invading your hearts and minds": Call of Duty® and the (re) writing of militarism in US digital games and popular culture. *European Journal of American Studies* (2).

Geyer, M. (1989). The militarization of Europe, 1914–1945. In J. R. Gillis (Ed.), *The militarization of the Western world* (pp. 65–102). New Brunswick: Rutgers University Press.

Giroux, H. (2012). The post-9/11 militarization of higher education and the popular culture of depravity: Threats to the future of American democracy. *International Journal of Sociology of Education, 1*(1), 27–53.

Gooskens, G. (2011). Beyond good and evil? Morality in video games. *Philosophical Writings, 1*, 37–44.

Gregory, D. (2011). The everywhere war. *The Geographical Journal, 177*(3), 238–250.

Grizzard, M., Tamborini, R., Sherry, J. L., Weber, R., Prabhu, S., Hahn, L., & Idzik, P. (2015). The thrill is gone, but you might not know: Habituation and generalization of biophysiological and self-reported arousal responses to video games. *Communication Monographs, 82*(1), 64–87.

Horne, J. (2019). A world at war: 1911–1949: Conclusion. In *A world at war, 1911–1949* (pp. 279–305). Brill.

Kim, C. (2009). Army displays draw crowds at Armed Forces Day event. Retrieved from http://www.army.mil/article/21252/Army_displays_draw_crowds_at_Armed_Forces_Day_event/

Lasswell, H., & Stanley, J. (2018). The garrison state hypothesis today. In *Essays on the Garrison State* (pp. 77–116). Routledge.

Leitenberg, M. (2006). *Deaths in wars and conflicts between 1945 and 2000*. Ithaca, New York.

Lenoir, T., & Lowood, H. (2005). Theaters of war: The military-entertainment complex. *Collection, laboratory, theater: Scenes of knowledge in the 17th century, 427*–456.

Leonard, D. (2004). Unsettling the military entertainment complex: Video games and a pedagogy of peace. *SIMILE: Studies In Media & Information Literacy Education, 4*(4), 1–8.

Lutz, C. (2018). Militarization. In H. Callan (Ed.), *The International Encyclopedia of Anthropology* (pp. 1–4). Wiley-Blackwell.

Mandelbaum, M. (2017). Pay up, Europe: What Trump gets right about NATO. *Foreign Affairs, 96*, 108.

Mariscal, J. (2003). "Lethal and compassionate": The militarization of US culture. *CounterPunch* (May 5, 2003) http://www.counterpunch.org/mariscal05052003.html

Martino, J. (2015). *War/play: video games and the militarization of society*. New York: Peter Lang.

Orr, J. (2004). The militarization of inner space. *Critical Sociology, 30*(2), 451.

Pinker, S. (2011). *The better angels of our nature: why violence has declined*. New York: Viking.

Poutvaara, P., & Wagener, A. (2007). To draft or not to draft? Inefficiency, generational incidence, and political economy of military conscription. *European Journal of Political Economy, 23*(4), 975–987.

Spigel, L. (2004). Entertainment wars: Television culture after 9/11. *American Quarterly, 56*(2), 235–270.

Susca, M. A. (2012). Why we still fight: Adolescents, America's Army, and the government-gaming nexus. *Global Media Journal, 12*(20).

Torres, N., & Gurevich, A. (2018). Introduction: Militarization of consciousness. *Anthropology of Consciousness, 29*(2), 137–144. doi:10.1111/anoc.12101

Turner, B. S. (2004). 14 Weber and Elias on religion and violence: Warrior charisma and the civilizing process. *The Sociology of Norbert Elias*, 245.

Turse, N. (2008). *The complex: How the military invades our everyday lives* (1st ed.). New York: Metropolitan Books.

Van Gestel, J. (2018). *Norbert Elias, social history and sport*. Routledge.

Wacquant, L. (2004). *Body and soul*. New York: Oxford University Press.

Wacquant, L. (2011). Habitus as topic and tool: Reflections on becoming a prizefighter. *Qualitative Research in Psychology, 8*(1), 81–92.

Chapter 10

Conclusion

The *Drumbeat* – Perpetual Social War

The *Drumbeat*

There is a drumbeat wringing out across the Western world – it has been doing so for more than six decades. Its origin is to be found in a huge military-industrial complex which came into existence at the height of the Second World War and has embedded itself within the fabric of everyday life. The existence of this set of structures, policies and practices has been facilitated by what social scientists have referred to as the neo-liberal political form. In the last decades of the 20th century and beyond, this political form and the intricate networks of social, economic and political power has been able, through the affordance made possible by digital technology, to re-write the culture and the consciousness of Western society through the "militarization" of everyday life.

This book was begun at the height of the Islamic State surge into the vacuum created by the American intervention in Iraq and the civil-war ravaged wastelands of Syria. This was the *Drumbeat* that attracted my attention and appeared to be a globe spanning conflict that was potentially the genesis for internal political conflict and a rise in authoritarianism. The focus of the public gaze and State actors at that time was on the rise of this movement and its reach across the globe into the "hearts and minds" of disaffected young people – particularly in the West. In the period leading up to the 2016 Presidential Election as well as the Brexit vote in the United Kingdom, another level of complexity emerged – the information war that IS had engaged in over a number of years to both inflict perceptual damage on the West, as well as to recruit new followers, was also employed by State actors as well as by a set of new non-State actors to achieve their political and ideological goals. The social war that I have described in this book is now an integral aspect of contemporary society – it has not diminished in both its real and potential impact on the lives of people living in the West. In many ways the insulation from risk in a physical sense that people had or believed that they had from their adversaries – violent religious extremists or rival State actors – evaporated with 9/11. The social war has created a contemporary landscape where information and kinetic warfare can easily overcome national boundaries and is conducted openly through a modern variant of proxy war – the lone-wolf attack and other forms of terror, and in a clandestine manner using all of the tools and affordances created by digital technologies.

Perpetual Social War

We are now in the midst of a perpetual social war. A war engaged in by a set of diverse actors – State and non-State, with conflicting agendas – but with a similar objective to create conflict, social disorder and hopefully the weakening of their opponents. The social war has been waged by extremist religious movements, the Alt-Right and State actors such as the Chinese and the Russian governments (Allcott & M.Gentzkow, 2017; Berger, 2015; Chung, 2016). The affordances created by new technologies have enabled these diverse actors to transcend national boundaries and inflict perceptual damage on their target subjects. The social war has harnessed new media and digital technology (the internet, social media, video games, and streaming media) to engage in algorithmic based perceptual warfare and has been applied both domestically and at transnational level.

The social war has been effective in targeting individuals and groups within Western society and projecting messages designed to spread disharmony and widen existing fissures within those societies. Applying this idea of the social war to events that have occurred over the past few decades helps us to understand how the process of militarization (the *Drumbeat* that the title of this book refers to) has re-constructed capitalist society. War and the preparation for war is an underlying and deeply embedded aspect of the culture of neo-liberal societies such as the United States, Britain, Europe, Australia, and other settler societies. This has been achieved through the creation of a series of enemies – both internal and external, real and contrived – to justify the maintenance of the machinery of war which emerged in the mid-20th century.

The amplification of social discord and the tapping into the strong current of cultural despair (Stern, 1974) found in our societies has enabled what I refer to as the "democratization" of this form of warfare. It does not require massive levels of human and military capital to inflict harm – to reach directly into target populations and inflict harm through symbolic violence. The hybrid-warfare model pioneered by the Russians in Ukraine has aided in the development of the social war, though as it is being applied in the West, without the "little-Green men" who applied kinetic back-up to the social media assaults (Monaghan, 2015; Rožukalne & Sedlenieks, 2017). The conduct of social war is not simply the project of IS or the Russians – this approach to inflicting perceptual damage has now become part of political conflict at a national level.

The techniques and technology of advanced warfare and its application to civil and communal conflict has become a part of everyday political struggle. This of course is by no means limited to the United States – in fact it is now a feature of the political landscape across the liberal-capitalist societies. Where we had once assumed that the danger faced by liberal-democracies was from armies of the disillusioned and alienated children of immigrants and adherents of the violent currents in the Islamic faith – in fact we are now aware of a much broader set of actors – State and non-State – in particular in the case of non-State actors from the extreme Right, who have adapted to the current digital landscape and have been adept at exploiting disharmony and social discord for their own purposes.

Non-State actors both from the religious extremists to the Alt-Right (such as neo-Nazis) share a common understanding that it is possible to undermine social cohesion in liberal democracies through the careful application of modern propaganda ideas through algorithmic technologies. Fake news and social media bots – generating rumors, lies and other forms of misinformation – are designed to sow conflict and add to a general sense of cultural despair and possible social collapse. What I think is clear is that the techniques and technologies developed and applied by the United States and its allies for use against its adversaries, first in the Cold War and then in the Gulf Wars I and II, have been adapted to enable the conduct information warfare inside Western society. The proxy wars conducted in Africa, Asia, the Middle East and Latin America – low intensity in nature but devastating nevertheless – are now the inspiration for an ongoing information war. The wars once conducted at arm's length and sometimes forgotten are now in a new form being brought home. The wars and conflicts on the periphery of the Empire are now being brought home to the suburbs and the cities.

Bringing the War Home

The enemy which had been identified in the early 2000s as a threat to the West – extremist religious adherents to particular interpretations of Islam – are still engaged in terror activities. However, they were never the existential threat that State actors in the United States and elsewhere in the West had portrayed them as being. They were and continue to be a threat because they have adapted to the existing social, cultural and political conditions in Western societies. They have taken lessons learnt in the insurgencies of Northern Ireland and the various guerilla and terror campaigns of the 1970s and 1980s and are now applying them in the West. In a sense they have created a "reverse" version of low-intensity conflict – attacking vulnerable targets in the West and recruiting small numbers of alienated young people to do their work. Lessons learnt in the wars that had been conducted on the periphery of the *Empire* were being applied to the conduct of a social war and amplified by and through the affordances created by our dependence on digital technology. Where the "Total War" of the 20th century was the outcome of an open declaration of war and the full mobilization of every aspect of life – economic, social, political and physical – to wage a global war, our current circumstances involve a form of war that is invisible yet has had a profound impact.

Over the past decade the interests of State (Russia and China), and non-State actors (extremist religious groups and the Alt-Right) have coalesced – they have a shared purpose, the bringing about of the destruction or at least weakening of liberal-democracy. At the same time, populist political movements and leaders were able to harness the affordances created by digital technology to engage in internal (and actively divisive) political campaigns. These campaigns were often related to the winning of elections or a particular plebiscite or referendum. What unites them in their strategies and actions is that they have adapted hybrid-warfare tactics to spaces which otherwise are not readily identified as war zones.

In the book I have worked towards an outline of the conditions which have created this perpetual form of war – the social war. Let me briefly reconsider some of the salient points outlined in the body of the book.

Radicals

As a part of the process of militarization and the extension of the perpetual social war has been the mainstreaming of extremist ideas – the Alt-Right now has a global audience and cheer squad. They are the "good people" to which Trump referred to in 2017. At the same time progressive ideas and the advocates in the anti-fascist and ecological movements have been lumped together with extremists from the Islamic State and other religious-inspired terror groups. The corruption of language, which Orwell had highlighted last century as being an integral element within the playbook of authoritarianism, has been clearly on display. A conscious effort has been made over the past decade to taint any genuine oppositional movement with a negative ascription of the term "radical", where in fact over the decades and centuries it has been radical movements which have led the efforts for emancipation based on color, gender, sexual orientation and class.

Habitus

In examining the vast panorama that is the post-Second World War era and the first decades of this century it has become evident that the creation of a militarized version of the liberal-democracies in order to conduct a "Total War" did not evaporate after the victory over the fascist states was declared. The machinery of war was not wound down and dismantled. The Iron Curtain and the Cold War which it symbolized ensured the maintenance of what Eisenhower described as the Military-Industrial Complex. The machinery of war and the expanding American Empire helped to establish what has been referred to as a process of militarization – the ongoing preparation for war and orientation of liberal societies to the use of violence and the conduct of war. This has been achieved through the creation of a societal process of pedagogy in order to create and sustain a mental-framework – a habitus which generates a socially disciplined subject population.

Hardening of Youth

An outcome of the emergence of this habitus and, in the service of militarization a cultural process which I have described as the "hardening" of youth, has evolved. This is the outcome of a cultural shift which has desensitized young people and more broadly the average citizen to violence and cruelty through exposure within various forms of media and the internet. This has led to a general hardening of attitudes in the broader society, workplaces and other social settings. Lack of humanity in the form of the degrading of any form of social safety net and the expendability of individuals, groups and entire segments of Western society as indicated by mass trenchant unemployment and inequality are reflective of this general hardening. The emergence of neo-liberalism as an economic, political and social force has underpinned this evolution in social attitudes. The dismantling of the welfare state, the abolition of good paying and long-term employment, the celebration of the individual and a societal commitment to putting the economic advancement of the individual at the forefront of social, economic and political decision making has been the driving force behind this.

Young people are being raised in a culture where the celebration of violence and cruelty has become embedded in everyday life. Violence permeates streaming media, YouTube channels, Facebook and Mixed Martial Arts, and the perennial military themed or oriented video games. The depiction of violence and cruelty is no longer even a point of contention – just like warfare, it is normalized. To challenge the current cultural obsession with violence, simulated and real as disseminated through new media and social media is often seen as a form of "moral panic" I reject this. At no stage in human history has the level of simulated and real cruelty and violence been so easily consumed – uncritically and with nonchalance. The consequences of this process are yet to fully emerge.

War-Play

Flowing on from both the creation of a militarized habitus, which has as its aim the construction of a population which is socially disciplined, is the instilling in young people of a set of skills and attitudes which help to fit them into roles within military structures and formations. These are soft skills, embedded in gameplay and game structures, scenarios and genres. The playing at war through video games and the construction of militarized forms of media and entertainment has been harnessed as a direct recruitment tool, as with *America's Army* and the Islamic Sate/Hezbollah versions of such game technology. But more than simply conducting ideological and propaganda campaigns through these technologies, it is my assertion that using games technology such as the *Xbox* and its control technology helps to develop a set of soft skills which don't prepare a young person for actual physical combat but do enculturate them into the use of play-like technology in actual war fighting. Playing a First-Person Shooter on an *Xbox* doesn't make you a soldier but it does help to develop and then engage the skills and attitudes that can be harnessed in an actual military training setting. Also, by extension, the reflexes and motor skills developed in playing video games does correlate with the control mechanisms used in the conduct of such methods of modern warfare as drone war (Macdonald, 2018).

Death Cults

It is not an outrageous thought to argue that IS has much in common with a death cult from the last century – the Nazi *Schutzstaffel*, or Protection Squad. Both groups saw death as an end in itself and also welcomed it. Both groupings used a concept of blood bonding or blood cement to adhere a recruit to the criminal undertakings of the organization. Both groups saw their work as being the application of violence to usher in a new era – at any cost. It is also possible to argue that the modern variant of the mid-century fascist movement – the Alt-Right – share a similar cult-like approach to the recruitment of their followers as well as in the obsession with an "End of Days" final conflict. Both IS and the Alt-Right long for a final conflict when either the godless West (as the IS perceives the world) or the multicultural and identarian United States and Europe, will end the "Great Replacement" (as the Alt-Right perceives the world) (Deem, 2019).

Militarization

This book has outlined the long-term process with which liberal democracy has had its underpinning logic undermined by a combination of militarization and the dominance of the neo-liberal economic model. The war economy that emerged in the mid-20th century in the liberal-democracies in order to combat the fascist Axis powers has, it is my assertion, never gone away. It has morphed into a self-perpetuating and ongoing process – militarization; which has re-configured capitalist social, political and economic relations to construct the foundations upon which a perpetual state of war can be maintained. Militarization is both a political and an economic process – a process which educates the population – it is pedagogic in the broadest sense of the term. If the adoption of manners and codes of conduct, the "civilizing process" to which Elias has referred, is integral to the economic and political evolution of Europe and settler societies such as the United States then I wish to re-assert that militarization is replacing this cultural form within the subject populations of the West.

This is being accomplished through the instilling of social discipline by the means of various forms of habitus – "ludic" (through military games) and the undermining of pro-social mental frameworks through the "hardening" of culture and of individuals. These processes have succeeded in configuring our mental framework to accept, as Geyer so eloquently put it, the process of militarization has embedded "the contradictory and tense social process in which civil society organizes itself for the production of violence" (Geyer, 1989). Militarization is the new civilizing process – it underpins almost every facet of our lived experience; in mass media, social media, video games, consumer culture and the gradual placing of war and warlike think at the core of capitalist culture. However, this is done in a way that is not overtly apparent, on the whole. It is, as Lutz has argued, a subtle process which leads to a "less visible deformation of human potentials into the hierarchies of race, class, gender, and sexuality, and to the shaping of national histories in ways that glorify and legitimate military action" (Lutz, 2002). Militarization has supplanted other elements of socialization in a manner which functions to create a political form which on the surface appears to be a continuation of the liberal-democratic political formation but it is in fact something quite different. Our political form is a neo-liberal war economy – primed to attack its opponents and to maintain a global *Empire*, much like its antecedents from an earlier age.

Conclusion

> Modern warfare has become very complex, especially during the last century. Wars are won not by a simple series of battles won, but by a complex interrelationship among military victory, economic pressures, logistic maneuvering, access to the enemy's information, political postures—dozens, literally dozens of factors.
>
> —Joe Haldeman, *The Forever War* (2017)

The social war has found fertile ground in Western society, which has been primed for conflict through more than half a century of militarization. The everyday life of the population of the liberal-capitalist societies has been militarized through both tangible and intangible ways. What has emerged from his process of militarization is a new form of war – social war, however since it is being waged in the metropolitan nations of the West it is happening without the recourse to guns. In this conflict the enemy is within – they are a neighbor, a co-worker or a classmate. The book you have just read has attempted to flesh out some of what I have observed as part of this ongoing process of militarization and its impact on the social fabric of the liberal democracies of the West. The extremist political movements that I have examined exist within the context of and are, in effect, beneficiaries of the decades-long process of militarization and the establishment of a perpetual state of war in the advanced nations of the West.

Young people are in many ways the focus of this social war – though the broader society is both impacted upon and provides the matériel for the extension and maintenance of the conflict. It is sobering to consider that we are only just becoming aware of how corrosive this conflict is and will continue to be. As Brecht wrote, in a time that echoes powerfully with our present condition,

> [w]e have sat, an easy generation In houses held to be indestructible. Thus we built those tall boxes on the island of Manhattan And those thin aerials that amuse the Atlantic swell. Of those cities will remain what passed through them, the wind! The house makes glad the eater: he clears it out. We know that we're only tenants, provisional ones And after us will come: nothing worth talking about.
>
> (Brecht, 1987)

References

Allcott, H., & M.Gentzkow. (2017). Social media and fake news in the 2016 election. *Journal of Economic Perspectives, 31*, 211–236.

Berger, J. M. (2015). The metronome of apocalyptic time: Social media as carrier wave for millenarian contagion. *Perspectives on Terrorism*. Retrieved from http://terrorismanalysts.com/pt/index.php/pot/article/view/444

Brecht, B. (1987). *Bertolt Brecht: Poems 1913–1956*: Theatre Arts Books.

Chung, A. (2016). Jihadism 3.0 the Islamic State's agenda of borderless radicalisation through the use of #social media. Retrieved from http://papers.ssrn.com/abstract=2760618

Deem, A. (2019). Extreme speech: The digital traces of #whitegenocide and Alt-Right affective economies of transgression. *International Journal of Communication, 13*, 20.

Geyer, M. (1989). The militarization of Europe, 1914–1945. In J. R. Gillis (Ed.), *The militarization of the Western world* (pp. 65–102). New Brunswick: Rutgers University Press.

Haldeman, J. W., Marvano, Haldeman, G., & Connery, C. (2017). *The forever war* (First edition. ed.). London: Titan Comics.

Lutz, C. (2002). Making war at home in the United States: Militarization and the current crisis. *American Anthropologist, 104*(3), 723–735.

Macdonald, C. (2018). US Army recruiting soldiers to enter professional video game contests to appeal to young Americans. *Mail Online*. Retrieved from https://www.dailymail.

co.uk/sciencetech/article-6381963/US-Army-recruiting-soldiers-enter-professional-video-games-contests.html

Monaghan, A. (2015). The 'war' in Russia's 'hybrid warfare'. *Parameters, 45*(4), 65.

Rožukalne, A., & Sedlenieks, K. (2017). The elusive cyber beasts: How to identify the communication of pro-Russian hybrid trolls in Latvia's internet news sites? *Central European Journal of Communication, 10*(1 (18)), 79–97.

Stern, F. (1974). *The politics of cultural despair: A study in the rise of the Germanic ideology*. Berkeley: University of California Press.

Index

24/7 news cycle 59, 73

accident porn 72
Adorno, T. 3
advertising 137
Afghanistan 19, 53, 131
African National Congress 89
Ahn, J.-K. 43
aims 6–7
Alexander, L. 116–117
algorithms x, 14, 161; manipulation 11
alienation 5, 113, 120–122
al-Qaeda 27, 51, 119, 121
Al-Rawi, A. 41–42
Alt-Right 2, 5, 14, 16, 74–75, 86, 98–99, 110, 113, 121, 122, 161; apocalyptic thinking 103–104, 119–121; attraction 120; audience 162; Death Cult 107–109, 164; end of days scenario 95–96, 96–98, 121; justification 108; legitimacy of violence 89; live streaming 59–60; mainstream alignment 97; propaganda 19–20, 106; white nationalism 118
American Family Foundation 108
American revolutionary War of Independence 87
America's Army 18–19, 23, 29–30, 30, 32, 34, 38, 42, 43–45, 164
Animal Liberation 95
anticipatory socialization 36
Anti-Defamation League 86
anti-heroes 79
anti-Semitism 5
anti-Vietnam War struggle 85, 90, 91–93
apocalyptic thinking 103–106, 109, 122; propagation of 14–15; understanding 119–121

Arab Spring 4, 88
architecture of fear 156
Arendt, H. 3, 7
asymmetrical warfare 14, 34, 39, 149
Aum Shinrikyo 105, 107, 110
Australia 2, 107, 110, 117, 156
Au, Wagner James 19

Baader-Meinhof 94
Barr, A. 73
Battlefield 32, 34
Battle Royale genre 43–45
battlespace: gamification 50–54
Beier, J. M. 136
Berger, J. M. 1
Berger, P. 14–15
Bittanti, M. 51–52, 154
Black September 57
Bloom, M. 40
Boggs, C. 131, 132
Boko Haram 107
Bourdieu, P. 6, 126–127, 132–133, 136, 146
boy scouts 64
Branch Davidians 107, 110
Brandon, J. 28
Braun, A. 147
bread and circuses 68
Brecht, B. 166
Brexit 14, 159
brutality 23, 69–70; image presentation 7
Bush, George W. 131
Butterworth, M. L. 137

Call of Duty 18, 19, 22, 28–29, 29–30, 32, 34, 36, 39, 51, 65, 154–155
Campbell, J. 79
Campbell's Soup 151

Index

capitalism 4, 5–6
Capra, Frank 18, 19, 55, 156
Card, O. S. 35
carrier wave 1
Castro, Fidel 94
Cetina 16–17
Charlottesville, North Carolina 89–90, 96, 99, 118, 121
China, People's Republic of 12, 23
Chinese Revolution 88
cinema 67; and war 31
civil collapse 76–77
civil disorder 24
civilian persona: breaking down 40
civilians: targeting 86
civilizing process: militarization 145–156, 165; pacification process 153; shift in attitudes 145–150
Civil Rights movement 90, 91
codes of conduct 154, 165
Cold War 12–13, 30–31, 33, 128, 130–131, 148, 162–163
collaborative working 44
Comet Ping Pong pizzeria terrorist attack 9
commodification 69
communications technology: sociality 16–17
community 122; sense of 40
Condis, M. 44, 58
conditioning 79–80
conflict: cinematic construction of 55–60
connectivity 11
Connor, J. W. 113
conspiracy groups 110
Conway, M. 56
Cost of War project 96
Covid-19 pandemic 24, 76–77, 110
Covid-19 Uprising 98
crime rates 74–75
criminality: allure of 63–64
crisis cults 110–113
Critical theory 3–6
cruelty 63–64, 65, 68, 163; culture of 70–72, 140
Cuban revolution 91, 94
cults 106–110, 164; attraction 120–122; characteristics 117; and cultural despair 110–113; *Schutzstaffel (SS)* case study 114–117; white nationalism 117–119. *See also* individual cults
cultural despair 76, 110–113, 160

cultural pessimism 75, 76–78
cultural tropes 60
culture 112
culture wars 122
cyber-espionage 15
cyberthreats 12
cyber-war 15

danger 74–75
Dark Web 106
Davey, J. 97
Death Cults 5, 85, 105–110, 114–117, 120–122, 164
Debord, G. 59, 69
Deep Web 106
Deleuze, G. 64
democratization 160
desensitization 40, 163
digital culture 54, 70
digital safe spaces 66–67
Dillon, J. 56
Dismounted Soldier Training System 34–35, 38
Disney 43
domestic terrorism 9
Doueihi, M. 70
drones 32, 58
drumbeat, the x, 1, 159–160
Duff, M. 60
Dunning, E. 146

Earth Liberation Front 95
Ebner, J. 97
economic structures 5
Eco-terror 86
Eisenhower, Dwight D. 129, 130, 163
Elias, N. 3, 6, 135, 145, 146, 153–154, 155, 156, 165
Empire 2–3, 6, 161–162, 165
empowerment 54–55
enculturation 29
Ender's Game (Card) 35
end of days scenario 85, 95–96, 96–98, 104, 105, 106, 109, 117–119, 120, 121, 122
enemy, the 161–162, 166
Enlightenment, the 85
Enloe, C. 136, 140, 150–151, 152
environmental movement 86, 90
Erikson, R. S. 92
everyday life: commodification of 69; militarization of 31

evil 63–64, 79
existential threats 96–98, 110–111, 128, 161
exploitation 5
Extremist Left political groups 93–94
extremists 1

Facebook ix, 10, 11, 23, 42, 56, 58, 66, 68
fake news 9–10, 24
Falciola, L. 95
fascism 4
fear 69, 74–75; architecture of 156
Field, A. 36–37
First Person perspective 51–52
First-Person Shooter (FPS) genre 18–19, 28, 29–31, 30, 45, 58, 64, 164; Battle-Royale styled 43; ludic military habitus 140–142; militarization through 38; military habitus 36, 38; *mise-en-scène* 59; pedagogic space 141; perception of power 32; perceptual damage 31–32, 39; perspective 51–52; production of violence 30; repertoire of mechanisms 30; Rules of Engagement 34; similarities to ISIS recruitment films 22; thrills 154–155
first-person thinkers 35
First World War 112–113, 148
Five Star 109–110
Floyd, George: murder of 76–77
foco theory of action 94
force: and violence 68–69
force amplifier 60
Fortnite 30, 43–45, 58
France: Nazi occupation of 68–69
Frankfurt School 6
French Revolution 85, 87, 87–88, 147, 148
Freud, S. 6
frictionless pipeline: internet 44–45
Friedman, T. L. 11
Fuchs, C. 5–6
Fukuyama, F. ix
Full Metal Jacket (film) viii–ix, 27
Full Spectrum Leaders 35

game aesthetics 39, 56, 57
game culture 39
Game of Thrones (TV series) 65, 70
game play language 35
gamer culture 60
games scenarios 18

gamification: battlespace 50–54; GoPro technology 50–53; heroization 53–54
Gardner, B. 15–16
Gat, A. 75
Gears of War 22
German liberalism: decline of 112
Geyer, M. 30, 127, 132, 145, 152, 165
Gill, Z. W. 34
Giroux, H. 66, 136, 137, 140, 142
Goffman, E. ix
Google ix
Gooskens, G. 155
GoPro live streaming 56, 57–58
GoPro technology 11, 23, 50–53, 55, 58, 59
Grand Theft Auto 41–42
Great Replacement threat 97, 164
Guattari, F. 64
Guevara, Ernesto "Che" 91, 94
Gulf War I 69, 149, 161
Gulf War II 19, 149, 156, 161

habitus 6, 77, 146, 149–150, 162–163; definition 126–127; layered 133–134; ludic military 140–142, 165; militarized form 132; nature of 132–135; and pedagogy 135–138; and social discipline 138–140
Haldeman, Joe 165
Halo 22
happy-slapping 65
hardening x, 40, 63–64, 64, 65–67, 71–72, 77–78, 79–80, 163, 165
Hardt, M. 2, 2–3, 6, 136
Hayden, T. 91
Hedges, C. 104, 110–111
Herfroy-Mischler, A. 73
heroization 53–54
Heyer, Heather: murder of 96
Hezbollah 41–42, 164
Hitler, Adolf 114, 116
Hitler Youth 64
Holocaust, the 55
Homer 68–69
Horkheimer, M. 3, 6
How ISIS Abducts, Recruits, and Trains Children to Become Jihadists 40
Huizinga, J. 29
humanity, lack of 163
human targeted acts: turn away from 94–95
Huntington, S. P. 105

Index

hybrid threats 13
hybrid warfare 13, 14, 15, 17, 52–53, 53–54, 160, 162

identity 4, 98
identity politics 16–17
ideological message 14
ideological vacuum 4
ideological war 115
imperialism, 5
Industrial Revolution 153
information: definition 10; dissemination 11; weaponization 11, 14–15, 28, 119
information bullets 57
information intangibles 10–11
Information Warfare 10, 11, 11–13, 15, 16, 23, 23–24, 50, 159
internet ix, 2, 106; culture. 58–59; frictionless pipeline 44–45; ubiquitous nature of 57
Internet Research Agency 15–16
internet soldiers 24
iPhones 11
Iraq 131
Islamic State ix, 3, 14, 16, 27, 58, 113, 121, 122, 164; apocalyptic thinking 103–106, 119–121; appeal 121; attraction 120; brutality 69–70; Death Cult 5, 105–106, 107–109, 164; emergence of 105; end of days scenario 105; extreme violence policy 72–73; justification 108; media strategy 72–73; murder as performance 54–55; political agenda 121; propaganda 1–2, 19–20, 22–23, 51, 106; recruitment 39–42, 104; recruitment films 23; rule 121–122; social media use 20; streaming technology 54; training methods 40; use of video games 41–42, 51; version of *Grand Theft Auto* 41–42; violence 65
Islamic terror 1
Israeli Olympic Team massacre, 1972 56–57
Italy 110

Jefferson, Thomas 87
Jensen, P 71
Jews 98
Jihadist movement ix, 89, 96; end of days scenario 95–96
Jowett, G. S. 18, 21

Kaempf, S. 52
Katz, J. 63–64, 78–79
killing: aversion to 36–37; pedagogic practices 36–39; simulated 141
King, Jay 22
Korean War 36, 128, 148
Krotz, F. 73

labelling 84
language: corruption of 84–99, 162; descriptive power 85; of existential threats 96–98; game play 35; labelling 84; mis-application 85–86; as political tool 84, 98–99; of radical movements 90–96; of radicals 88–90, 162; of revolutionaries 86–88
Late Barbarian Society 145–150
Lenin, V. I. 147
liberal triumphalism x
lifeworld: militarization and 150–153, **151**
Lifton, R. J. 108
live streaming 54, 54–55, 56, 57–60
Lone Wolf attackers 24, 118–119
low-intensity conflicts 12
ludic military habitus 140–142, 165
Lutz, C. 127, 135, 140, 165

McCauley, C. 89
McCuen, 13
McDonald, K. 119
Macedonia, M. 35
Magnanville, France: terrorist attack 56
Mandela, Nelson 89
Marcuse, H. 6
Marega, S. 104
Mariscal, J. 152
Marshall, S. L. A 36–37
Marvel 43
Marvel Avengers 43
Marx, K. 6, 121
masculinity 136
mass-mobilization 20
May '68 radical student movement 85, 90–91, 92–94
Mead, M. 13
media technology 73
mediatization 65–66, 71–72, 73–74
media tropes 76
memes 58
Mennell, S. 146
mental architecture ix, 133
message amplification 14, 96–97, 122

Index

Michael, G. 98
microblogging 11
militarism 127
militaristic foundations: masking 43–44
militarization 17, 18, 35–36, 45, 67, 160, 164–165, 165–166; civilizing process 145–156, 165; as a cultural and political form 131–132; definition 19, 30, 126, 132; drift towards 127–128; effectiveness 140; emergence of 6–7; enculturation 29; of everyday life 31; habitus of 77; lifeworld and 150–153, 151; ludic military habitus 140–142; and masculinity 136; nature of 127–132; normalization 42; pedagogic practices 39; pedagogy 78, 142; as pedagogy 132, 135–136, 137–138; as response to existential threats 128; and social discipline 139–140; through First-Person Shooter (FPS) genre 38; of Western society 2
militarized pedagogy 132, 135–136, 137–138
military doctrine: shift in 31
military expenditure 150, 151
military habitus 36, 38
military-industrial complex x, 7, 45, 126, 128–129, 129–131, 159, 163
military-industrial-entertainment complex 149, 150
military service: recruitment 32–36
military thinking 28–29
military training 27, 45; in killing 36–39; simulators 38; video games as 33–35
military values and culture 141
millenarianism 109, 120
Mineau, A. 116
mise-en-scène 59
misinformation 24
Mixed-Martial Arts 65, 67–68, 70–71, 77–78, 155, 163
modding 41–42, 59
modes of behavior 147
Mohandesi, S. 93
moral dilemmas 155
morality 145–150
moral panic 163
Moskalenko, S. 89
Moskal, S. D. 137
movies 67
murder: as performance 54–55
murder rates 75

Nazi Germany 6, 18, 21, 68–69, 76, 112, 113, 114–117, 128
Negri, A. 2, 2–3, 6, 136
neo-liberalism 112, 128–129
neo-liberalist economics 109
neo-Nazis 89–90
Netflix 72
Network of Excellence for Research in Violent Online Political Extremis 56
New Left movement 91
New Yorker Magazine 22
New York Times (newspaper) 58
New Zealand mosque massacres 57–58, 59–60, 68, 97
non-linear warfare 15
non-state actors 1, 12, 16, 159, 161, 162; live streaming 55–60; political messaging 52–53; propaganda 19–20; recruitment 39–42, 44–45
North Atlantic Treaty Organization (NATO) 13
nostalgia 75

objectualization 16–17
O'Donnell, V. 18, 21
Oestreich, G. 138–139
oil shock, the 128
Oklahoma bomber, the 121
One Nation 110
online forums 66
On Photography (Sontag) 54–55
Orban, V. 4–5
Orr, J. 152
Orwell, G. 84, 99, 162
Other, the: fear of 74–75

pacification process 153
Pantucci, R. 107, 120, 121
Passeron, J.-C. 136
peace dividend 30
peak digital violence 68
pedagogic practices: killing 36–39
pedagogic space 141
pedagogy 78; definition 136–137; forms of 135; and habitus 135–138; of militarization 78, 142; militarization as 132, 135–136, 136; militarized 132, 135–136, 137–138; public 142
people-centrism 16
perception 3; tools of 9–10; weaponization 31–32
perceptual damage 6, 31–32, 39, 119, 160

perceptual weaponry 27–28, 45
performative violence 59
perpetual social war 160–161, 166
perpetual warfare: entrenchment of 7
photography: political power 54–55
Pinker, S. 75
play 29, 140, 141, 163–164
Player Unknown Battle Grounds 43, 43–44, 44
PlayStation 28
pleasures of evil 63–64
police deaths 71–72
political-ideological messages 17
political interests 18
political messaging 1, 50, 52–53
political reform 112
political violence 68
Pollard, L. T. 131, 132
pop culture 42
pop culture propaganda 22–23
popular culture ix–x, 111
populism 113
populist movements 4–5, 97, 112, 162
Port Huron statement 91
Post-Truth period 24
power: perception of 32
problem solving 44
propaganda 1, 17–22, 50, 51, 55, 156; Alt-Right 19–20, 106; definition 17–18, 20–21; democratization 52; game aesthetics 39; Islamic State 1–2, 19–20, 22–23, 106; materials 21; Nazi Germany 21; non-state actors 19–20; personalized ix; pop culture 22–23; Second World War 18, 20, 21; video game messages 28–29
prosocial attitudes 37
proxy wars 128, 160, 161
public pedagogy 142
pugilistic habitus 134–135

quest for excitement 155

race and racism 98, 115–117
race baiting 74–75
race war 107
radical: contemporary use of the 84–99; mis-application of the term 85–86
radical action 95
radicalization 17
radical movements 85, 90–96
radical politics 95

radicals 88, 88–90, 162; mis-application of the term 87
recruitment 27, 137, 141, 149; *Fortnite* and 43–45; Islamic State 39–42, 104; non-state actors 39–42, 44–45; state actors 32–36, 33, 42, 44
Red Army factions 93, 94
Red Brigades 94
refugees 117
Reid-Henry, S. 128–129
revolution and revolutionaries 86–88
Richard, B. 69
Riefenstahl, Leni 18, 21, 55
rightness: belief in 117
Rousseau, J.-J. 87
Rules of Engagement 32, 34
Russian Federation 12, 13, 15, 23, 53–54, 58, 160; Internet Research Agency 15–16; use of GoPro technology 50–53
Russian Revolution 88, 148

Salon.com 19
Salter, M. 65
Salvaing, Jean-Baptiste: murder of 56
Schutzstaffel (SS) 106, 110, 114–117, 122, 164
science-fiction 35
Scientology 110
Second World War 18, 19, 20, 21, 31–32, 36, 42, 111, 128, 130, 132, 148
self: breaking down ix
self-censorship 53
self-constraint 146, 147
sexual violence 70
Shock and Awe x, 23, 51, 69, 105, 119, 122
Signal 10
skills development 28–29, 29, 164
Skocpol, T. 87–88
snuff films 42
Snyder, T. 114–115
social cohesion: decline of 109
Social Contract, the 87
social discipline 77, 79–80, 138–140, 163, 165
socialization 30, 40, 146–150, 165; anticipatory 36
social media: leveraging 16; manipulation 9; tools 14; weaponization ix, 14–15, 20
social reproduction theory 138
social solidarity: dismantling of x
Social War, the 7, 13, 23–24, 126, 159–160, 165–166; actors 160;

definition 10, 15; and information intangibles 10–11; people-centric 16; perpetual 160–161, 166; propaganda 17–23; strategies 17; and tools of perception 9–10
societal collapse: fear of 112
society: pacification of 145–150
society of the spectacle 59
soft power 18, 31, 32
soft skills 29, 164
soldierization 34, 40
Soldier's Creed, the 33
Sontag, S.: *On Photography* 54–55
South Africa 117
Soviet Union: collapse of 11, 30, 131, 148
spectacle 40, 59, 68–73
Spencer, R. 2
sports and sports training 134–135, 153–154
Stalin, Joseph 130
Star Wars 43
state actors 1: political messaging 52–53; recruitment 32–36, 33, 42, 44
Stern, F. 76, 112–113
Stoker, L. 92
Stott, N 36
streaming technology 54, 54–55, 55–60
Students for a Democratic Society 91
Surkov, V. 15–16
Symbionese Liberation Army 93, 94
symbolic violence 138
Syrian conflict 54, 105; Russian incursion 50–53

target audience 67
targets 86
Telegram 10
Television War 53
terror: cinematic construction of 55–60
terrorism 9; domestic 9
theoretical framework 3–6
thrills 154–155
Tigerland (film) 27
TikTok 10, 23, 42
Toffler, A. 10–11
Toffler, H. 10–11
Tomsen, S. 65
total institutions ix
Total War 20, 42, 128, 152, 162
toughening up 63–64, 155–156
toughness 78–79
Tourish, D. 108

training methods: Islamic State 40
Triumph of the Will (film) 18, 21, 55
Trolling 15, 58
Trump, D. 4–5, 5, 98, 99, 118, 131, 150
Turse, N. 149
Twitch 66
Twitter 11, 22, 56, 64, 66, 69

Ukraine 13, 15, 52, 53–54, 160
Ultimate Fighting Championship 67–68, 70–71
United States Army: Soldier's Creed 33
United States of America: civil collapse 76–77; Cyber Command 11–12; empire 131; military expenditure 150, 151; Presidential election campaign, 2016 9, 14, 24, 159; war economy 130–131; white nationalism 117–119
Urban guerrillas 94
US Cyber Command 11–12
US Marine Corps 36

video fights 65
video game controllers 27, 28, 59, 155
video games: IS use of 41–42; ludic military habitus 140–142; as military training 34–35; mods 41–42; pedagogic characteristics 28; propaganda messages 28–29
Vietnam War 30–31, 33, 53, 55, 70, 128, 148; opposition movement 85, 90, 91–93
violence 23, 150; celebration of x; channeling 154; cultural obsession with 70, 163; and danger 74–75; decline in 75; desensitization to 40; economy of 64; exposure to 64; and fear 74–75; and force 68–69; graphic depiction of 67, 70; image presentation 7; justification 108; as legitimate 89; mediatization 65–66, 71–72, 73–74; normalization 31, 65–66, 139, 153; performative 59; and pleasure 63–64; political 68; prevalence of 72–73; production of 30, 58; resort to 138; sexual 70; social reproduction theory 138; spectacle 68–73; state monopoly of legitimate 146–147; symbolic 138; voyeuristic consumption 64–68
Virilio, P. 3, 6, 31–32, 69
virtual communities 2–3

virtual conflict 31
visual culture 57–58
von den Hoff, R. 54
voyeuristic consumption 64–68

Wacquant, L. 133–135, 155
war: boundaries of 32; and cinema 31–32; definition 13; gamification 50–54; ideological 115; normalization 42, 139, 153; preparation for x, 27; simulated 27–29; traditional notions 32
war culture: extension of 30
war economy 130, 164–165
WarGames (films) 38
War on Terror 19, 33, 53, 96, 109, 131
war-play 60, 163–164
War/Play: Video games and the Militarization of Society (Martino) 2
wartime culture 19
war weariness 5
weapons 59
Weather Underground 89, 93, 94, 95
web culture 58–59

Weil, S. 68–69
Weimar Germany 111–113
Welch, Edgar M. 9
Western society: militarization of 2
West, the: victory of 4
White nationalism 98–99, 117–119
Why We Fight (film) 18, 19, 21, 55, 156
Wikileaks 53
Wild Bunch, The (film) 70
Williams, R. 89
Wohlforth, T. 108
world views ix
Worsham, L. 135, 136–137
Wright-Mills, C. 129–130, 130–131

Xbox 28, 45, 164

young people 166; hardening 63–64, 64, 65–67, 78, 79–80, 163; marginalization 66; voyeuristic consumption 64–68
youth sub-cultures 78–79
YouTube 23, 39, 42, 51, 53, 54–55, 55, 56, 58, 64, 65, 66, 68, 69, 73

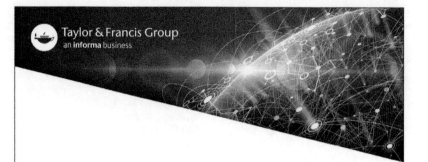